THE HISTORY
ESSENTIALS™

U.S. & WORLD TIMELINE

©2015 Hexco Academic

Disclaimer notice: The content of the History Bee or any other contest is not limited to the events in this book. There is no guarantee that this material will appear in the National History Bee or any other competitions. Dates and facts have been verified by at least two reliable sources, however, we encourage you to contact us if any information contained in this book is historically inaccurate. We do not claim to have all world events and history listed in this abbreviated timeline book and encourage all to use this book as a starting point for his/her own research.

Printed in the United States of America

First printing, 2015
ISBN: 978-0-578-15630-9

Hexco Academic
P.O. Box 199
Hunt, TX 78024
www.hexco.com

Contributing authors - Shannon Barker, Nancy Barnard, and Keisha Bedwell
Editors - Linda Tarrant, Noel Putnam, Eric Huff, and Nick Clusserath
Cover and internal design - Jennifer King

ORDERING INFORMATION
Special discounts are available on quantity purchases by schools, corporations, associations, etc. For details, contact the publisher at the address above. Bookstores and wholesalers interested in resale options for this publication are encouraged to contact Hexco at (800) 391-2891, or email hexco@hexco.com.

The farther backward you can look,
the farther forward you are likely to see.

~ Winston S. Churchill

Tips for your Journey

1. Take note of new concepts.

When a topic or fact in this book is shown in **boldface type** or has you scratching your head saying, "Huh?" ... make a note! That is probably a good topic to look up! Remember, there is not enough room to cover all the interesting details in this one little book.

2. As you're reading, think deeper.

Where would a small change in history have had the biggest impact on where we are today? What if there had been no Magna Carta? What if Lincoln had lived? Or what if the South had won? Imagine if Russia had not sold Alaska. How might our world be different? Ponder questions of your own to share with your coach or team to really make the facts "stick."

3. Become an expert in one or more areas!

Take note of things that interest you, such as music, art, wars, Native American studies or famous documents and start your own notebook or spreadsheet of your favorite areas of study. "Rabbit" down different paths as you research to broaden your scope and knowledge base!

This time-saving historical summary is designed to
help you organize your studies by listing basic historical themes
in the order in which they happened.

The History Essentials lists monumental events and noteworthy individuals in U.S. and world history based on official study guides and encyclopedic references. Use this guidebook in conjunction with your contest guide and do more research on your own! Read books, refer to maps, visit museums, use search engines, watch reputable documentaries and history shows, and talk with experts whenever you have the opportunity. And, most of all, have fun!

Navigation

CHAPTER TITLE   **PAGE**

Prehistory of the World....................................7

Western Hemisphere - PART 1: United States.................11

Western Hemisphere - PART 2: Canada,
    Central America, and South America.....................83

Eastern Hemisphere - PART 3: Europe.....................103

Eastern Hemisphere - PART 4: Asia.......................157

Eastern Hemisphere - PART 5: Africa.....................191

Bibliography..217

Index...220

Have a wonderful journey.

PREHISTORY OF THE WORLD

- Prehistory
- Stone Age
- Bronze Age
- Iron Age

Prehistoric Periods

Prehistory - Time before recorded history was divided by an archeological system based on human technology into three periods: the **Stone Age**, the **Bronze Age** and the **Iron Age**. The beginning of life on Earth has generally been used as the starting point, and the period continued until written records were made. Dates varied from place to place in civilization.

Stone Age - This lasted nearly 2½ million years, ending about 3000 BCE. During this period, prehistoric people used stone to make tools with sharp edges, points or hammering surfaces. They also used bone in making tools, but there are few artifacts that have survived. This period saw people controlling fire for their use and creating art on pottery and on cave walls. The geologic ages that were part of the Stone Age are the **Paleolithic**, **Mesolithic**, **Neolithic** and **Chalcolithic** periods.

Bronze Age - This period saw bronze used in making tools as opposed to the use of stone. This era began around 3000 BCE and ended between 1200 BCE and 600 BCE. These people were able to smelt copper to form an alloy with tin, which produced bronze. Making improved tools and weapons enabled the rise of warfare.

Also typified in this era was the development of trading networks as celestial navigation improved. Writing systems and mathematics were developed. The potter's wheel was used to create improved vessels. Centralized governments developed with social stratification and slavery. The end of the era was heralded by the ability to use iron for making tools and weapons.

Iron Age - This age was marked by widespread use of iron and then use of steel by combining iron with carbon to make superior cutting tools and weapons, ultimately with elaborate designs. Iron tools and weapons were not necessarily better than those made of bronze, but iron was in greater supply than copper and tin. The Iron Age began around 1000 BCE. The introduction of alphabetic characters allowed history and literature to be written down. Ending of this age varied from 500 BCE to 700 CE.

· ·

AGES OF MAN - The first mention of putting history into ages was by the Greek poet Hesiod around 700 BCE. He listed the ages as the Golden Age, the Silver Age, the Bronze Age, the Heroic Age and the Iron Age. These were related to gods of mythology.

WESTERN HEMISPHERE

Part 1
United States

- Migrations from Asia
- Prehistoric Cultures
- Norse Explorations
- Exploration by Columbus
- Columbian Exchange

Early Cultures & Explorations

Migrations from Asia to North America - Around 15,000 BCE, a land bridge across what is now the **Bering Strait** probably allowed people to go from northeast Asia to what is now Alaska during the **Stone Age**.

Prehistoric Native American cultures (c. 9000 BCE-1500 CE) - The earliest cultures included the **Clovis** and **Folsom** cultures during the **Stone Age**, which spread from northern New Mexico into the Great Plains. Cultures along the Ohio and Mississippi River valleys were classified as **Mound Builders**, and included **Adena**, **Hopewell** and others. The **Anasazi** or ancient Pueblo culture occupied the Four Corners region of the U.S. (parts of Arizona, New Mexico, Colorado and Utah). This group later moved to cliff dwellings, such as those in Mesa Verde, Colorado. Descendants built the **Pueblo** village of **Acoma** in New Mexico. Acoma was one of the oldest, continuously occupied U.S. settlements.

Norse explorations - **Leif Erikson** and the Norse arrived on the coast of Canada around 1014 CE and created a small colony in **L'Anse aux Meadows**, in Newfoundland. He is thought to have explored along the St. Lawrence River to the Great Lakes and along the New England coast during the **Bronze Age**.

Christopher Columbus' exploration - In 1492, an Italian explorer from Genoa, Columbus, sailed under the flag of Spain for **Queen Isabella** and **King Ferdinand** with three ships, **Niña**, **Pinta** and **Santa María**. Italy, Portugal and France refused to back his expedition. He landed on Hispaniola, a Caribbean island, and he ultimately made four voyages to the **New World**.

Columbian Exchange - Around 1493, soon after settlers had come to the New World, the Columbian Exchange was created to trade goods. Ships from Europe and Africa brought wheat, bananas, rice, horses, pigs, goats and cows, as well as smallpox and typhus to the Americas. Ships returned with animal pelts and new foods, such as sweet potatoes, maize, beans, squash, tomatoes and cocoa.

* *

MAMMOTH HUNTING? - Evidence of the Clovis people was first found in the form of an arrowhead point inside a mammoth.

• European Exploration Continues

Early Cultures & Explorations

Northwest Passage - **John Cabot** was an Italian from Venice who sailed under the English flag for **Henry VII** in 1497. Cabot was seeking a northwest passage to Asia. He probably landed in Newfoundland.

Fountain of Youth - Sailing for Spain in 1513, **Juan Ponce de León** was searching for the mythical **Fountain of Youth** in the New World. He traveled through Florida around the area near present-day **St. Augustine**.

Exploration of the Gulf of Mexico - In 1519, **Alonzo Álvarez de Pineda**, a Spanish explorer and mapmaker, circled the Gulf and explored several miles up the Mississippi River.

Exploration of the Hudson River - Italian **Giovanni da Verrazano** sailed under the French flag for **Francis I**. He explored the east coast of North America from Cape Fear to Nova Scotia, including the mouth of the Hudson River in 1524.

Exploration of Canada - A French explorer, **Jacques Cartier** made three voyages to the New World between 1534 and 1542. He sailed up the St. Lawrence River to what is now Montreal. He named **Canada** and claimed it for France.

Exploration of the Mississippi River - A Spanish explorer, **Hernando de Soto** was first to explore deep into the territory of the U.S. He went up through Florida and then explored westward to the Mississippi River between 1538 and 1542.

Search for the Seven Cities of Cibola - A Spanish explorer, **Francisco Vásquez de Coronado,** traveled through the southwestern U.S. in 1540 in search of the fabled Seven Cities of Cibola, which was also called the **Seven Cities of Gold**. He saw the Grand Canyon and explored part of the Colorado River.

FOUNTAIN OF YOUTH? - *Ponce de Leon's Fountain of Youth is located near present-day St. Augustine in Florida. The area has been converted into a park, and anyone can drink from the fountain. Beware though, it smells like rotten eggs! While safe to drink, the smell is attributed to a high sulfuric content.*

- St. Augustine Colonized
- Iroquois Confederacy
- Roanoke Colony
- Introduction of Horses
- St. Lawrence Exploration

Early Cultures & Explorations

St. Augustine colonized - A Spanish explorer and admiral, **Pedro Menéndez de Avilés,** traveled to Florida for **Philip II**. He founded **St. Augustine** in 1565, and it was the oldest continuously occupied city in America settled by Europeans.

Iroquois Confederacy - Also called the **Iroquois League** or **Five Nations**, this group was brought together by **Dekanawidah** and **Hiawatha** around 1580. The group included the Mohawk, Oneida, Onondaga, Cayuga and Seneca, and all spoke the Iroquois language. The Tuscarora joined in 1722, and the group became the **Six Nations**. They developed a constitution called a **Great Binding Law**. All decisions required unanimity, and each tribe had one vote. They originated **lacrosse** and shared the game with colonists.

Roanoke Colony - Called the **Lost Colony**, Roanoke was first colonized under the English flag in 1585 by Sir **Walter Raleigh**. It soon collapsed, and it was reestablished in 1587 under **John White**, who served as governor. **Virginia Dare**, a granddaughter of White, was born in this colony and was the first English child born in America. The colony disappeared again by 1590.

Introduction of horses - A Spanish conquistador, (**Don**) **Juan de Oñate**, founded **Santa Fé de Nuevo México** as a Spanish province in present-day New Mexico in 1598. Oñate brought a large herd of horses. When the Spanish were driven out of the area, the horses were left. The local **Apache** people mastered the use of horses and began trading them with other native nations.

St. Lawrence River exploration - Exploring for France in 1603, **Samuel Champlain** traveled down the St. Lawrence River along the coast to what is now Massachusetts. He established **Quebec**, or Kebec in the **Algonquin** language, meaning, *where the river narrows.*

. . . .

LOST COLONY? - *Governor White went to England to get supplies and ask for aid. When he returned, he found Roanoke deserted. Not only were the colonists gone, but their cabins and livestock as well. The only remaining evidence was a pair of graves and a post with the word "Croatan" carved into it. What could have happened?*

- Jamestown Colony
- New York Colonization
- *Mayflower Compact*
- Plymouth Colony
- Treaty with Wampanoag

Colonial Times

Jamestown Colony - The **British Virginia Company** established this colony in 1607. It survived mainly because Captain **John Smith** enforced a *no work-no food* policy. He established trade relations with natives and became a friend of Chief **Powhatan**, father of **Pocahontas**. A colonist, **John Rolfe**, later married Pocahontas. Rolfe grew tobacco and exported it to England, and this ultimately became a major cash crop.

Colonization of New York - Englishman **Henry Hudson** explored along the Hudson River in 1609. He traveled with the **Dutch East India Company** and represented the Netherlands. He established the **Fort Orange** trading post at present-day Albany.

Mayflower Compact - The **Separatists** and **Strangers**, who were religious refugees, came on the *Mayflower* in 1620, and these groups were later called **Pilgrims**, collectively. Before they reached North America, they signed a covenant, which was a set of rules to govern everyone equally, called the *Mayflower Compact*.

Plymouth Colony - The *Mayflower* landed at Cape Cod, Massachusetts and established the Plymouth Colony. A Separatist, **William Bradford** was the leader of this colony. Many of the Strangers were skilled laborers and military leaders, such as **Myles (Miles) Standish**. This colony ultimately merged with the **Massachusetts Bay Colony**. This group set the stage for religious tolerance and government for the betterment of all.

Pilgrim-Wampanoag peace treaty - In 1621, this was the first treaty between colonists and Native Americans. Pilgrims conferred with Wampanoag Native Americans with the aid of **Squanto** and **Samoset**, who were natives who had learned English from earlier explorers. The group agreed not to harm one another. Anyone who broke the treaty would be punished by the other group.

. . . .

LIFESAVING ACT OF KINDNESS - Some historians believe that Pocahontas befriended Captain Smith and perhaps saved him from execution and hunger. Pocahontas and her attendants were said to have brought Smith provisions once every four or five days.

1621 - 1636

- New Netherland
- Massachusetts Bay Colony
- Antinomian Controversy
- Providence, Rhode Island

Colonial Times

New Netherland - Established in 1624 by the **Dutch West India Company**, this colony was located on **Manhattan Island**. Their interest was in fur trade, not agriculture. **Peter Minuit** became director of the colony two years later, and he purchased Manhattan Island from the natives and ordered the building of **Fort Amsterdam**. The city outside the walls became **New Amsterdam** and was later renamed **New York**.

Massachusetts Bay Colony - Founded by owners of the **Massachusetts Bay Company** in 1630, this English colony was primarily **Puritan**. There was little tolerance for other religions, which caused friction and slow growth. The Puritans considered education important for all.

Antinomian Controversy - A Puritan spiritual adviser, **Anne Hutchinson**, conducted religious discussions in her home in the Massachusetts Bay Colony around 1634. Her belief in the **covenant of grace** philosophy was opposed to the Puritan's **covenant of works** philosophy. This created the Antinomian Controversy between these two different religious views. She was exiled, and with a group of people, founded **Portsmouth** on Aquidneck Island in **Rhode Island**.

Providence, Rhode Island - After **Roger Williams** was exiled from the Massachusetts Bay Colony for his religious beliefs, he founded this colony

in 1636 as a refuge for persecuted religious dissenters. Williams was a Puritan chaplain. This was the first colony to guarantee religious freedom. Williams returned to England to seek recognition for the area as an English colony. It became known as **Providence Plantations** and included several colonies. The area became one of the original 13 colonies.

* *

THE NEED TO READ - The Puritans felt that education was necessary to read the Bible as well as to read and understand the capital laws of the country.

- Languages of America
- Connecticut Colony
- Pequot War
- Fort Christina
- New England Confederation

Colonial Times

Key into the Languages of America - Written by **Roger Williams**, this was the first study of Native American customs and languages.

Connecticut Colony - In 1636, **Thomas Hooker**, a Puritan leader who disagreed with leaders in Massachusetts, founded this colony at **Hartford** in Connecticut. He established the First Church of Hartford and opened his sermons with, "the foundation of authority is laid in the free consent of the people."

Pequot War - The first open conflict in colonial times was between settlers and the native **Pequot**, who lived in southeast Connecticut. After the death of **John Oldham**, a trader, the colonists demanded revenge and took extreme action. They burned villages and killed hundreds of natives. The Pequot declared war and united with several other tribes. The English colonies united and prevailed in battle in 1636 and 1637.

Fort Christina - The first Swedish colony in North America was named after their queen in 1638. Peter Minuit, who originally sailed for Holland, now sailed for the **New Sweden Company**. He established a settlement in Delaware Bay which expanded to both sides of the Delaware River into modern Maryland and Pennsylvania. They traded peacefully with the **Lenni Lenape**. Swedes governed their towns until 1681, when **William Penn** obtained a charter for an English colony.

New England Confederation - This group was formed in 1643 by English colonists who were united against the Dutch, French and Native Americans. The agreement was that each colony would remain independent, but join together for mutual defense. This was the first formal attempt at colonial unification; it ended in 1684.

• •

UNSETTLED ARGUMENT - Historians still argue about the causes of the Pequot War. Why not look it up and share what you determine to be the cause with your coach or teacher?

- Comanche Migration
- Navigation Act of 1651
- Mississippi Exploration
- King Philip's War
- Nathaniel Bacon's Rebellion

Colonial Times

Comanche migration - Around the mid-1600s, this group of Native Americans migrated from Wyoming to the **Great Plains** and acquired horses. They went from a weak tribe to a powerhouse in the Great Plains within two generations.

Navigation Act of 1651 - This act was Britain's first attempt in the colonies to ban shipments of goods going to England or to English colonies in ships that were not owned by the English. It was designed to cripple Dutch trade in the colonies, but it also caused problems for the colonists.

Mississippi River exploration - In 1673, **Louis Jolliet** and Father **Jacques Marquette** explored the **Mississippi River** south to the Arkansas River under the flag of France. French colonization was disorganized, but French trappers and traders thrived. They created numerous small outposts.

King Philip's War - This conflict was started in 1675 when **Metacomet**, who was a Wampanoag chief, called King Philip by the colonists, sought justice for the killing of one of his people. He did not receive the justice sought, and the Native Americans' unrest over English expansion and religious conversions boiled into a full-scale war. Colonies united to defeat the Wampanoag and Narragansett alliance. The conflict lasted two years, and colonists prevailed.

Nathaniel Bacon's Rebellion - In 1676, a group of settlers fought back against Native Americans in Virginia. Unfortunately, they attacked the wrong group. **William Berkeley**, governor of Virginia, had Bacon arrested as a traitor, and he pled guilty. Berkeley pardoned him. Bacon then raised an army against friendly tribes. He felt Berkeley was putting trading interests above colonists' safety, and he eventually burned **Jamestown** in a revolt against Berkeley. New York Governor **Edmund Andros** sent troops in support of Berkeley to defeat Bacon.

. . . .

FUR FAD - From about 1600 to 1850, the fad in Europe was wearing beaver fur. When the supply of beaver grew thin, the traders turned to America. At first, it was the natives who traded with men from fishing ships. Beaver hats and fur stayed in vogue until silk became the fashion in Europe.

- Penn's Colony
- Great Pueblo Revolt
- Salem Witch Trials
- New Orleans Founded
- Georgia Colony

Colonial Times

Penn's colony - A devout **Quaker** who believed in religious tolerance, William Penn was granted a charter in 1681 for a colony. His tolerance extended to all settlements within the charter, including the Swedes and Finns. The Lenni Lenape and other natives in this area were treated fairly. Penn's treaty with the **Delaware** was never broken, and **Philadelphia** became a melting pot of diversity and compromise. Rhode Island was the only other state to accept Quakers, who were also called the **Society of Friends**.

Great Pueblo Revolt - This was also called **Popé's Rebellion**. In 1680, the Pueblo Native Americans rebelled against the Spanish in New Mexico, killing 400 and causing some 2,000 settlers to move out of the area. The natives won, and the missions were abandoned. This freed thousands of horses left by the Spanish, and these animals thrived on the Plains.

Salem witch trials - Salem was the site of many witch trials in Massachusetts. Trials had occurred previously, but these became rampant **witch-hunts** around 1692. The daughters of Reverend **Samuel Parris** started these accusations. By the end of the year, 140 people had been accused, dozens were convicted and 18 were executed. The governor was alarmed, and by 1693, a person could no longer be arrested for witchcraft.

New Orleans - **Jean-Baptiste le Moyne de Bienville** founded this city at the mouth of the Mississippi River in 1718 for a private company. It became the capital of **Louisiana**, which included all of France's territory. By 1763, the unprofitable port was ceded to Spain by France in the **Treaty of Paris**.

Georgia Colony - In 1732, **James Oglethorpe** gained a charter to establish this 13th colony. It was settled by people from **debtors' prisons**.

. . . .

TOXIC TOMATOES? - *Some colonists believed tomatoes were poisonous and refused to eat them. This was a belief carried from Europe; it was said that aristocrats died after ingesting the fruit. However, the wealthy ate from pewter plates with a high lead content. The acid of the tomatoes probably absorbed the poisonous substance.*

- *Poor Richard's Almanack*
- **First Great Awakening**
- **Bering Sea and Strait**
- **Horses across the Plains**
- **French and Indian War**

Colonial Times

Poor Richard's Almanack - This almanac was first published in 1732 by **Benjamin Franklin** in Philadelphia.

First Great Awakening - This religious movement was begun by **John Wesley** and lasted from the 1720s-1740s. **Jonathan Edwards**, a participant in this movement, gave a speech that was entitled *Sinners in the Hands of an Angry God*. This period questioned the Puritan religion, and some suggested that an individual could determine what was true or untrue, rather than a preacher.

Bering Sea and Strait - In 1741, **Vitus Bering** explored the seas between Asia and present-day Alaska and determined that these land areas were not connected. The Bering Sea and Bering Straits were named after this explorer.

Horses across the Plains - By 1749, horses lived throughout the **Great Plains**, from Texas to Canada. Like the Comanche, once the Arapaho, Cheyenne and Lakota acquired horses, their loosely organized tribes developed into complex military societies. They left their semi-permanent settlements to avoid contact with the whites and conflicts with other nations, and they moved west as nomads following the buffalo.

French and Indian War - This war was fought in America between 1754 and 1763. The conflict began when **George Washington** evicted French trespassers from **Fort Duquesne** near present-day Pittsburgh. Some Native American nations sided with either the French or British, and the French were defeated by 1758. The **Treaty of Easton** was established with the tribes, and the treaty defined that there would be no more settlements west of the **Allegheny Mountains**. The treaty was quickly broken by land-hungry settlers. The **Treaty of Paris** in 1763 ended the war between the European factions.

. . . .

MOVING DAY - Native Americans did not know about wheels, and they had no vehicles. To transport goods while following the bison, they used the travois: two long sticks joined at one end and strapped on either side of a dog at the other end. These were dragged by dogs until the arrival of horses. Horses were then used with harnesses to drag larger loads.

- Plan of Union
- Criticism of British Policies
- Pontiac's Rebellion
- Proclamation of 1763
- Taxation without Representation

Revolutionary Period

Plan of the Union - **Benjamin Franklin** proposed a plan at the **Albany Congress** to unite colonies for defense against the French and Native Americans in 1754.

Criticism of British search and tax policies - **James Otis** wrote "The Rights of the British Colonies" which criticized the tax policy that the British Parliament had levied on the colonists and the policy that allowed a search without a reason in 1764. Otis coined the phrase, "a man's house is his castle."

Pontiac's Rebellion - Pontiac was a war chief of the **Ottawa**. He called for a united attack against further European settlers. Most participants were from the **Algonquin** tribes in the region of Detroit. Settlers who crossed the treaty lines were their main targets. Atrocious brutalities were committed by all, including the deliberate spread of smallpox among Native Americans. Pontiac agreed to peace in 1764 with a new treaty that established new boundaries.

Proclamation of 1763 - This act of **King George III** established a boundary along the **Appalachian Mountains** that settlers were not supposed to cross. This extended the original boundary set by the **Treaty of Easton**, and, like that treaty, the Proclamation was ignored by settlers.

Taxation without representation - Colonists reacted strongly against acts passed by Parliament starting in 1764. The **Sons of Liberty** was formed to organize protests against the British. Colonists were being taxed, but they had no voice in the government that was levying the following taxes:
Sugar Act - This taxed molasses in 1764.
Stamp Act - In 1765, this taxed all paper products, such as newspapers, documents, playing cards and dice. It was the first direct tax on the colonies and was an effort to raise money for the British military in the colonies. It required a stamp to be on paper products to prove the tax had been paid.
Townshend Acts - In 1767, this taxed glass, paint and tea.

. . . .

JOIN, OR DIE - This political cartoon was published by Franklin in 1754 in the Pennsylvania Gazette. *The cartoon appeared along-side a story concerned with the lack of unification of the colonies. It became a symbol of colonial freedom.*

- Cumberland Gap
- Boston Massacre
- Philip Freneau's Writings
- Boston Tea Party and Intolerable Acts

Revolutionary Period

Cumberland Gap - In 1767, **Daniel Boone** widened the pass that made it easier for wagons to cross the Appalachians. This allowed a large migration of Scottish and Irish settlers from the eastern colonies. The route became known as the **Wilderness Road**, and **Boonesborough** was established in Kentucky.

Boston Massacre - This was a conflict in 1770 between colonists and British soldiers. The British, surrounded by a mob of colonists, opened fire and killed five colonists and wounded six. The soldiers retreated, but eventually eight were arrested. Explaining that everyone deserved a fair defense, **John Adams** defended the soldiers. Six were acquitted, while the other two were convicted of manslaughter and given a reduced sentence.

Writings of Philip Freneau - "The Rising Glory of America," an epic patriotic poem, was coauthored by Philip Freneau and **Hugh Henry Brackenridge**. In 1771, Freneau was termed the "poet of the Revolution" and many regard him as the "Father of American Literature."

Boston Tea Party - A political protest in 1773 was started by the Sons of Liberty to protest the **Tea Act**, which had given the **East India Company** a monopoly on tea imports to the colonies. Many colonists felt Parliament had no right to impose taxes on the colonies.

Intolerable Acts - After the Tea Act, these three British laws were enacted.
Boston Port Act - This specified that no trade could be done through the Boston port until the colonists paid for the destroyed tea.
Administration of Justice Act - This was also called the **Murdering Act.** It enabled Crown officials, accused of crimes in colonies, to be tried in England.
Massachusetts Government Act - This prohibited general assembly by colonists, changed some elective offices to appointive ones and strengthened the **Quartering Act**, which forced civilians to house British soldiers.

. . . .

TEA HARBOR? - *Participants of the Boston Tea Party destroyed a ludicrous amount of tea. As a matter of fact, the tea thrown overboard could have filled about 18½ million tea bags.*

- First Continental Congress
- *Give Me Liberty* Speech
- Lexington & Concord
- Second Continental Congress

Revolutionary Period

First Continental Congress - In 1774, representatives from 12 colonies met in Philadelphia. They formally declared that Parliament had no authority to legislate for the colonies in any manner. A **Continental Association** was formed to present grievances to Parliament. The **Declaration of Rights and Resolves** was written by **John Adams**. King **George II** declared the colonists in a state of rebellion after months of correspondence with them in which they asked for self-government within the protection of the British Empire.

Give me Liberty or Give me Death! - This was a slogan that was picked up from a speech in 1775 by **Patrick Henry** as a call to arms. Henry was a lawyer from Virginia, and he became Virginia's first governor after independence.

Battles of Lexington and Concord - These battles in 1775 marked the beginning of the **American Revolution**. It was the first armed conflict between the British and the colonists. The militia at Lexington was defeated, but those in Concord pushed the British back to Boston. These conflicts occurred in April when the British marched toward Concord from Boston. **Paul Revere**, a Boston silversmith, and **William Dawes** sounded the alarm through the countryside. Both made it to Lexington where Dr. **Samuel Prescott** joined them. Dawes and Revere were stopped by the British at a roadblock, but Prescott rode on to Concord, spreading the alarm. The ride was immortalized in the **Henry Wadsworth Longfellow** poem, "**The Midnight Ride of Paul Revere**," in 1861.

Second Continental Congress - This group met in May 1775 and established the **Continental Army** under **George Washington**. In July, the **Declaration of the Causes and Necessity of Taking Up Arms**, or **Olive Branch Petition**, was written by **Thomas Jefferson** and **John Dickinson**. It was sent to King George, asking for fair treatment. The king again referred to the colonists as rebels and hired **Hessian** mercenaries to control them. The Continental Congress became a *de facto* government. A committee worked on the *Articles of Confederation*.

. . . .

"CONCORD HYMN" - *This poem was written by Ralph Waldo Emerson for the dedication of the monument in Concord of the battle that began the Revolutionary War. It is best known for its reference to the 'shot heard round the world.'*

1775 - 1776

- **Battle of Bunker Hill**
- *Common Sense*
- **Independence Declaration**
- **American Spy**
- **Battle of Trenton**

Revolutionary Period

Battle of Bunker Hill - This conflict occurred in 1775 when colonial troops arrived at Breed's Hill by mistake, which was very close to a British encampment. Sir **William Howe**, a British general, led his forces uphill to charge the Americans who refused to yield. Three attempts were made before the British succeeded, but the British lost half their troops and realized that the Americans were not going to run.

Common Sense - This pamphlet was published by **Thomas Paine** in 1776. It challenged British colonial rule in general and the concept of hereditary rule. In *Common Sense,* Paine discussed the American situation and why the colonies should seek independence. The pamphlet had a great impact on the public, and several hundred thousand were eventually sold and distributed.

Declaration of Independence - **Thomas Jefferson** was selected to write this document. He was assisted by John Adams, Benjamin Franklin, Robert Livingston and Roger Sherman. The document was discussed, amended and finally adopted on July 4, 1776. The *Declaration of Independence* proclaimed the independence and separation of the colonies from Britain.

American spy - **Nathan Hale** served as an intelligence gatherer, or spy, in the New York City area for the Continental Army. He was caught by the British and ultimately hanged in 1776 at 21 years old. It is rumored that he said the following: "I only regret that I have but one life to lose for my country."

Battle of Trenton - This battle occurred as George Washington crossed the Delaware River into New Jersey and defeated the Hessian soldiers in 1776. The crossing was hazardous due to the icy, winter weather. It is immortalized in a famous painting by **Emanuel Leutze**. The original painting of *Washington Crossing the Delaware* is in the Metropolitan Museum of Art in New York.

. . . .

SUMMER SOLDIERS - *"These are the times that try men's souls: The summer soldier and the sunshine patriot will, in this crisis, shrink from the service of his country..." ~ Thomas Paine from* Common Sense *(This famous excerpt attempted to bolster morale and shame those against the Revolution.)*

- Battle of Saratoga
- Battle of Yorktown
- *Articles of Confederation*
- Treaty of Paris
- Northwest Territory
- Northwest Indian War

Revolutionary Period

Battle of Saratoga - This battle in 1777 was a victory and a turning point for the colonists. American generals **Horatio Gates** and **Benedict Arnold** defeated British forces led by General **William Howe** and **John Burgoyne**. Arnold felt his accomplishments were undervalued. He later turned traitor and attempted to hand **West Point**, a fortified fort, over to the British.

Battle of Yorktown - This battle in 1781 was also called the **Siege of Yorktown**. French officers Marquis **de Lafayette**, Admiral **François-Joseph de Grasse** and Comte **de Rochambeau** aided patriots in defeating Lieutenant General **Charles Cornwallis** on the Yorktown Peninsula of Virginia to end the Revolution.

Articles of Confederation - This document was written in 1777 and adopted in 1781. This served as a constitution and guideline for governing the colonies.

Treaty of Paris - This treaty officially concluded the war in 1783. It was signed between American representatives, Ben Franklin, John Jay, John Adams and Henry Laurens, and the British representative of King George III, David Hartley. The result was that Britain kept part of Canada, but turned over all claims of land west to the Mississippi River.

Northwest Territory - Between 1785 and 1795, this referred to a region encompassing Ohio, Indiana, Illinois, Michigan and Wisconsin. Natives traded furs for guns with the British in Canada. The Americans continued pushing west. Widespread conflicts occurred in this area.

Northwest Indian War - This conflict was between the U.S. and British, who were supported by a confederacy of North American tribes. On the Confederacy's side were the Shawnee and Miami under chiefs **Blue Jacket** and **Little Turtle**. Battles included **Wabash** and **Fallen Timbers**. The British and Native Americans were defeated. Little Turtle supported the peace effort and aided in keeping his people out of the future Shawnee alliance led by **Tecumseh**. The conflict lasted from 1785 to 1795.

. . . .

NO GOOD WAR - *"In my opinion, there never was a good war or a bad peace."*
~ *Benjamin Franklin (Written in a letter to Josiah Quincy in 1783)*

- Northwest Ordinance
- *U.S. Constitution*
- *Federalist Papers*
- Election of 1789
- Second Great Awakening

Young Republic

Northwest Ordinance - Written in 1787 while the ***Articles of Confederation*** was in effect, this legislation outlined how new states and territories would be created from recently acquired areas. It prohibited slavery in new territories. It protected religious freedom and trial by jury, and it stipulated that states were to be responsible for public education.

Constitution - The *U.S. Constitution* was drafted amid much discussion and debate. It was designed to replace the *Articles of Confederation,* which had no power to raise money, borrow money or raise an army. Ratification began in late 1787, and by 1788, it was officially adopted. Delaware was the first state to ratify the *Constitution*, and Rhode Island was the last.

Federalist Papers - These individual essays were written in 1788 to support the new *Constitution* and to encourage states to ratify the document. The chief authors were **Alexander Hamilton**, **James Madison** and **John Jay**. "Essay Number 10" was written by Madison, and it explained why a republican government would work for a large country. All the essays were later published together as a book, *The Federalist Papers*.

Election of 1789 - In the first U.S. presidential election, **George Washington** won by a unanimous vote, and **John Adams** became vice-president.

Second Great Awakening - The rise of evangelical ministries and preachers, such as **Charles Finney**, promoted revivals as a way to reach the people between 1790 and 1840. His premise was that people were transformed by grace, not merely saved as dictated by Anglicans and Puritans. His main point was the idea that people could change and then defeat sin. To enable people to defeat sin, his plan included eliminating alcohol, illiteracy, slavery and suppression of any people. This led to the temperance and suffrage movements.

. . . .

AN ARM & A LEG - During colonial times, there were no cameras. A person's image was either sculpted or painted. One painting of Washington shows him behind a desk with one arm behind his back, and another shows both legs and arms. Prices charged by painters were based on how many arms and legs were to be visible in the painting. Hence the expression, "Okay, but it'll cost you an arm and a leg."

- *Bill of Rights*
- Cotton Gin
- Whiskey Rebellion
- Jay Treaty

Young Republic

Bill of Rights - The first ten amendments to the *Constitution*, or the *Bill of Rights*, were ratified in 1791. The *Constitution* did not guarantee personal freedom for individuals. It did not limit the government's power in judicial proceedings, and it failed to reserve some powers for the states and the public. The *Bill of Rights* addressed these issues. These amendments guaranteed freedom of speech, choice of religion and the press. They ensured the rights to assembly, to bear arms, to have trials by jury, to due process and to reasonable bail. It precluded quartering of soldiers during peacetime and unreasonable searches and seizures. Rights not mentioned were not allowed to be denied. State governments assumed rights not given to the national government.

Invention of the cotton gin - **Eli Whitney** invented and patented the mechanical cotton gin in 1793 to make large scale processing of cotton possible. Thus, farmers increased the amount of land they devoted to the cotton crop.

Whiskey Rebellion - This revolt began in 1791 when **Alexander Hamilton**, Secretary of the Treasury, proposed a tax on "spirits distilled within the United States." Hamilton wanted to use the money to help reduce the debt incurred during the Revolutionary War. Frontier farmers felt this was an unfair tax because it affected Westerners more than Easterners. By 1794, the protests became violent. President Washington led a militia to western Pennsylvania, and the rebels dispersed. The tax was repealed in 1802.

Jay Treaty - A 1794 agreement between the U.S. and Great Britain, this treaty resolved some of the issues remaining since the **Treaty of Paris** and was the beginning of ten years of peaceful trade between the countries. According to the treaty, British Army units left their forts in the Northwest Territory, and the U.S. was granted limited rights to trade with other British colonies.

· ·

AMENDMENTS - The U.S. Constitution has 27 amendments that have been adopted and ratified. The Constitution of Texas, however, has 653 amendments, and it is one of the longest state constitutions. The Alabama Constitution is longer and has been amended 800 times even though it is 25 years younger than Texas' document.

- XYZ Affair
- Alien and Sedition Acts
- Election of 1800
- *Marbury v. Madison*

Young Republic

XYZ Affair - This was an attempt by U.S. diplomats to negotiate with French diplomats concerning trade in 1797. **Charles Talleyrand**, the French Foreign Minister, demanded bribes before starting the talks or attempting to control French "pirates" harassing American ships. When the American public learned of the bribes, they were enraged and ready for war. France dropped their demands and stopped the piracy. The French diplomats' names were replaced by "X", "Y" and "Z" in documents released by the Adams' administration.

Alien and Sedition Acts - These acts were adopted in 1798 and evolved from a French emissary trying to stir up trouble in the U.S. He wanted the Americans to aid France with its fight against Britain. The acts, however, greatly limited free speech, free press and free assembly. They also allowed states to nullify laws that they deemed unconstitutional, which eventually resulted in the **Nullification Crisis** leading up to the **Civil War**.

Election of 1800 - **Thomas Jefferson** was elected as the third U.S. president with **Aaron Burr** as vice-president. Originally, when votes were cast for president, the person receiving the most became president and the runner-up became vice-president. The result of this election was a tie that required 36 separate votes to break. The **12th Amendment** was passed requiring separate ballots for president and vice-president.

Marbury v. Madison - This Supreme Court case of 1803 established that a federal law, such as the **Judiciary Act of 1789**, could be ruled invalid because it violated the *Constitution*. Chief Justice **John Marshall**, a Federalist, formally established the Supreme Court's responsibility for **judicial review**.

• •

XYZ EMBARGO *- The political cartoon above shows the 'French' turtle snapping at the American shipper. The shipper has named the turtle,* OGrabMe, *which is the word* Embargo *spelled backwards.*

- Louisiana Purchase
- Lewis and Clark Expedition
- Chesapeake-Leopard Affair

Expansion & Turmoil

Louisiana Purchase - When France regained control of the **Louisiana Territory** from Spain in 1802, it refused to allow the U.S. access to the port of **New Orleans**. This created problems with Americans that France did not need. They already had trouble with the Caribbean Islands and Britain. U.S. negotiators, **Robert Livingston** and **James Monroe**, went to France and purchased this territory for $15 million. This doubled the size of the U.S. and included the port of New Orleans. The U.S. took formal possession in 1803.

Lewis and Clark Expedition (1804-1806) - This group mapped the western part of the U.S. with the **Corps of Discovery**, a unit of the U.S. Army. President Thomas Jefferson authorized the mission that started at St. Louis, Missouri and proceeded up the Missouri River. They met **Toussaint Charbonneau** and his wife **Sacajawea**, a Shoshone, in a Mandan-Hidatsa village in the Dakotas, and both joined them and agreed to act as translators. They arrived at the Pacific Ocean in 1805. The group returned after winter, having recorded more than 170 plants, 120 birds and animals previously unknown to Europeans, as well as having encountered more than 50 Native American tribes. This expedition gave Americans a claim to the **Pacific Northwest**.

Chesapeake-Leopard Affair - This was a naval engagement near Norfolk, VA. The **HMS *Leopard***, a British ship, fired on the **USS *Chesapeake*** while it was in port. This violated American sovereignty. The American ship surrendered, and the British boarded to retrieve deserters. This led to passage of the **Embargo Act of 1807,** which closed American ports to export shipping and placed restrictions on imports from Britain. It ultimately hurt the U.S. more than the British or French.

· ·

LATER GATORS - Louisiana boasts a large population of Cajuns, *many of whom are descendants of the French who moved to Acadia in Canada in the early 1600s. Those who wouldn't pledge allegiance to the King of England when the British took over were deported out of Canada in the 1700s. Originally known as* Acadians, *their name was eventually shortened to* Cajuns.

- *Clermont*
- **War of 1812**

- **Tecumseh's War**

Expansion & Turmoil

Clermont - This was the first functional steamboat, which was launched in 1807 by **Robert Fulton**, the builder. It was named the ***North River Steamboat*** and nicknamed ***Fulton's Folly***. The name *Clermont* has long been used for this steamboat, but it was not the name given by Fulton.

War of 1812 (1812-1814) - There were multiple causes of this war. American sailors were impressed into the British Navy, settlers on the western frontier were upset that the English in Canada were giving weapons to Native Americans, and a war with Britain meant war with Spain with the U.S. possibly acquiring Florida from Spain. This war ended in 1814 with the **Treaty of Ghent**, but it did not address the issues that had triggered the war.

President **James Madison** and the **Federalists** did not want a war, but **Henry Clay** and the **War Hawks**, who favored war, prevailed. The war united the eastern and western portions of America and helped give the nation a sense of unity and its own identity. The war also crushed the weakening alliance of Native American nations in the Ohio Valley, who had sided with the British in an effort to remove western settlers.

Tecumseh's War - A coalition of Ohio Valley Native Americans led by a Shawnee, **Chief Tecumseh**, fought this war against American settlers under General **William Henry Harrison** at **Tippecanoe** in 1811. It was costly on both sides, although Harrison claimed a victory. Tecumseh tried to rebuild the coalition. He also had a loose alliance with the British. His war continued during the **War of 1812**. The **Battle of the Thames** in 1813 was the last major battle between eastern Native Americans and settlers. The British allies were defeated near Moraviantown, and the battle ended with the death of Tecumseh and the destruction of the Native American coalition.

. . . .

CLERMONT - *Robert Fulton's first steamboat was 150 feet long with paddle wheels on either side of the hull. It traveled less than five miles per hour, leaving New York on the Hudson River and arriving at Albany 32 hours later, a distance of 150 miles.*

1814 - 1815

- Creek Wars
- Battle of Fort McHenry
- Hartford Convention
- Battle of New Orleans

Expansion & Turmoil

Creek Wars - The Creeks of Alabama, Georgia, Florida and Mississippi were divided about whom to support, the Shawnee and British or the Americans. The **Red Sticks** supported Tecumseh and the Shawnee. The **White Sticks** and **Cherokee** supported the Americans under **Andrew Jackson**. The Red Stick Creeks were defeated in 1814. The **Treaty of Fort Jackson**, also called **Treaty of Horseshoe Bend**, ended the Creek Wars. It took 23 million acres from ALL of the Creek peoples, including the Creek and Cherokee, who had been allies. The path was cleared for American settlements westward.

Battle of Fort McHenry - This battle took place in 1814 after the British had burned the White House and occupied Washington, D.C. **Francis Scott Key** wrote the poem "**Defense of Fort McHenry**" while watching the British Navy in the Chesapeake Bay bomb the fort. The poem was set to the music of a popular British tune. Woodrow Wilson used the song in 1916, and it became the national anthem in 1931.

Hartford Convention - This meeting was held in secret by the **New England Federalist Party** between 1814 and 1815 to discuss grievances concerning the **War of 1812** and problems with the increasing power of the federal government. The convention concluded after the signing of the **Treaty of Ghent**; its secrecy made many people distrust the Federalists, and this party faded away.

Battle of New Orleans - This conflict was actually part of the **War of 1812**, but it occurred after the Treaty of Ghent was signed. News traveled slowly, and those near New Orleans did not know the war had ended. General **Andrew Jackson** soundly defeated the British led by General **Edward Pakenham**. The battle was fought just south of New Orleans in 1815.

. . . .

"BATTLE OF NEW ORLEANS" - *This was a song written by Jimmy Driftwood, a school principal in Arkansas with an interest in history. It was popularized by singer Johnny Horton in 1959 and became the Number 1 song on the Billboard charts. The lyrics provide a comical version of what happened at the battle.*

- **Convention of 1818**
- **Adams-Onis Treaty**
- **Panic of 1819**

- *McCulloch v. Maryland*
- **Missouri Compromise**

Expansion & Turmoil

Convention of 1818 - The 49th parallel from the **Great Lakes** to the **Rocky Mountains** was defined as the border between the U.S. and Canada during this convention.

Adams-Onís Treaty (1819) - Also called the **Purchase of Florida Treaty**, this was signed by **John Quincy Adams**, Secretary of State, and the Spanish foreign minister, **Luis de Onís**. Ratified in 1831, the U.S. gained Florida and Oregon. Mexico kept Texas and the area west to California, because of the treaty.

Panic of 1819 - This was the first major depression in U.S. history. It was triggered in part by the debt America owed as a result of the War of 1812. People of the South and West were hurt more than Easterners. This ultimately caused increased feelings of "separateness" between the different areas.

McCulloch v. Maryland - This case was heard by the Supreme Court in 1819. The issue was whether the Federal Government had sovereign power over states. Chief Justice **John Marshall** handed down the court's decision in favor of federal employee **James McCulloch**. As the head of the Baltimore Branch of the Second Bank of the U.S., McCulloch had refused to pay a Maryland state tax. The Court ruled that a state could not tax the Federal Government.

Missouri Compromise (1820) - This agreement served as a temporary fix to the question of slavery. When Missouri asked to enter the Union as a slave state, the balance between slave and non-slave states would change. To make states even, Maine entered the Union as a free state, that is, one that did not allow slavery. The remaining section of the Louisiana Territory was divided. Slavery could exist south of the line marked by the 36° N parallel, and there would be no slavery north of the line. The Compromise remained in effect until the **Kansas-Nebraska Act**.

. . . .

SCHOOL OF HARD KNOCKS - When the English factory system was introduced in the 1820s, education was not mandatory. Instead of going to school, many children were forced to work six days a week from dawn to dusk. Women were paid about ¼ of what men were paid.

- English Factory System
- Monroe Doctrine
- Election of 1824
- Election of 1828
- Underground Railroad

Expansion & Turmoil

English factory system - This process grew at the beginning of the **Industrial Revolution** in England, and it was introduced to the U.S. in 1823. This method of manufacturing used machinery, unskilled labor and more centralized factories. This increased employment and production. The abundance of jobs also increased immigration, especially from Ireland.

Monroe Doctrine - This policy, initiated by President **James Monroe** in 1823, was intended to keep Spain from reclaiming newly independent **South American** nations and to prohibit Russians, who controlled present-day Alaska, from encroaching into the **Pacific Northwest**. The policy stated that any attempt to interfere with states in the Americas would be considered aggression. It also stated that the U.S. would not interfere in Europe's internal affairs.

Election of 1824 - **John Quincy Adams** was ultimately elected president, besting **Andrew Jackson**. There was no majority reached in the election process, and the House of Representatives was called to resolve the issue. The Speaker of the House, **Henry Clay**, gave support to Adams, and when Adams won, Clay was appointed Secretary of State. Jackson and his supporters labeled the whole affair a *corrupt bargain*.

Election of 1828 - After a campaign rife with mudslinging, Andrew Jackson beat John Quincy Adams to become president. Citizens from the South and West were happy because they viewed Jackson as a common man. He was a populist and united the **Democrats**. He promoted the removal of the native populations in the east to the Oklahoma territory.

Underground Railroad - This transportation route, not really a railroad, began around 1830 to help slaves reach freedom in the northern U.S. and Canada. It was managed by freed or escaped slaves. **Harriet Tubman** escaped from slavery and then made numerous trips to the South to help others.

. . . .

RAILROAD CODE - Slaves heading north via the Underground Railroad sought safety in stations *or* depots *which included barns, caves, riverbanks and churches. The abolitionists who assisted were known as* conductors. *Some conductors posed as slaves to help other slaves escape at night.*

1830 - 1832

- Indian Removal Act
- Nat Turner's Rebellion
- Black Hawk's War
- Nullification Crisis

Expansion & Turmoil

Indian Removal Act - Supported by President Jackson, this act was passed in 1830. However, good land in the South belonging to Native Americans was traded to Americans while the Native Americans received land west of the Mississippi in exchange, requiring them to move. Many of the natives had agreed to the removal; others were bitter landholders and farmers with extensive properties that they did not want to leave. This paved the way for the mass relocation known as the **Trail of Tears**.

Nat Turner's Rebellion - A group of rebellious slaves led by **Nat Turner** began a killing spree in Virginia in 1831. They went from farm to farm, killing around 60 people. By the next day, the mob of slaves had expanded to more than 40. The whites formed vigilante-like posses and eventually killed more than 100 of the rebels and other slaves. The Virginia legislature, by a very narrow margin, voted to retain slavery the next year.

Black Hawk's War - A **Sauk** leader, Chief **Black Hawk** led his people back to Illinois after the U.S. failed to keep the promises made to them when they moved across the Mississippi River. Black Hawk and his people returned to find their cornfields overrun by cattle and much of their village destroyed by new settlers in 1832. A four-month long war ensued. It ended at the **Battle of Bad Axe** with the total defeat of Black Hawk and his few remaining people.

Nullification Crisis - South Carolina passed an **Ordinance of Nullification** in 1832, which declared that federal tariffs were unconstitutional within the state. These tariffs placed on British goods benefitted northern states. Tariffs favored manufacturing concerns, which were primarily in the North, over the commerce and agriculture of the South. Rather than uphold a states' rights position, President Jackson asked Congress to use force. A judge ruled that the Ordinance violated a treaty with Britain and was unconstitutional. This foreshadowed the **American Civil War**.

. . . .

ALL MINE - In 1828, gold was discovered on Cherokee lands. Ignoring the boundary lines, white settlers helped themselves, and the Georgia Gold Rush ensued. The state of Georgia 'protected' the Cherokees by forbidding them to mine for gold on their own land. The Indian Removal Act of 1830 and the Trail of Tears followed.

- Farm Tool Improvements
- Trail of Tears
- Great Migration
- Invention of the Telegraph

Expansion & Turmoil

Farm tool improvements (1834-1836) - **Cyrus McCormick** patented a reaper to cut and gather grains mechanically. Soon after, **John Deere** perfected the cast-steel plow. These inventions allowed farmers to expand operations on the hard-packed, but fertile prairies of the **Great Plains**. Farming became a big business, and immigrants flocked westward.

Trail of Tears - Shortly after enactment of the **Indian Removal Act**, more than 45,000 Native Americans were forcibly relocated to Indian Territory in present-day Oklahoma. Thousands perished during the marches due to cold, disease and hunger. The removal continued from 1831 to 1840.

Great Migration - Having returned from Oregon to St. Louis, **Marcus Whitman** started a return trip and joined a wagon train traveling the **Oregon Trail** with about 1,000 settlers in 1843. The settlers were told the trail was not suitable for wagons, but Whitman agreed to lead the wagons. He felt they could build whatever road improvements were necessary on the way. This was the beginning of a mass westward migration. The Oregon Trail covered 2,000 miles. Migrations continued until a transcontinental railroad was finished.

Invention of the telegraph - Though invented a few years earlier, it wasn't until 1844 that **Samuel Morris** was able to get Congress to support a line from Baltimore to Washington and allow him to prove what the telegraph could do. His code, a series of dots and dashes, was used to send the first message, "What hath God wrought?"

. . . .

OREGON TRAIL - *It took approximately one week to travel 85 miles by wagon.*

1845 - 1846

- Autobiography of a Slave
- Texas Annexation
- Manifest Destiny
- Knickerbocker Rules
- Mexican-American War

Expansion & Turmoil

Autobiography of a slave - In 1845, **Frederick Douglass** wrote his autobiography, *Narrative of the Life of Frederick Douglass, An American Slave* to prove that he had, in fact, been a slave named **Frederick Bailey**. He spent two years in Britain promoting the abolitionist cause and bought his freedom upon his return. He advised **Abraham Lincoln** to make the abolishment of slavery a focus of the **Civil War** and allow blacks to fight for the Union army.

Texas annexation - The Texas territory was annexed to the U.S. in 1845. The area covered land from the Louisiana border west to present-day Central Texas. In the agreement, Texas was allowed to keep its public lands and enter the Union as a slave-holding state.

Manifest Destiny - In 1845, **John L. O' Sullivan** wrote for the *New York Post* and was the first to use the term *Manifest Destiny* to describe America's westward expansion and the restless need of people to settle new frontiers to populate the entire continent.

Knickerbocker Rules - In 1845, **Alexander Cartwright** formalized the rules of baseball. The "Knickerbocker Rules" elevated the children's game to an official sport for grown men.

Mexican-American War (1846-1848) - This war was fought between the U.S. and Mexico primarily over the disputed southern border of Texas. The U.S. invaded Mexico in 1847. By fall, **Winfield Scott**, U.S. general, had captured Mexico City. The **Treaty of Guadalupe Hidalgo** was signed, giving the U.S. title to the lands that eventually became the states of New Mexico, Utah, Nevada, Arizona, California and part of Colorado. It established the **Rio Grande River** as the southern border of Texas.

. . . .

REMEMBER THE ALAMO! - *Santa Anna, the commander of the Mexican Army, successfully defeated the Texas rebels at the Alamo in 1836. This was the Texians' cry, rally troops to remember their defeat, not their win. The saying inspired the Texians to get revenge and finally defeat Santa Anna.*

1846 - 1850

- Mormon Migration
- Seneca Falls Convention
- Transportation Expansion
- Compromise of 1850

Expansion & Turmoil

Mormon Migration (1846-1847) - **Brigham Young** became the leader of the Mormon congregation after the murder of **Joseph Smith**, the religion's founder. There was conflict between the Mormons and other settlers of the area. Young decided they should leave Illinois and find land no one else wanted. They moved to the area around the **Great Salt Lake** in Utah.

Seneca Falls Convention - In 1848, this convention was the first that was concerned with women's rights. Its intent was to discuss social, civil and religious rights of women, marking the beginning of the women's rights movement. **Elizabeth Cady Stanton** and **Lucretia Mott**, both abolitionists, led the convention and then the movement. **Susan B. Anthony**, a delegate, began forming grassroots organizations in New York championing women's rights.

Transportation expansion - The **Baltimore and Ohio Railroad (B&O)** connected the East Coast to Chicago. In 1848, another railroad was opened from Chicago to Galena, Illinois, which was a hub on the Mississippi River. In the same year, the **Illinois and Michigan Canal** opened, enabling navigation between the **Great Lakes** and the **Mississippi River**. Chicago was thus becoming a major transportation hub for most goods, finished and raw, that crossed the nation.

Compromise of 1850 - This was a collection of five bills drafted by **Henry Clay** and promoted by **Stephen Douglas**. States were given power to create their own constitutions and decide the slavery question for themselves. California would be admitted to the Union without becoming a territory first. Slave trade in the District of Columbia was banned. The Fugitive Slave Laws were strengthened. Debts of Texas were absorbed by the U.S. No one was completely happy, but the Union was preserved.

. . . .

☑VOTE *19TH AMENDMENT - In 1872, Susan B. Anthony was arrested for voting in a national election. Anthony told the judge that she refused "to pay a dollar" for the unjust penalty, presenting the argument that her 'natural rights' had been denied. Her case was won, but the battle was far from over. The 19th Amendment, which would allow women to vote, was not passed until after Anthony's death at 86 years old. Susan B. Anthony was both loved and hated for most of her life. Why? How were women viewed at that time?*

- *Uncle Tom's Cabin*
- Kansas-Nebraska Act
- Central Park
- *Dred Scott v. Sanford*
- Discovery of Oil

Expansion & Turmoil

Uncle Tom's Cabin - This book, written by **Harriet Beecher Stowe** was published as a newspaper serial and later as a book. Stowe used stories from former slaves to create the characters in the story. She aimed to make a difference and did. Her book inspired people to join the **abolitionist movement**.

Kansas-Nebraska Act - This act of 1854 adopted by Congress annulled the **Missouri Compromise of 1850** and confirmed the concept of **popular sovereignty**. Kansas and Nebraska became U.S. territories and were permitted to decide whether they would allow slavery in their areas. However, pro-slavery and anti-slavery groups both moved to the Kansas Territory. These groups opposed each other violently in what was termed *Bleeding Kansas.*

Central Park - **Frederick Law Olmsted** and **Calvert Vaux** were among the first to use landscape architecture when they began designing this public park in New York City in 1857. It was officially completed in 1876 and has been used as a model for urban parks around the world.

Dred Scott v. Sanford - **Dred Scott**, a black slave, attempted to sue for his freedom in 1857. He claimed he and his wife should be free because they had lived in a free state. The Supreme Court decided that Scott did not have the same rights as white Americans and therefore could not file a lawsuit. The court also declared the **Missouri Compromise of 1820** unconstitutional because Congress had no power to prohibit slavery in territories.

Discovery of oil - By the mid-1800s, whale oil was the most common lamp fuel, and it was expensive. In Austria, a lamp was created that could burn **kerosene**, a substance produced from oil shale. **George H. Bissel** and **James Townsend** bought land in Titusville in Pennsylvania and sunk a well, that hit oil at 69 feet. For the first time, oil was tapped at its source.

• •

STAR STRUCK *- Central Park was the setting for a scene in* Home Alone 2: Lost in New York *and was the backdrop of the movie,* Ghostbusters. *The Strawberry Fields Memorial in the park honors the life of former Beatles rock band member, John Lennon, who lived just across the street from Central Park with his wife, Yoko Ono, just before he was assassinated.*

- **Harper's Ferry**
- **Pony Express**
- **Election of 1860**
- **Beginning of Civil War**

U.S. Civil War

Harper's Ferry - Abolitionist **John Brown** led a raid in 1859 to get weapons from the arsenal at Harper's Ferry in Virginia. His intent was to start a slave uprising throughout the South. After the raid, they attacked plantations and freed the slaves. They were captured by forces led by **Robert E. Lee**. Brown was convicted of treason and hung. This was one of the catalysts for the **Civil War**.

Pony Express - Begun in 1860, this mail service was one of the most colorful pieces of American history, although it was short-lived and a financial failure. It lasted only a year and a half. It took 24 days for mail to travel from Missouri to California. The Pony Express covered 2,000 miles in ten days. Each rider rode about 100 miles. The transcontinental telegraph ended the need for the service 18 months later.

Election of 1860 - The winner was **Abraham Lincoln**, a Republican. Some 81% of the voting population cast their votes, and this was the second highest turnout in history. The issues centered on expansion of slavery and rights of those who owned slaves. The runner-up was **Stephen A. Douglas**, a Democrat. The famous **Lincoln-Douglas Debates** were held two years before, and Lincoln published the debates. The debates vaulted him into the presidency.

Beginning of the Civil War - Major **Robert Anderson** was the commander of 85 men in South Carolina at **Fort Sumter**, which was on an island in Charleston Harbor. The state had seceded in December of 1860, so Anderson and the **Union Army** were in enemy territory in 1861. Anderson had refused to surrender the fort, and General **P. G. T. Beauregard** began firing and continued for about 34 hours. The fort officially surrendered on April 14. Union soldiers were allowed to return to Union ships located outside of the harbor. This **Battle of Fort Sumter** was the initial conflict of the **American Civil War**.

. . . .

SPEAKING OF LINCOLN - The Lincoln-Douglas Debates consisted of seven debates between Lincoln and Douglas. The subject they debated was slavery, and each lasted for 90 minutes. Today, there is a national competition called Lincoln-Douglas Debate *that is hosted by the National Speech and Debate Association.*

- Secession
- Civil War
- Confederate Victories
- Union Victories

U.S. Civil War

Secession - Between Lincoln's election and inauguration, seven southern states seceded from the U.S. They were disgruntled by Lincoln's anti-slavery expansion platform. These states formed the **Confederate States of America (CSA)**. After the war started, six more states and two territories joined the CSA. The South was primarily agricultural, and many depended on slaves to farm their properties. Limitation on owning slaves threatened their way of life.

Civil War (1861-1865) - After Fort Sumter, the war between the U.S., or **Union**, and the CSA lasted four long, bloody years. It left over 600,000 Union and Confederate soldiers dead, and it destroyed much of the South. Ultimately, the Confederacy collapsed, slavery was abolished, and the very difficult period of **Reconstruction** in the South began.

Confederate victories - The **First** and **Second Battles at Bull Run** were victories for the South. During the second battle, **Robert E. Lee** was the commander for the CSA, and General **Thomas J. Jackson** earned his nickname of **Stonewall**. Other victories during the early years included the **Seven Days Battle**, the **Battle of Fredericksburg** and the **Battle of Chancellorsville**. The Battle of Fredericksburg in 1862 was considered the Union's worst defeat.

Union victories - Victories for the Union included the **Battle of Antietam**, which was part of the Maryland campaign fought in 1862. It was the bloodiest single day of conflict in U.S. history with more than 22,000 dead. **Gettysburg** was fought in 1863 over a three-day period. It was the costliest battle of the war with more than 50,000 dead. Gettysburg is considered the turning point as it was General Lee's last opportunity to try to win a Confederate victory on Union soil. General **George Meade** was the victorious Union commander. Other critical battles were fought at **Shiloh**, **Vicksburg** and **New Orleans**.

· ·

HORSEHAIR - When the Confederates ran out of silk thread for suturing wounds, they used horsehair instead. As a result, the success rate of recovering from wounds was greater in the South. Why? Because the horsehair was sterilized by boiling -- the silk thread was not.

- Homestead Act
- Emancipation Proclamation
- March to the Sea
- Sand Creek Massacre

U.S. Civil War

Homestead Act - During the Civil War, this act was passed in 1862 to allow citizens to apply for federal land grants of 160 acres of land. They could keep the land if they built a house and lived there for five years. Congress wanted to encourage independent farmers, rather than wealthy planters who would develop it with slave labor. More than 500,000 homesteads and 80 million acres had been claimed by 1900.

Emancipation Proclamation - Issued by **Abraham Lincoln** in 1863, this official executive order freed slaves in the states that were 'in rebellion.' It did not apply to slaves in border states or areas occupied by the Union since they were not rebelling. The proclamation had no legally binding effect on the southern states, but it allowed the Union to recruit black soldiers. It did not make the ex-slaves citizens.

March to the Sea - A Union general, **William Tecumseh Sherman,** was considered one of the key designers of modern warfare strategy. He used the *scorched earth policy* in his march from Atlanta to Savannah in 1864. Sherman defeated armies and destroyed or burned anything that could be used by the South in a war capacity, including railroads, grain stores, cotton facilities, crops, industry, supplies, bridges and personal properties. He ignored the impact this had on the civilian population.

Sand Creek Massacre - Colonel **John M. Chivington** led an army in a surprise attack on a peaceful camp of Cheyenne and Arapaho on Sand Creek in Colorado in 1864. The Native American camp was in peace negotiations with the commander at Fort Lyon. Chief **Black Kettle** raised an American flag and a white flag of surrender, but Chivington continued the attack, killing about 100 Native Americans, most of whom were women and children. This incident triggered a war between the U.S. and Cheyenne-Arapaho alliance.

. . . .

TIP YOUR HAT - President Lincoln had 18 months of formal schooling. He established Thanksgiving as a national holiday. Lincoln kept his important documents inside his hat. He was the first president with a beard, and he used the telegraph like email to communicate with generals.

- Battle of Appomattox
- Lincoln's Assassination
- Reconstruction Era

U.S. Civil War

Battle of Appomattox Courthouse - After several skirmishes, Confederate General **Robert E. Lee** launched an attack in 1865 to break through Union forces, thinking he was facing cavalry alone. However, Union General **Ulysses S. Grant** had his cavalry backed by two corps of infantry. Ending the fighting near Appomattox Courthouse, Lee finally asked to surrender. Though not the end of the Civil War, this battle heralded the end. Grant gave the Confederate troops generous terms, allowing them to return to their homes with their mounts and with food. This served as a model for the remaining armies.

Assassination of Lincoln - Actor **John Wilkes Booth** assassinated Lincoln in 1865 at **Ford's Theatre**, and **Andrew Johnson** became president. This produced a backlash of anger at the South. Lincoln was remembered for his famous **House Divided speech**, which forewarned the nation that civil war was likely. His **Gettysburg Address**, which dedicated a cemetery on part of the Gettysburg battlefield, was his most quoted speech. His **Second Inaugural Address** ended with the paragraph whose initial statement began "With malice toward none; with charity for all..."

Reconstruction Era (1865-1877) - Lincoln and then Johnson had a moderate approach to the rebuilding the South. The **Radical Republican** group in Congress stymied their moderate direction and called for radical changes. They planned a free labor economy in the South using the U.S. Army and **Freedmen's Bureau**, an agency created to protect legal rights of freed slaves.

Thousands went south as missionaries, teachers, politicians and businessmen. Southerners termed many **Carpetbaggers**, who preyed on Southerners by buying up lands and businesses at desperation prices. Biracial governments were made up of Carpetbaggers, freedmen and **Scalawags**, who were white Southerners who supported Reconstruction. Most consider Reconstruction a failure because it left the South in a poverty-stricken condition.

REAL AMERICANS - Grant's adjutant was Ely S. Parker, a Native-American of the Seneca tribe. Parker recorded the terms of surrender in a document. Lee, upon discovering Parker to be a Seneca remarked, "It is good to have one real American here." Parker replied, "Sir, we are all Americans."

- Ku Klux Klan
- 13th Amendment
- Civil Rights Bill of 1866
- National Labor Union

Reconstruction

Ku Klux Klan - From 1865 through the 1870s, this hate group consisted of small bands that were not organized and is often referenced as the **KKK** or **Klan**. They considered the new biracial governments to be corrupt, and they fought to restore white supremacy to the South. Their means were violence coupled with burning crosses and terrorism of the blacks and the whites who supported the Reconstruction movement. This type of group with the same name cropped up again in 1915 and again in the 1950s.

13th Amendment - This Amendment was adopted in 1865 to abolish slavery throughout the nation, except as punishment for a crime. It was the first of three **Reconstruction Amendments** that followed the Civil War.

Civil Rights Bill of 1866 - This bill was passed overriding two vetoes by President **Andrew Johnson**. It defined U.S. citizenship and gave all people, except Native Americans, "full and equal benefit of all laws..." of the U.S. Johnson thought the Federal Government should be less involved in state affairs, but others felt that the Federal Government should assist in molding a multiracial southern society. Congressmen **John Bingham** and others argued that Congress did not have the power to pass this bill. After passage of the **14th Amendment**, it was reenacted.

National Labor Union - In 1866, this Union was comprised of skilled and unskilled workers, farmers and reformers. It was formed to try to persuade Congress to address labor issues, such as working conditions and work hours. The organization fell apart by 1873, but created a greater awareness of work-related issues among the public and paved the way for future change.

. . . .

JIM CROW - The Compromise of 1877 marked the end of military Reconstruction and became a significant factor in ushering in the Jim Crow Laws. These laws introduced a 'separate, but equal' clause that allowed a type of legal discrimination that separated blacks and whites in public places, forbade intermarriage, and restricted the voting rights of African Americans. The name Jim Crow dated to a once-popular song-and-dance act about a black slave, performed by a white man in the 1830s. Jim Crow came to be a derogatory term, reminiscent of segregation.

- **Goodnight-Loving Trail**
- **Bozeman Trail**
- **Indian Problem**
- **Alaska**

Growth of U.S.

Goodnight-Loving Cattle Trail - This trail was blazed when **Charles Goodnight** and **Oliver Loving** decided to bring longhorn cattle north from Texas to the settlers, soldiers and Navajos in New Mexico in 1866. The trail was extended to Denver and on to Cheyenne in Wyoming. Former Civil War soldiers and drifters thus became trail-riding cowboys to move the cattle north.

Bozeman Trail - Active from 1863 to 1868, this connected the gold rush area of **Montana Territory** to the **Oregon Trail**. It was widened by **John Bozeman** and **John Jacobs** so that wagons could get to the goldfields in Montana. This territory had been given to the Sioux, Cheyenne and others by the **Treaty of Fort Laramie** in 1868. The military built forts across Indian Territory to protect the trespassers. **Lakota** Chief **Red Cloud** began a two-year conflict to remove the forts by ambushing soldiers' hunting parties and supply trains. This route was eventually abandoned. The area was returned to the natives.

The Indian Question (1866-1876) - After the Civil War, many from the South and some from the North headed west, which increased conflicts between settlers and natives. White settlers and miners refused to acknowledge the treaty boundaries set for Native American lands. The government felt obligated to protect the settlers and miners in spite of their trespassing onto Native American lands. Wars on the Great Plains between Native Americans and the U.S. cavalry began in earnest.

Alaska - In 1867, **William H. Seward**, U.S. Secretary of State, persuaded President Johnson to approve the purchase of the Russian territory of Alaska from Emperor **Alexander II** to protect borders in the far northwest. The cost was more than $7 million or about two cents per acre. The purchase was also called *Seward's Icebox*, or *Seward's Folly* by the press.

. . . .

ANOTHER PATH - Oliver Loving was shot in the arm by Comanche Indians on the trail bearing his name and died from gangrene caused by the wound. Charles Goodnight later went on to produce the first cattalo *by breeding buffalo with cattle. As a result of his business and pioneering ventures, Goodnight died a wealthy man in his nineties.*

- First Impeachment
- 14th Amendment
- Transcontinental Railroad
- 15th Amendment
- Gilded Age

Growth of U.S.

First impeachment - President **Andrew Johnson** was impeached in 1868 by the House of Representatives after continuous battles over government policy concerning the southern states after the Civil War. **Radical Republicans** wanted immediate and strict changes while Johnson favored a slower approach. The impeachment proceedings failed in the Senate by one vote, and Johnson was allowed to complete his term.

14th Amendment - In 1868, this second of the **Reconstruction Amendments** gave citizenship to all people 'born or naturalized' in the U.S., 'equal protection under the laws.' The Amendment guaranteed citizenship to African Americans and emancipated slaves; it excluded Native Americans.

Transcontinental Railroad - The connection of the existing **Union Pacific** and **Central Pacific** railroads at **Promontory Point** in Utah occurred in 1869. This completed the transcontinental railroad across the U.S. It was celebrated by driving a **'golden spike'** into the last railroad tie.

15th Amendment - Adopted in 1870, this Amendment guaranteed the right to vote for all male citizens regardless of race, but did not include Native Americans. It was the third and last of the **Reconstruction Amendments**.

Gilded Age (1870s-c. 1900) - This was an era of rapid economic growth, particularly in the North and in the West. Immigration accelerated with available high wages. Industrialization was spurred. However, this was a period of poverty with many of the immigrants being very poor. There were two depressions during the period, the **Panic of 1873** and the **Panic of 1893**. *The Gilded Age: A Tale of Today* was a book by **Mark Twain**, the pen name for Samuel Clemens. The characters reflected the materialism and corruption of the times, and the book's title eventually became the name of the period.

· ·

WIT & WISDOM - Mark Twain was said to have used pictures when he delivered some of his famous speeches and was convinced that drawing pictures could help children learn and remember history. He was known for his wit and sense of humor: "A man who carries a cat by the tail learns something he can learn in no other way." ~ *Mark Twain*

1870 - 1876

- **Great Chicago Fire**
- **Yellowstone Park**
- **Red River War**
- **Invention of Telephone**

Growth of U.S.

Great Chicago Fire - A raging fire in 1871 leveled the entire business district of Chicago, killing 300 and leaving more than 100,000 people homeless. In rebuilding its business district, Chicago established new building standards and increased the use of brick. It also developed one of the nation's top fire-fighting forces.

Yellowstone National Park - Signed into law by President **Ulysses S. Grant** in 1872, this was the first national park, and it was located primarily in Wyoming. This suggested a remarkable shift in thinking about the use of land. The idea of setting aside land to be preserved in its natural state for recreational use and for appreciation of plants and animals living there was a new concept that later became a worldwide phenomenon.

Red River War - This series of battles took place in the panhandle of Texas along the Red River from 1874 to 1875. The U.S. Army was trying to remove Kiowa, Comanche, Southern Cheyenne and Arapaho from the Plains. Native Americans were angry with the **Medicine Lodge Treaty of 1867**, which had relegated them to reservations. An early battle ensued when **Quanah Parker** attacked the outpost at **Adobe Walls** in the **Second Battle of Adobe Walls**.

The major Army victory came with a surprise attack by Colonel **Ranald S. Mackenzie** and the **4th Cavalry** on the Native Americans' village at the **Battle of Palo Duro Canyon**. The village was burned, the horses were taken and shot, and the food stores were destroyed. The Native Americans had no recourse but to submit to moving to reservations. The southern buffalo herds were nearly extinct, and the Texas Panhandle was finally open to white settlers.

Invention of the telephone - The inventor of this device is disputed, but **Alexander Graham Bell** was the first to patent it in 1876, thus revolutionizing communications in the U.S.

. . . .

FIRE FIBBER? - The newspaper reported that the Great Chicago Fire started in Catherine O'Leary's barn. One account reported that it was caused by a cow kicking over a lantern while being milked which caught straw in the barn on fire. The reporter, however, later recanted the story.

- Battle of Little Bighorn
- Election of 1876
- Dull Knife Fight
- Chief Joseph's Surrender

Growth of U.S.

Battle of the Little Bighorn - This battle in 1876 was often called **Custer's Last Stand**. This was the most prominent battle of the **Sioux War** between the U.S. cavalry under General **George Armstrong Custer** and the Lakota, Cheyenne and Arapaho. A surprise attack on the Native American encampment on the Little Bighorn River in Indian Territory of Montana was a disastrous defeat for Custer. All of his men died. Historians contend that Custer made multiple strategic errors and grossly underestimated the enemy.

The U.S. rallied. Many felt all Native Americans should be on reservations, and previous treaties should be discarded. This battle signaled the beginning of the end for the Native Americans of the Great Plains.

Election of 1876 - In one of the most contentious and controversial elections in history, **Rutherford B. Hayes** was elected president by a margin of one electoral vote. His opponent, **Samuel J. Tilden**, received over half of the popular vote. Twenty electoral votes were questioned. The **Compromise of 1877** decided the election by awarding all contested votes to Hayes.

Dull Knife Fight - In 1876, this battle was in Wyoming during the Sioux War. It was another surprise attack on an encampment of **Dull Knife** and **Little Wolf** by Colonel **Ranald Mackenzie**, much like that at Palo Duro. The village of 173 lodges and all its contents were entirely annihilated. The battle essentially ended the Cheyenne's ability to wage war.

Chief Joseph's surrender - In 1877, a group of **Nez Perce** did not want to go to a reservation. This group of around 750 people, 1,400 horses and several chiefs left their home in Oregon to go to Montana and then the Canadian border. When they were about 40 miles from freedom in Canada, over 1,000 miles from their homes, there were less than 400 people left. Chief Joseph surrendered to General **Nelson Miles**, explaining, "...I am tired. My heart is sick and sad. From where the sun now stands, I will fight no more forever."

TAKE NOTE - "Please Mr. Custer" is a novelty song about a cowardly soldier in the Battle of Little Bighorn. In 1960, it was the number one song in the U.S.A.

- Free Silver Movement
- Tuskegee Institute
- American Red Cross

Growth of U.S.

Free Silver Movement - Silver miners and Southern farmers wanted both gold and silver as the U.S. backing for currency. They advocated unlimited minting of silver coins. They were known as **Silverites**. Congress passed an act that omitted the silver dollar from the official list of acceptable coins. This was referred to as the **Crime of '73** by the Silverites.

The movement eventually led to the **Bland-Allison Act** of 1878, which restored the silver dollar and required the government to buy and mint millions in silver coinage. With a decline of gold in the U.S. Treasury, a panic developed. To restore the economy, Congress ultimately passed the **Gold Standard Act** in 1900. Gold again became the only standard for currency.

Tuskegee Institute (1881) - **Booker T. Washington**, son of a slave and white father, worked as a laborer in West Virginia while attending school to become a teacher. He was asked to head an industrial and agricultural school in Alabama. The school became known as the Tuskegee Institute. His leadership promoted the education of black Americans. The school soon had programs in business education, veterinary medicine and nursing. He emphasized economic self-sufficiency for all and stayed away from political issues.

American Red Cross - In 1881, **Clara Barton**, a former teacher, founded the **American Red Cross**, which she patterned after the **Red Cross** in Europe. She had been one of the first women to work for the Federal Government. In 1861, she had begun caring for troops during the Civil War while working as a recording clerk. She was instrumental in getting Congress to permit her to attend servicemen on the battlefield, which earned her the nickname of **Angel of the Battlefield**. She continued to care for servicemen and their families after the war. Barton was instrumental in getting the U.S. to ratify the **Geneva Convention**, also called the **Red Cross Treaty**.

. . . .

INSULT TO INJURY - In the 1860s, Joseph Lister had pioneered use of sterile instruments and cleaning wounds. James A. Garfield, the 20th president, was shot in the back in 1881 and died. Had Lister's antiseptic methods been used to treat the wound, he likely would not have died. Happenstance, Abraham Lincoln's son was present when he was killed.

- Surrender of Geronimo
- Haymarket Affair
- Election of 1888
- Oklahoma Land Rush

Growth of U.S.

Surrender of Geronimo - The **Apache Wars** were fought between the Apache and the U.S. from 1849 until 1886 in the Southwest. **Geronimo**, one of the most famous Apache warriors of all time, was a leader of the **Chiricahua Apache**, but not a chief. It took roughly 8,000 American and Mexican soldiers to find Geronimo and his people and take them to the San Carlos Reservation. Geronimo fled again with over 100 people, but was caught and surrendered.

Haymarket Affair - Labor leaders and anarchists gathered at Chicago's Haymarket Square in 1886 to discuss labor issues and an eight-hour workday. As they left, the police arrived to disperse the crowd and then someone threw a homemade bomb into the police patrol. It caused a riot. The resulting **Red Scare**, enhanced by the press, publicized activity of anarchists in the U.S. The **American Federation of Labor** (**AFL**), created by **Samuel Gompers** as a collective bargaining organization, was promoted as a less radical, non-political way for laborers to improve working conditions.

Election of 1888 - This was notable as it was the third of four presidential elections in which the winner of the electoral vote did not win the popular vote. **Benjamin Harrison** became the 23rd President. **Grover Cleveland** preceded Harrison, and in the following election of 1892, the two men again faced each other at the polls and Cleveland won. Cleveland was the only president to have served two terms that were not consecutive.

Oklahoma Land Rush - Most of the Oklahoma Indian Territory was sparsely farmed, but in a few areas, farming was very profitable. White settlers trespassed to set up their own farms in Indian Territory. Unable to stop settlers who wanted land, the U.S. decided to open two million acres within Indian Territory to settlers. This land rush began officially in 1889, but hundreds had previously crossed the line to hide in order to claim the best lands. These people were known as **Sooners**, and their actions resulted in disputed land lawsuits.

. . . .

GROWTH SPURT - The AFL grew from 150,000 people to more than three million by the time Samuel Gompers passed away. Gompers was originally an immigrant from England.

• **Wounded Knee Massacre**   • **Progressive Era**

Progressive Period

Wounded Knee Massacre (1890) - After Chief **Sitting Bull** was killed in a scuffle by reservation police, hundreds left the Pine Ridge reservation and moved into the Badlands to an area called the **Stronghold**. General **Nelson A. Miles** ordered Colonel **James W. Forsyth** to bring in the Lakota. The Lakota were commanded to surrender all weapons. A fight ensued between a young, deaf warrior and soldiers. His weapon discharged and killed a soldier. Troops with rifles and Hotchkiss machine guns fired into the group and chased the unarmed survivors down Wounded Knee Creek. Some 300 Lakota were massacred, with about half being women and children. Thirty soldiers died.

Poet **Stephen Vincent Benet** wrote a poignant poem ending with the phrase, "*Bury my heart at Wounded Knee.*" Historian **Dee Brown** wrote a best-seller in 1970 with the same title. This brought awareness to atrocities committed against Native Americans. The site of the massacre at Wounded Knee became a rallying point for the 20th century **American Indian Movement** (**AIM**).

Progressive Era (1890s-1920s) - This lengthy period was characterized by social activism and political reform. Government corruption was addressed. Laws were passed to regulate corporate monopolies with antitrust laws, such as the **Sherman Antitrust Act**. The roots of prohibition and women's suffrage were found in the early parts of this period. It was a period of new scientific methods and new technology as well as economic growth.

Awareness of living conditions was brought to the surface in the early part of the **Progressive Era**. **Jacob August Riis**, a Danish immigrant who became a reporter, had struggled in the slums of New York before he wrote *How the Other Half Lives* that exposed the terrible conditions of the slums of New York through pictures and words. He felt people would take action if the truth were known. **Theodore Roosevelt** thought the book "an enlightenment."

BROWSER WARS - In 1998, Internet Explorer came 'free' with Micro-soft Windows, and 90% of the computers sold at the time came with Windows. Other companies selling browser software lost significant sales, and Microsoft was accused of violating the Sherman Antitrust Act. Today, most browsers are free and there are many choices.

- Chicago World's Fair
- Hawaiian Monarchy's End
- *Plessy v. Ferguson*
- Spanish American War

Progressive Period

Chicago World's Fair - Also termed the **Columbian Exposition**, this event took place in 1893 to celebrate the 400th anniversary of Columbus' arrival in the New World. **Frederick Law Olmsted**, who had been the landscape architect for Central Park, laid out the fairgrounds and **Jackson Park**. Many of the buildings were made of white stucco and referred to as the **White City**. The first **Ferris wheel**, invented by **George W. Ferris**, was built here. Other 'firsts' included **Cracker Jacks**, **Juicy Fruit** gum, **Quaker Oats**, **Hershey chocolate**, moving walkways and extensive usage of electricity.

End of the Hawaiian monarchy - A group of Americans and Europeans formed the **Committee of Safety** in 1893 to overthrow the Hawaiian monarch, Queen **Liliuokalani**. The group feared she would repeal the **Bayonet Constitution**, which had been forced on the prior monarch at gunpoint. It limited the monarch's power in favor of foreign interests who controlled the sugar and pineapple industries. U.S. President **Grover Cleveland** considered the overthrow, which occurred without his authority, an act of war and refused to annex the islands. A group of foreign businessmen ran the islands until 1900 when President **William McKinley** annexed the islands as a territory.

Plessy v. Ferguson - The Supreme Court upheld states' laws requiring racial segregation in public areas under a doctrine of '**separate but equal**' in 1896. The Supreme Court determined that segregation did not mean discrimination and was therefore not unconstitutional. This case was later overturned by *Brown v. Board of Education of Topeka* in 1954.

Spanish-American War (1898) - This conflict began when an explosion of unknown origin occurred on the **USS *Maine*** while it was in Cuba's **Havana Harbor**. The U.S. demanded that Spain leave Cuba, and Spain declared war against the U.S. During this war, **Theodore Roosevelt** and his **Rough Riders** conquered **San Juan Hill**. By the end of the war, the U.S. had annexed the Philippines, Samoa, Guam and Wake Island. Cuba was held until 1902. Cuba, however, maintained that it became independent when Spain left in 1898.

. . . .

CHEW ON THIS - *During WWII, Juicy Fruit gum was taken off the market because all that was produced was given to solders in their C-rations.*

- McKinley's Assassination
- Square Deal
- Steel Production
- Ford Motor Company
- Invention of Airplane

Progressive Period

Assassination of McKinley - Elected president in 1900, **William McKinley** was fatally wounded a year later by an anarchist. He died eight days later from gangrene. His vice-president, **Theodore (Teddy) Roosevelt**, became president. Congress passed legislation to charge the **Secret Service** with protection of the president.

Square Deal - Known for his exuberance, President **Theodore Roosevelt** was a foe of corruption during his term from 1901 to 1909. His Square Deal domestic policy centered on conservation of natural resources, consumer protection and regulation of corporations. He became known as the **trust-buster**. He strove to aid the middle class and at the same time protect businesses from the extreme demands of organized labor.

Steel production - A way to mass produce steel created by **Andrew Carnegie** changed the industry. It combined the full advantage of the **Bessemer steel process** with Carnegie's innovative mass production of steel rails used by the railroad companies. He based his company in Pittsburgh, Pennsylvania, and eventually sold all steel operations to **U. S. Steel** in 1901.

Ford Motor Company - Founded in 1903 by **Henry Ford** to make custom automobiles, this company has been family owned and operated for over 100 years. Ford's vision was to produce affordable vehicles for the common man. He began the concept of assembly-line production. By 1908, the **Model-T** rolled off the line as a car many Americans could afford. Ford's assembly lines transformed mass production.

Invention of the airplane - Brothers **Wilbur** and **Orville Wright** built the first plane in 1903. They flew it at Kitty Hawk in North Carolina. They patented the system of aerodynamic control that enabled a pilot to control the aircraft.

THE 'WRIGHT' TOY - As children, the Wright brothers had received a toy helicopter from their dad after one of his trips. It was made of bamboo, paper, cork and a rubber band. They were intrigued with it, and played until they broke it. They then 'manufactured' a new one.

- Panama Canal
- Pure Food Acts
- NAACP

Progressive Period

Panama Canal - The U.S. supported Panama's independence from Columbia in an effort to gain control of land needed to build the Panama Canal. The **Hay-Bunau-Varilla Treaty of 1903** gave the U.S. control of a 10-mile wide swath of land that was to become the **Canal Zone** for perpetuity. The treaty was officially approved by Congress in 1904 with strong support from President **Roosevelt**, and the canal was completed by 1914.

Pure Food Acts - The **Pure Food and Drug Act** and the **Federal Meat Inspection Act** were laws passed by Congress in 1906 under **Roosevelt** to protect consumers from adulterated or mislabeled food products. It required all food and drug products be labelled with ingredients. This led to the creation of the **Food and Drug Administration**.

The book by **Upton Sinclair**, entitled *The Jungle,* revealed exploitative and inhumane conditions faced by immigrant stockyard workers. It ultimately revealed the unsanitary nature of the meatpacking industry. The book became a hallmark of the **muckraking** movement driven by writers who revealed corruption, slum conditions, labor horrors and other social wrongs. Sinclair's exposé of revolting conditions in the meat industry led directly to Congress' passing the **Pure Food Acts**. The term *muckraker* was coined by Theodore Roosevelt and referenced a muckrake, which was a tool used to clean filth off of floors.

National Association for the Advancement of Colored People - The **NAACP** was founded in 1909 to promote the rights of African Americans. It has become the most influential and successful black organization in American history. **W. E. B. DuBois**, the first African American to hold a doctorate, was one of the early leaders. The organization initially began challenging laws and legal rights and later expanded to promote education and economic success in the black community.

• •

POISON SQUAD - Before the Pure Food and Drug Act there were 12 government taste testers called the 'poison squad.' The squad would drink and eat toxic food until the Act made using humans as guinea pigs illegal. A toast published in 1903, reads, "Oh here's to good old germs, Drink em down!"

53

- 16th Amendment
- Federal Reserve Act
- Clayton Antitrust Act
- Entrance into WWI
- Selective Service Act

World War I

16th Amendment - Under President **Woodrow Wilson**, this Amendment was adopted in 1913 and established a federal income tax. Specifically, none of this tax would be apportioned to states.

Federal Reserve Act - This act passed by Congress in 1913 under President Wilson created the **Federal Reserve System**, a system of public and private entities. There were 12 private regional **Federal Reserve** banks created. The governing board consisted of seven people appointed by the president.

Clayton Antitrust Act - This act of 1914 closed the loopholes of the **Sherman Antitrust Act** of 1890. Both acts were intended to regulate business monopolies that prevented fair competition. Both acts were enforced by the **Federal Trade Commission**. This commission was created by the **Federal Trade Commission Act** to regulate monopolies and trusts.

Entrance into World War I - After winning a reelection on the slogan, "He kept us out of war," President **Wilson** was reluctant to enter **WWI**. The war actually began in Europe in 1914. In 1915, the Germans sunk the *Lusitania*, a civilian British ship, killing 124 Americans. The **Zimmerman Telegram** was intercepted and decoded by the British. It proposed that the Germans would ally with Mexico against the U.S. to reclaim territory Mexico had lost to the U.S. if the U.S. entered the war. News of the communication enraged the populace, and paved the way for Congress to pass Wilson's war declaration request in 1917.

Selective Service Act - This 1917 act authorized the government to raise an army for WWI through conscription and gave the president power to draft soldiers into service. All males between 21 and 30 were required to register for military service. This range was changed to be age 18 to 45 a year later.

. . . .

SIGNIFICANT SHIP - *When the* Titanic *hit the iceberg it created a 300 foot gash below the waterline. On April 15, 1912, over 1500 passengers lost their lives, and just over 700 survived the sinking. The Titanic was longer than three football fields, took three years to build, and sank in three hours. Eerily, a fiction book called* The Wreck of the Titan *was released 14 years earlier and told a very similar story.*

- Spanish Influenza
- Treaty of Versailles
- 18th Amendment
- 19th Amendment
- Roaring Twenties

World War I & Aftermath

Spanish influenza pandemic - A two-year, worldwide pandemic of Spanish Flu began in 1918 and infected a fifth of the global population. Around 20 to 40 million people perished, making it the deadliest epidemic of recorded history. More people died of this infection than were killed in WWI.

Treaty of Versailles - Peace negotiations to end hostilities between Germany and the **Allies** were held at the **Paris Peace Conference** from 1919 to 1920. The **Big Four** of the Allies included the U.S., Britain, France and Italy. President **Wilson** promoted his **Fourteen Point Plan.**, suggesting free trade, international disarmament, a **League of Nations** and other things. Wilson presented his plan in a speech to the country rather than to Congress. Congress did not get behind the plan, and the Senate never ratified it. It failed by seven votes. Wilson considered this a great failure, and it plagued him until his death.

18th Amendment - This amendment was passed in 1919 and prohibited making, distributing or consuming alcohol. Prohibition had long been a political issue. It was a triumph for **Temperance Unions** and the prohibition movement that had been working since the Civil War to ban the evil alcohol from society. This amendment was repealed by the **21st Amendment** in 1933.

19th Amendment - Passed in 1920, this Amendment gave women the right to vote in all states. This had been implied in the 14th Amendment, but states continued to hinder women's suffrage. This made it a federal law.

Roaring Twenties - The 1920s saw social, artistic and cultural dynamism. Normality returned to politics after the war, jazz music evolved, and the **flapper** redefined the modern woman. **F. Scott Fitzgerald** helped define the 1920s as the **Jazz Age** in his first book, *This Side of Paradise*. His most famous work, *The Great Gatsby*, published in 1925, reflected not only the society of the times, but also the development of America as a nation.

· ·

CUTTING LOOSE - Hair and hemlines got considerably shorter in the 1920s. It was a time of social change with more women in the workplace and a growing disdain of the 'norms' of previous generations.

- Teapot Dome Scandal
- Peanut Butter
- Indian Citizenship Act
- Scopes Trial

World War I & Aftermath

Teapot Dome Scandal - This derived its name from a rock formation near an oil field. This scandal in 1921 involved the U.S. Secretary of the Interior, **Albert Bacon Fall**. He secretly leased the oil reserves on federal land in Wyoming to the **Mammoth Oil Company** for bribes. When this was discovered, the prior decision of President **Warren G. Harding** to take supervision of the naval oil reserve from the Navy and give it to the Department of the Interior was found to be illegal, though he was not directly implicated in Fall's illegal dealings.

Peanut butter - The mother of **George Washington Carver** was a slave and disappeared during a Civil War raid. Her son, Carver, eventually traveled to the Midwest and worked his way through segregated schools. He accepted a teaching position at the Tuskegee Institute in Alabama. He used his position as a platform for his agricultural research to find uses for low cost crops, such as sweet potatoes, soybeans and peanuts. Carver developed 105 food recipes using peanuts, including peanut butter. He was an ingenious man whose scientific creativity improved the lives of black and white southern farmers.

Indian Citizenship Act - Also called the **Snyder Act**, this 1924 legislation finally gave all Native Americans U.S. citizenship and all the rights associated with citizenship. It was signed into law by President **Calvin Coolidge**. It was enacted in part to recognize the thousands of Native Americans who served in WWI.

Scopes Trial - Also called the **Monkey Trial**, this 1925 litigation occurred in Tennessee after the arrest of **John T. Scopes**, a biology teacher. Scopes taught the **theory of evolution**, and this teaching violated Tennessee law. Though the prosecution prevailed and Scopes was fined, the Tennessee Supreme Court overturned the decision on a technicality and the case was never further reviewed. The conflict of teaching evolution versus biblical theory as part of school science class has continued.

FIELDS OF GOLD - George Washington Carver realized that the cotton fields were stripping the soil of nutrients, and farmers could not keep growing crops where cotton had previously been planted. He discovered that planting peanuts where cotton had grown added important nutrients back into the soil. Search the internet for a list of George Washington Carver's inventions, and prepare to be amazed!

- Transatlantic Flight
- Great Depression
- Bootleggers

Depression Era

Transatlantic flight - The first successful solo flight from the U.S. to Europe was accomplished by **Charles W. Lindbergh**, who was nicknamed **Lucky Lindy** and the **Lone Eagle**. He flew from New York to France in 1927 and inspired a new age in aeronautical development, especially commercial aircraft. His plane was called the *Spirit of St. Louis*.

Though he was a pacifist and isolationist, he served his country as a pilot in **World War II (WWII)**. His infant son was kidnapped and killed in what was termed the **Crime of the Century** in 1932. An avid environmentalist in his later years, he did not support the development of supersonic transportation as he feared negative environmental impacts.

Great Depression - A massive economic depression was caused by the **Stock Market Crash of 1929** that lasted roughly ten years. It happened on what came to be known as **Black Tuesday**. Many people and businesses had borrowed money to enter the stock market. When the market started to fall, people and companies panicked. Banks called in loans; people lost their homes and businesses. The ripple effect caused people who had never participated in the market to be hurt. Mobilization of the U.S. as they prepared to enter **WWII** probably served to hasten the end of the depression.

Bootleggers - The **18th Amendment** (ratified in 1919), which prohibited the making or selling of alcohol, provided more incentive for state and local authorities to track down bootleggers making alcohol at home. Mountain people of Appalachia had always made **moonshine** for personal use and minor sales. Now they began widespread selling. Law enforcement cracked down on this illegal activity. Transporting their products over rough, curvy, mountain roads was often done at night in cars without headlights. Races would take place among the various drivers to see who was fastest. Thus, the seeds of **NASCAR** racing were sown.

• •

EQUESTRIAN STATUES - Some claim a statue of a man on horseback indicates that the person died in battle if the horse is rearing with both front legs in the air. If only one of the horse's legs is in the air, it indicates that the rider was wounded in battle and died afterward. If all four hooves are on the ground, this indicates that the rider died outside battle. However, there are many statues that do not follow this generalization.

1930 - 1937

- Transatlantic Flight
- New Deal

Depression Era & Aftermath

New Deal - During the Great Depression, **Franklin D. Roosevelt** became president and set up a series of policies between 1933-1939 to stabilize the economy and ease unemployment. This collection of policies and government programs were called the New Deal. During his first hundred days in office, Roosevelt saw the passage of more than a dozen acts designed to help people and improve the economy. Several pieces of legislation were passed. The **Tennessee Valley Authority** (**TVA**) was intended to reduce flooding and generate cheap electricity by building a dam on the Tennessee River. The **21st Amendment** ended **Prohibition**.

The **Agricultural Adjustment Act of 1933** paid farmers to leave some fields unplanted to avoid overproduction and sustain prices. Overproduction, a reduction in exports and a severe economic depression were crippling American farmers. The idea was to pay farmers to limit production, which would then increase prices for the crops that were produced. This act was later declared unconstitutional.

The new **Agricultural Adjustment Act of 1938** revived the subsidy provisions and used money from the government to pay for the program. The payments, called price support, were mandatory for corn, cotton and wheat, while other agricultural products, such as butter, dates, and figs could be added as needed.

Transatlantic Flight - Emulating an earlier flight of **Charles Lindbergh**, **Amelia Earhart** became the first female aviator to complete a solo transatlantic flight. In 1937, she undertook her final challenge, becoming the first woman to fly around the world. She completed all but 7,000 miles of the 29,000 mile journey before vanishing. Neither she nor her plane were ever found. No evidence of what occurred was ever determined.

BABE RUTH (1895-1948) - An outfielder and pitcher who played 22 seasons of major league baseball, George Herman Ruth, Jr. was nicknamed the 'Sultan of Swat.' He was one of the first five inductees into the National Baseball Hall of Fame. Many have dubbed him the "greatest baseball player of all time."

- *Hindenburg*
- *Grapes of Wrath*
- Start of WWII

- **Axis Powers**
- **Allied Powers**

World War II

Hindenburg - A large German airship, which was over 800 feet long and built to carry passengers, burst into flames in 1937 above its destination in Lakehurst, New Jersey. Thirty-six of the 97 passengers on board were killed when the **zeppelin** exploded. The cause of the explosion was never determined.

Grapes of Wrath - This novel was written by **John Steinbeck** in 1939. He told the story of millions of Americans affected by the **Great Depression** and **Dust Bowl**, which was a period of severe drought and dust storms on the Plains of the central U.S. in the 1930s. Many migrated to California from the Plains to take minimal jobs as migrant farm workers. The book won a **Pulitzer Prize**.

Start of World War II - The second **Great War** began in 1939 when France and Britain declared war on Germany because Germany had invaded Poland. For the first few months, the majority of the war involved the German and British Navies. In April 1940, Germany invaded Norway and occupied Denmark, widening the land battle. It soon became a global war.

Axis powers - This included Germany, Japan and Italy. Germany was led by **Adolf Hitler** and his **Nazi** regime. They had superior military strength, and their **blitzkrieg**, or lightning war, was fast and decisive as they made their way across Europe. They could literally run over the towns of their enemies with their **panzer**, or tank, divisions. Italy was led by **Benito Mussolini**, called **El Duce**, who was head of the **National Fascist Party.** Led by **Hirohito**, Japan fought China and took over European colonies in the Far East.

Allied powers - Initially, this group consisted of France, Poland and Great Britain. Soon, many countries of the British Commonwealth joined, including Canada, Australia, New Zealand, Newfoundland and South Africa. Later, China, India, the Netherlands, Norway and Yugoslavia joined, plus the U.S, finally. Together these were called the **United Nations**, and they formed the official group with the same name in 1945 after the war.

• •

MEIN KAMPF - The title of this book means my struggle. It was written by Adolf Hitler. He initially wanted to name it My Long Struggle against Lies, Stupidity and Cowardice, *but his publisher chose a shorter title.*

1941 - 1942

- **Attack on Pearl Harbor**
- **Holocaust**
- **Battle of Midway**

World War II

Attack on Pearl Harbor - On **December 7, 1941**, the U.S. joined the Allies after the Japanese dropped bombs on Pearl Harbor, a U.S. naval base in Hawaii. Most of America's battleships were severely damaged or destroyed. The **USS Arizona** remained under the waters of Pearl Harbor, and the **USS Arizona Memorial** was built as a war memorial for those who died.

President **Franklin D. Roosevelt** delivered a speech the next day to a joint session of Congress, asking them to declare war on Japan. He referred to the date of the attack as "a date which will live in infamy..." It took Congress less than an hour to formally declare war on Japan. Germany and Italy retaliated, declaring war on the U.S., thus bringing the U.S. into the **European theatre**.

Holocaust - This was Hitler's methodical extermination of Jews, Romani, Jehovah's Witnesses, and other groups. He was intent on making Germany an entirely **Aryan nation**. More than six million were killed in extermination camps. Some people were literally worked to death, and others were killed in large groups in gas chambers.

Battle of Midway - In 1942, Japan engaged the U.S. Navy and Army Air Force at **Midway Atoll**. Unlike the surprise attack at Pearl Harbor, the U.S. defeated Japan. It was Japan's first naval defeat in almost 80 years. The American code breakers had been successful at intercepting and translating Japanese messages, but Japan didn't know Americans knew of their plans. The U.S. Navy was led by three admirals, Chester W. Nimitz, Frank Jack Fletcher and Raymond A. Spruance.

• •

EXCERPT FROM THE DIARY OF ANNE FRANK - *"...I still believe, in spite of everything, that people are truly good at heart...I see the world being slowly transformed into a wilderness, I hear the approaching thunder that, one day, will destroy us too, I feel the suffering of millions. And yet, when I look up at the sky, I somehow feel that everything will change for the better, that this cruelty too shall end, that peace and tranquility will return once more." ~ Anne Frank (This diary was written while in hiding from the Germans before her internment in a camp.)*

- Japanese Internment
- D-Day
- Election of 1944
- End of WWII in Europe

World War II

Japanese Internment - Camps were created in 1942 by the U.S. War Department under **Executive Order 9066** following the bombing of Pearl Harbor. About 120,000 people of Japanese descent, including many who were American citizens, were forced to sell their homes and businesses and relocate to one of ten camps in six states. Though this directive was challenged in ***Korematsu v. U.S.***, Fred Korematsu lost the case, and camps were not closed until 1946.

D-Day - On June 6, 1944, the Allied Forces landed at the **Normandy** beaches in France, each of which had a code name. The mission was called **Operation Overlord**. Americans landed on **Omaha** and **Utah Beaches** as Canadians and British troops stormed the beaches of **Gold**, **Juno** and **Sword**. There were many casualties, but the Allies pressed on and the landing was a success. This was considered one of the greatest amphibious landings in military history.

Election of 1944 - **Franklin Delano Roosevelt (FDR)** won the 1932 and 1936 presidential elections by landslides of both electoral and popular votes while the **Great Depression** harnessed the country. He ran for an unprecedented third term in 1940. In 1944, FDR sought the office for a fourth term with **Harry S Truman** as the vice-presidential candidate. Again, FDR succeeded, but he died from health issues about a year later, and Truman took office.

End of WWII in Europe - The Allies forged through France. The **Battle of the Bulge** was a decisive victory, which **Winston Churchill** described as "undoubtedly the greatest American battle of the war and will be regarded as an ever-famous American victory." From this point the Allies swept across Germany and Italy, and the Soviets came down to Austria and Germany. In Italy, **Mussolini** was stripped of power, and Italy surrendered in 1943. The **Battle of Berlin** was the final major offensive of the European theatre with the Soviets taking the city. Before the battle was over, **Hitler** and many of his followers committed suicide. Germany surrendered on May 7, 1945.

TO BOMB OR NOT TO BOMB - *FDR died, leaving Harry Truman with a big decision: whether or not to use the atomic bomb. Truman, however, had no idea about the Manhattan Project since FDR had never mentioned it.*

1945 - 1953

- Atomic Bombs
- Cold War
- Election of 1948
- Korean War

World War II & Aftermath

Atomic bombs - War continued with Japan until the U.S. dropped atomic bombs on **Hiroshima** and **Nagasaki** nearly three months after the end of the war in Europe. Around 200,000 people were estimated to have been killed or injured from the bombs' destruction. Japan surrendered on September 2, 1945. The **Manhattan Project** had begun in 1942 after **Albert Einstein** discussed the possibility of harnessing nuclear fission to create an atomic bomb.

Cold War - This refers to the strained relationship between the capitalist U.S. and communist **Union of Soviet Socialists Republics** (**USSR** or **Soviet Union**) between 1945 and 1989. After WWII, the Soviet Union began to communize the countries it controlled. During this time both nations built strong militaries. The Cold War ended in 1989 with the disintegration of the Soviet Union. Neither side really won this war.

Election of 1948 - This was an upset victory by President **Harry S Truman**, a Democrat, against **Thomas E. Dewey**, a Republican. Truman had become president upon the death of Roosevelt. However, virtually every poll reported that Dewey would win. The Democrats garnered the presidency and also gained control of both houses of Congress. Though Truman had many successes, his and his party's popularity declined throughout his term.

Korean War (1950-1953) - This conflict began when **North Korea** invaded **South Korea**. North Korea had support from the **Soviet Union**. South Korea had the support of the U.S. and forces from the **United Nations** (**UN**). President Truman called the war a **police action**. The UN forces, led by the U.S., made an amphibious landing at **Incheon** in South Korea. They were able to recapture the capital city of **Seoul** and turn the tide of the war. A truce was signed that created a demilitarized zone. The peninsula remains divided, as of 2015, and the 38th parallel remains the border just as it was when the conflict started. The war was the backdrop for the popular television series *M.A.S.H.*

. . . .

THE 'TRU' WINNER - *Few thought Truman would win. The* Chicago Daily Tribune *went to press before all results were in and declared Dewey the winner. Later newspapers showed the now famous picture of victorious Truman holding the* Chicago Daily Tribune *with the "DEWEY DEFEATS TRUMAN" headline.*

1953 - 1962

- Warren Court
- *Brown v. Board of Education*
- Conservative Movement
- *Engel v. Vitale*

Civil Rights Era

Warren Court (1953-1969) - Led by Chief Justice **Earl Warren**, this period of the **Supreme Court** indicated a shift in priorities. It began to focus more on personal rights instead of property cases. The majority of the important cases were decided based on the ***Bill of Rights***.

Brown v. Board of Education of Topeka - In 1954, this case of the **Warren Court** declared **segregation** in public schools unconstitutional. This overturned a previous case, ***Plessy v. Ferguson*** of 1896, in which the court declared 'separate but equal' to be legal. However, a timetable for school integration was not set, and many schools remained segregated into the 1960s.

Conservative Movement - There were many different conservative groups in the United States, and the Conservative Movement tried to bring them all together. The values supported by this political group include small or limited government, free enterprise, a strong military and school prayer. It was also clearly anti-communist. The movement became a strong political force when **Ronald Reagan** was elected president.

Engel v. Vitale - This Supreme Court case in 1962 concerned prayer in schools. The court stated that New York's policy of beginning the school day with a prayer was unconstitutional. The court determined that it violated the **Establishment Clause** of the **1st Amendment**, which stated that Congress could not make any law respecting an establishment of religion. Since then, there have been three other significant cases, and conflict has continued to the present. Even the 'moment of silence' has been challenged.

• •

PEACEFUL PROTESTER - Martin Luther King received the Nobel Peace Prize in 1964. Gunnar Jahn, president of the Nobel Committee, said of King, "He is the first person in the Western world to have shown us that a struggle can be waged without violence. He is the first to make the message of brotherly love a reality in the course of his struggle, and he has brought this message to all nations and races." Jahn remarked that King "never abandoned his faith" and, in spite of being imprisoned and of having his own life and his family's life threatened, King "has never faltered."

- **Cuban Missile Crisis**
- **Kennedy Assassination**
- **Vietnam War**

Civil Rights Era

Cuban Missile Crisis - The U.S. learned that the Soviet Union had placed nuclear missiles in Cuba. President **John F. Kennedy (JFK)** and Soviet leader **Nikita Khrushchev** engaged in a 13-day standoff in 1962. The U.S. set up a naval blockade of Cuba and offered a three-part deal. The publicized part dictated that the U.S. would not invade Cuba if missiles were removed. Two parts were private. One specified that the U.S. would withdraw missiles in Turkey if the offer were accepted. The other part stated that the U.S. would attack Cuba within 24 hours if the offer were rejected. Khrushchev accepted the offer.

Assassination of Kennedy (11/22/1963) - Preparing for his next campaign, President Kennedy was in a motorcade that was driving from the airport through downtown Dallas. When his car passed the **Texas School Book Depository**, gunfire began and Kennedy was struck. He was pronounced dead at 1 p.m., and Vice President **Lyndon B. Johnson** was sworn in as president on **Air Force One**. A Texas School Book Depository employee named **Lee Harvey Oswald** was arrested for the shooting, but he himself was shot and killed while being transferred from one jail to another by **Jack Ruby**.

Vietnam War (1965-1973) - The war started because the U.S. government felt it had to protect South Vietnam from communist North Vietnam. Most Americans did not support the war, but anti-war protests and violence did not start until the late 1960s. Originally, President Kennedy sent in troops to train the Vietnamese, then President Lyndon Johnson sent in combat troops in 1965, and, finally, **Richard Nixon** ended the war and brought the troops home. The nation treated returning soldiers harshly. The war was costly and nothing was gained or prevented, as North Vietnam claimed the entire peninsula two years later.

DUCK AND COVER - During the Cuban Missile Crisis, the U.S. felt so threatened by the nuclear missiles in Cuba that school children performed 'duck and cover' drills. Conducted just like a fire drill, an alarm would sound and the children would immediately hide under their desks covering their heads with their arms.

- **Great Society**
- *Miranda v. Arizona*
- **Civil Rights Movement**
- *Apollo 11*

Civil Rights Era

Great Society - This term was first used in a speech at Ohio University. It became Johnson's agenda for Congress in 1965. He outlined plans for expanded social welfare programs supporting education and care for the elderly, as well as social security and strong enforcement of the **Civil Rights Act**. Congress supported his plan and passed almost all of the associated legislation.

Miranda v. Arizona (1966) - This case was tried because **Ernesto Miranda** was interrogated by the police based on circumstantial evidence. He signed a confession but was never told he had the right to legal counsel. He filed a suit insisting that the interrogators had coerced him to confess. This landmark case ended in a 5-4 decision at the Supreme Court under **Warren**. As a result, the police have since been required to give a **Miranda warning** to anyone they interrogate to preserve admissibility of their statements in trials.

African-American Civil Rights Movement - This movement lasted from around 1955 to 1968 and was a series of non-violent protests aimed at securing the rights and privileges given to African-Americans under the **14th** and **15th Amendments**. The movement ended segregation of public facilities and helped create new civil rights legislation that was passed in 1964 and 1965. In 1955 in Montgomery, Alabama, **NAACP** activist **Rosa Parks** refused to give up her seat on a bus to a white man. A mass bus boycott followed. **Martin Luther King, Jr.** was one of the leaders of this movement before his assassination. He is well known for his **"I Have a Dream"** speech delivered at Lincoln Memorial during the **March on Washington for Jobs and Freedom**.

Apollo 11 - In 1969, astronauts **Neil Armstrong** and **Edwin E. "Buzz" Aldrin** became the first men to walk on the moon during this mission of the **National Aeronautics and Space Administration** (**NASA**). They spent just over two hours walking on the moon, setting up equipment and gathering samples of lunar material. As of 2015, no other nation has landed a man on the moon.

. . . .

THE LAST WORD - *The Miranda warning states, "You have the right to remain silent. Anything you say or do can and will be used against you in a court of law. You have the right to an attorney. If you cannot afford an attorney, one will be appointed to you. Do you understand these rights as they have been read to you?"*

- **Kent State**
- **Watergate Scandal**
- *Roe v. Wade*
- **American Promise**

Civil Rights Era

Kent State - An anti-war protest at **Kent State University** turned violent and destructive in 1970. The **Ohio National Guard** was called in. The gathering was considered an illegal protest, and the crowd was seriously agitated. The National Guard used tear gas, but these were lobbed back at the Guard. Students refused to disperse. Ultimately, the troops opened fire on the crowd and killed four students and wounded nine. It was never determined why the Guard opened fire. Such protests highlighted the divisive nature of the Vietnam War and the need for improved tactics for crowd control.

Watergate Scandal - This was the political scandal of the decade. In 1972, burglars were caught trying to wiretap phones and steal important documents from the **Democratic National Committee Headquarters**, which was located in the **Watergate Building** in Washington. President **Nixon** and his close aides attempted to cover up the crime, destroy evidence and interfere in the FBI investigation. The conspiracy led to Nixon's resignation in 1974. He was the first and only U.S. president to resign.

Roe v. Wade (1972) - This case remains one of the most controversial heard by the Supreme Court. At issue was whether a woman had a constitutional right to end her pregnancy through abortion, if she so chose. The Court ruled that abortion fell within the right to privacy protected by the **14th Amendment**. The case affected laws in 48 states. **Right to Life** and **Pro-Choice** groups continue to lobby for their causes.

American Promise - In 1976, President **Gerald R. Ford** repealed FDR's **Executive Order 9066** ordering the internment of Japanese Americans. The camps had long been closed, but the Order had never been cancelled. Ford also made an official apology and the promise "...to treasure liberty and justice...and resolve that this kind of action shall never again be repeated."

. . . .

THE FAR-OUT '70s - Disco was the popular dance and millions owned 'pet rocks.' The Vietnam War ended and, for the first time ever, Sky-lab was manned for 28 days. Mother Teresa was awarded the Nobel Peace Prize, and the World Trade Center was completed. The first, successful video game, Pong, was invented. "Have a nice day."

- Death of Elvis Presley
- Iran Hostage Crisis
- *Challenger* Disaster
- Exxon *Valdez*
- Persian Gulf War

War & Turmoil

Death of Elvis Presley - Known as the **King of Rock and Roll**, Presley died at his home, **Graceland**, in Memphis. His popularity crossed generations. He thrilled teens and shocked their parents with his provocative hip swivel dance style.

Iran hostage crisis (1979-1981) - The U.S. gave temporary asylum to the deposed **Shah of Iran** and broke diplomatic ties to Iran after the overthrow of the Shah's government in 1979. Angry students responsible for the coup then took 52 Americans hostage at the U.S. Embassy in Tehran in protest. They wanted the Shah to be returned for trial and execution for crimes committed during his reign. The hostages were held 444 days before being freed. As of 2015, the U.S. and Iran have maintained no formal diplomatic ties.

***Challenger* Disaster** - In 1986, this space shuttle blew up 73 seconds after lift-off. The entire crew died, including **Christa McAuliffe**. She had been selected from 11,000 applicants in the **Teacher in Space Project**. It was intended that she be the first teacher in space.

Exxon *Valdez* - The oil tanker *Valdez*, owned by Exxon, ran aground in **Prince William Sound** in Alaska in 1989. It spilled 11 million gallons of crude oil. While it was not the largest spill, it had the worst impact due to the remoteness of the environment and abundance of wildlife in the region. Litigation ensued, and **Exxon Mobil** was charged over $507 million for damages plus interest.

Persian Gulf War (1990-1991) - The code name for this war was **Operation Desert Storm**. The U.S. along with 34 other nations responded to Iraq's invasion and annexation of Kuwait and their oil reserves. The Iraqis were expelled, but set the Kuwaiti oil wells on fire before leaving, which burned for ten months causing pollution and possibly the **Gulf War syndrome** and associated severe health issues. The U.S. government came under criticism for allowing **Saddam Hussein** to remain in power rather than depose him.

. . . .

THE AWESOME '80s - Sally Ride was the first woman in space, the Rubik's Cube was a favorite pastime, and AIDS was feared and little understood. President Ronald Reagan was shot and wounded, and in 1989 he delivered his famous, "Tear Down this Wall" speech.

- Storm of the Century
- Waco Siege
- NAFTA
- Oklahoma City Bombing

War & Turmoil

Storm of the Century - Also called the **'93 Superstorm**, this was a large cyclonic storm that began in the Gulf of Mexico and moved up the coast into Canada in 1993. Cuba saw tornadoes. More than ten million people were left without power, nearly 40% of the nation's population. The storm is responsible for the deaths of 318 people.

Waco siege - In 1993, a group of **Branch Davidians** led by **David Koresh** was suspected of weapons violations. The **Bureau of Alcohol, Tobacco and Firearms (ATF)** attempted to serve an arrest warrant. A battle ensued, killing four agents and six Davidians. A 51-day standoff followed. The **Federal Bureau of Investigation (FBI)** became involved. Ultimately, the FBI launched a tear-gas assault. A fire from unknown origin broke out, killing all 76 Davidians, including children. The government was hotly criticized for their handling.

North American Free Trade Agreement - The 1992 **NAFTA** agreement between Canada, the U.S. and Mexico was created to eliminate tariffs and trade barriers between the nations. The policy was inspired by some of Europe's trading partnerships. Some of the tariffs were removed immediately and others gradually disappeared over a period of 15 years.

Oklahoma City bombing (1995) - Two Americans, **Timothy McVeigh** and **Terry Nichols**, who were disgruntled with the government and its handling of the Waco siege, set off a bomb at the **Alfred P. Murrah Federal Building**. This killed 168 people and injured 680+, including children at the day-care center for federal employees. Buildings were damaged in a 16-block radius.

· ·

GENERATION GADGET - In the 1990s, the World Wide Web exploded, and a home computer was finally perceived as a necessity instead of a luxury. In the year 1999, many feared Y2K (the idea that computers would not be able to change from 1999 to the year 2000). Some anticipated global shutdown and stockpiled food and water. The new year rolled in without mishap. The Java computer language and the DVD were invented in '95.

- Defense of Marriage Act
- Columbine Shooting
- 9/11 Terrorism
- War on Terror

War & Turmoil

Defense of Marriage Act (DOMA) - In 1996, Congress passed this act that specified that states were not required to recognize same-sex marriages from a different state. Section 3 stated that **marriage** referred only to a legal union between one man and one woman and **spouse** only referred to a partner in a marriage. The **Supreme Court** ruled that Section 3 was unconstitutional.

Columbine High School shooting - In 1999, seniors **Eric Harris** and **Dylan Klebold** used guns in an attack on their high school. Twelve students and a teacher were murdered. Some 21 were injured in this suicidal attack.

9/11 Terrorism - Terrorists hijacked four planes in 2001. Two were flown into the twin towers of the **World Trade Center**, and one was flown into the **Pentagon**. Passengers on a fourth plane, alerted by cell phone calls from relatives, forced the hijacker of their plane to crash into a field in Pennsylvania, and all were killed. The **Twin Towers** collapsed, heavily damaging other buildings around them. Nearly 3,000 people were killed. This was the deadliest incident for firefighters and law enforcement officers in the history of the U.S. The terrorist group **al-Qaeda** claimed responsibility. Civilian air-traffic was closed for two days in the U.S. and Canada. Wall Street and the New York Stock Exchange closed for six days.

War on Terror - U.S. President **George W. Bush** declared a global War on Terror after the 9/11 attack. **Osama bin Laden**, a Saudi national in exile in Afghanistan, was the leader of the terrorist group **al-Qaeda** that claimed responsibility for the attack. The U.S. launched an attack against al-Qaeda in Afghanistan. The U.S. also opposed the **Taliban**, the oppressive government of Afghanistan who allowed al-Qaeda to operate from their country.

• •

TALLEST TOWERS - One World Trade Center, or Free-dom Tower, now stands as a memorial to the victims of 9/11 and their families. Freedom Tower is taller than the Willis Tower (formerly Sears) in Chicago, but only if you count the antenna. The jury is still out on which building then is actually the 'tallest' in America.

- Iraq War
- *Columbia* Shuttle Disaster
- Hurricane Katrina
- Tea Party
- *Deepwater Horizon* Spill

New Millennium

Iraq War (2003-2011) - Also called the **Second Persian Gulf War**, this conflict was begun because Iraq was not cooperating with the original conditions that ended the **Persian Gulf War**. Many believed that Iraq had not destroyed their chemical weapons. The U.S., Great Britain and several other countries ordered Saddam Hussein to leave Iraq. When he did not leave, a two-phase war started. He was eventually removed from power and, once the major revolts had been calmed, the coalition forces left. Hussein was hanged in 2006 for crimes against humanity.

Columbia **Shuttle disaster** - The **Space Shuttle** *Columbia* disintegrated in 2003 as it reentered Earth's atmosphere. The entire crew was lost in a fireball over Texas that spread debris from California to Louisiana.

Hurricane Katrina - This 2005 storm devastated the U.S. **Gulf Coast** from Florida to Louisiana. The worst damage occurred in **New Orleans**. Levees between the city and **Lake Ponchartrain** broke and water flooded into the city that is below sea-level. Nearly 2,000 people died, and tens of thousands of people along the coast lost their homes and businesses. As of 2015, it was the costliest natural disaster in U.S. history.

Tea Party - This new political party surfaced in 2009. It was named after the Boston Tea Party. Most considered it a splinter group of the Republican Party. It promoted a political platform based on reduction of the national debt, the federal budget deficit and government spending and taxes.

Deepwater Horizon **oil spill** - An oil rig owned by **British Petroleum (BP)** exploded in the Gulf of Mexico in 2010. The spill was also called the **BP oil spill**. It dumped nearly five million barrels of oil over an 87-day period. This was the largest oil spill in the history of the petroleum industry.

WHERE IN THE WORLD? - *Iraq is about 437,000 square miles, which is approximately the size of California or twice the size of Idaho. It shares a border with six nations: Iran, Jordan, Kuwait, Saudi Arabia, Syria and Turkey. Beneath the land, Iraq is rich in oil reserves.*

- Matthew Shepard Act
- Death of Osama Bin Laden
- STS-135
- Boston Marathon

New Millennium

Matthew Shepard Act - In 2009, this act made discrimination based on sexual orientation, gender identity, sex or disability a criminal act; enforced in 2010.

Death of Osama bin Laden - This **al-Qaeda** leader was responsible for the **9/11 terrorist** attacks on the Twin Towers. He was killed by U.S. Navy SEALs in Pakistan in a raid code-named **Operation Neptune Spear** in 2011. The Pakistani government knew nothing of the raid, and this caused problems between the U.S. and Pakistan government.

STS-135 (2011) - The final mission of the **U.S. Space Transportation System (STS)** ended the American Space Shuttle program. The last U.S. visit to the **International Space Station (ISS)** was by the **Shuttle *Atlantis***. Since the end of the shuttle program, the U.S. has relied on private companies or the Russians to visit the ISS.

Boston Marathon bombing - The **Tsarnaev brothers** were born in Chechnya, a republic of Russia, but they had lived in the U.S. most of their lives. They detonated bombs at the finish line of the Marathon in 2013. Three people were killed and 283 injured. The oldest brother, **Tamerlan**, was shot by police and died. Younger brother, **Dzhokar**, was still awaiting trial in 2014. The Boston Marathon in the subsequent year was dedicated to the victims.

• •

NO BULLYING - Due to numerous suicides in the news, bullying is now a crime in some states. Bullying can be verbal or physical, and includes any words or actions that could hurt or intimidate a person. Emails, texts, and hurtful posts on websites are all forms of cyber-bullying. The website www.stopbullying.gov can help students and schools learn how to prevent bullying and recognize bullying behavior.

• •

TMI? - In 2013, National Security Agency (NSA) Contractor Edward Snowden released to the press details on the existence and use of a mass electronic data surveillance program that is managed by the government. Since the leak, 'government data collection' has been a subject of controversy. Should the government be able to view your Internet, phone and social media accounts? Does the idea of government monitoring make you feel safer or do you feel it encroaches on your freedom?

U.S. Presidents 1789 - 1817

George Washington (1732-1799)
- **Two Terms** (1789-1797) No party affiliation
- **Nickname** - Father of His Country

Oddly enough, he bowed to guests because he felt presidents should not shake hands, he wore dentures, but they were not wood as is commonly thought, and his six white horses had their teeth brushed every morning.

John Adams (1735-1826)
- **Term** (1797-1801) Federalist
- **Nicknames** - Atlas of Independence and Old Sink or Swim

Oddly enough, his ancestors included John and Priscilla Alden who arrived at Plymouth Rock in 1620. He and Thomas Jefferson were the only two presidents to sign the Declaration of Independence.

Thomas Jefferson (1743-1826)
- **Two Terms** (1801-1809) Democratic-Republican
- **Nicknames** - Man of the People and Sage of Monticello

Oddly enough, Jefferson was the first president inaugurated in Washington, D.C. He was right-handed, but he taught himself to write with his left. He invented the swivel chair, a pedometer and a lazy Susan. He kept bears in cages on the White House lawn.

James Madison (1751-1836)
- **Two Terms** (1809-1817) Democratic-Republican
- **Nicknames** - Father of the Constitution, Little Jemmy and His Little Majesty

Oddly enough, Madison was the first president to wear long pants. Previous presidents wore knee-breeches. He was the shortest and lightest president at 5'4" and about 100 pounds.

U.S. Presidents 1817 - 1841

James Monroe (1756-1831)
- **Two Terms** (1817-1825) Democratic-Republican
- **Nicknames** - Era-of-Good-Feeling President and the Last Cocked Hat

Oddly enough, he was the first president to have been a senator, his daughter had the first wedding in the White House, and the U.S. Marine Band played at an inauguration for the first time; this tradition continues today.

John Quincy Adams (1767-1848)
- **Term** (1825-1829) Democratic-Republican
- **Nicknames** - Old Man Eloquent and the Abolitionist

Oddly enough, he was the first president elected without receiving a majority of either the popular vote or the Electoral College vote. He regularly swam without clothes in the Potomac River at 5 a.m. He was the first president to be photographed.

Andrew Jackson (1767-1845)
- **Two Terms** (1829-1837) Democrat
- **Nicknames** - Old Hickory and the Hero of New Orleans

Oddly enough, Jackson fought in the Revolutionary War, but he was only 13 at the time. He also fought in the War of 1812. He was a noted duelist and carried a bullet in his chest close to his heart from a duel in 1806 until he died.

Martin Van Buren (1782-1862)
- **Term** (1837-1841) Democrat
- **Nicknames** - The American Talleyrand, the Careful Dutchman, the Little Magician, the Mistletoe Politician and the Red Fox of Kinderhook

Oddly enough, he was the first president born in the country of the United States of America. The term okay (OK) evolved from the abbreviation for Old Kinderhook, which was Van Buren's home.

U.S. Presidents 1841 - 1850

William Henry Harrison (1773-1841)
- **Term** (1841) Whig
- **Nicknames** - Tippecanoe, Old Tippecanoe, Washington of the West and General Mum

Oddly enough, Harrison and Tyler are the only president and vice president to be born in the same county. Harrison's father signed the Declaration of Independence.

John Tyler (1790-1862)
- **Term** (1841-1845) Whig
- **Nickname** - His Accidency

Oddly enough, he was one of five presidents, Tyler, Fillmore, Johnson, Arthur and Ford, who were never inaugurated. When the South seceded, he served as a member of the Confederate States Congress from 1861 to 1862.

James Knox Polk (1795-1849)
- **Term** (1845-1849) Democrat
- **Nicknames** - Napoleon of the Stump and Young Hickory

Oddly enough, Polk's wife, a devout Presbyterian, banned dancing, card-playing and alcohol in the White House. She also held the first White House Thanksgiving dinner.

Zachary Taylor (1784-1850)
- **Term** (1849-1850) Whig
- **Nicknames** - Old Rough and Ready

Oddly enough, Taylor was a soldier, and, consequently, he never had a place of residence. Therefore, he was not registered to vote and did not vote in his own election. His election was the first to be held on the same day in every state.

U.S. Presidents 1850 - 1865

Millard Fillmore (1800-1874)
- **Term** (1850-1853) Whig
- **Nickname** - The American Louis Philippe

Oddly enough, he helped found the University of Buffalo and served as its Chancellor. He was one of five presidents never inaugurated.

Franklin Pierce (1804-1869)
- **Term** (1853-1857) Democrat
- **Nicknames** - Young Hickory of the Granite Hills and Handsome Frank

Oddly enough, he defeated his former commander, Winfield Scott, to become president. He chose to affirm rather than swear his oath of office. He had no turnover among his cabinet members.

James Buchanan (1791-1868)
- **Term** (1857-1861) Democrat
- **Nicknames** - Old Buck, Bachelor President, Ten-Cent Jimmy and Old Public Functionary

Oddly enough, Buchanan used his niece, Harriet Lane, as primary hostess in the White House because he was an unmarried president.

Abraham Lincoln (1809-1865)
- **One+ Terms** (1861-1865) Republican
- **Nicknames** - Honest Abe, Illinois Rail Splitter, the Ancient One and the Great Emancipator

Oddly enough, Lincoln was the first president to be assassinated, the first to be born outside the original colonies and the only president to receive a patent. He and his wife held séances in the White House.

U.S. Presidents 1865 - 1881

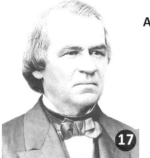

Andrew Johnson (1808-1875)
- **Term** (1865-1869) Democrat
- **Nickname** - The Tennessee Tailor

Oddly enough, he was the first U.S. president to be impeached by the House, but it was overturned in the Senate. He was another of the five presidents who was never inaugurated.

Ulysses Simpson Grant (1822-1885)
- **Two Terms** (1869-1877) Republican
- **Nicknames** - Unconditional Surrender Grant and Hero of Appomattox

Oddly enough, the office of the President received a pay raise from $25,000 to $50,000 in 1873 during his second term.

Rutherford Birchard Hayes (1822-1893)
- **Term** (1877-1881) Republican
- **Nicknames** - Dark-Horse President, Rutherfraud and His Fraudulency

Oddly enough, he won the presidency by one electoral vote. His wife refused to serve alcohol and was called Lemonade Lucy. Hayes had the first telephones installed in the White House.

James Abram Garfield (1831-1881)
- **Term** (1881) Republican
- **Nickname** - Boatman Jim

Oddly enough, Garfield could write in Latin with one hand while writing in Greek with the other. He campaigned in two languages, English and German.

U.S. Presidents 1881 - 1897

Chester Alan Arthur (1829-1886)
- **Term** (1881-1885) Republican
- **Nicknames** - Chet, the Gentleman Boss and the Dude President

Oddly enough, his wife had died prior to his becoming president so he hired Louis Tiffany, a famous designer, to refurbish the White House in high style.

Stephen Grover Cleveland (1837-1908)
- **First Term** (1885-1889) Democrat
- **Nicknames** - The Veto President and His Obstinacy

Oddly enough, he is the only president who served two terms that were not consecutive. He vetoed 414 bills during his first term. He is the second president to marry while in office and the first to be married in the White House.

Benjamin Harrison (1833-1901)
- **Term** (1889-1893) Republican
- **Nicknames** - Little Ben, the Front Porch Campaigner and the Human Iceberg

Oddly enough, he was the grandson of President William Henry Harrison and great-grandson of Benjamin Harrison V who had signed the Declaration of Independence.

Stephen Grover Cleveland (1837-1908)
- **Second Term** (1893-1897) Democrat
- **Nicknames** - The Veto President and His Obstinacy

Oddly enough, Cleveland had surgery in secret to treat an epithelioma on his upper jaw. The surgery was performed on a friend's yacht off Long Island, and the press was told he was on vacation.

U.S. Presidents 1897 - 1921

William McKinley (1843-1901)
- **One+ Term** (1897-1901) Republican
- **Nicknames** - The Idol of Ohio and the Napoleon of Protection

Oddly enough, he was the first president to run a 'front porch' campaign.

Theodore Roosevelt (1858-1919)
- **Two Terms** (1901-1909) Republican
- **Nicknames** - Teddy, TR, the Trust-Buster, the Lion and the Hero of San Juan Hill

Oddly enough, he was the first president interested in conservation, and dozens of national parks, monuments and wildlife refuges were created during his term. He was thought to have inspired the "Teddy" bear.

William Howard Taft (1857-1930)
- **Term** (1909-1913) Republican
- **Nicknames** - Big Chief and Big Lub

Oddly enough, he served on the U.S. Supreme Court for nine years after his presidency. He is one of only two presidents buried at Arlington Cemetery with John F. Kennedy being the other. His wife arranged to have 3,000 cherry trees planted in Washington, D.C.

Woodrow Wilson (1856-1924)
- **Two Terms** (1913-1921) Democrat
- **Nicknames** - Schoolmaster of Politics and the Phrasemaker

Oddly enough, he was the only president to earn a doctorate degree. His second wife, Edith, was called his 'co-president' when she assumed his duties after his stroke, and his Cabinet was called the 'Kitchen Cabinet.'

U.S. Presidents 1921 - 1945

Warren Gamaliel Harding (1865-1923)
- **Term** (1921-1923) Republican
- **Nickname** - Wobbly Warren

Oddly enough, he had a nervous breakdown at 24 years of age. His advisors were known as the 'Poker Cabinet' because they played together twice a week.

Calvin Coolidge (1872-1933)
- **One+ Terms** (1923-1929) Republican
- **Nicknames** - Silent Cal, Cool Cal and Cautious Cal

Oddly enough, Coolidge was the first president to use radio to address the American public.

Herbert Clark Hoover (1874-1964)
- **Term** (1929-1933) Republican
- **Nicknames** - The Great Engineer, the Great Humanitarian and the Chief

Oddly enough, he was orphaned and lived with relatives in Oregon. He later became a self-made millionaire. He was an engineer in China when the Boxer Rebellion broke out. He was the first president born west of the Mississippi River. The Star Spangled Banner *became the national anthem under him.*

Franklin Delano Roosevelt (1882-1945)
- **Four Terms** (1933-1945) Democrat
- **Nickname** - FDR

Oddly enough, he was the only president elected to four terms. He also was known for his 'Fireside Chats' that addressed the nation on various issues. His wife Eleanor was an outspoken activist and wrote a daily newspaper column.

U.S. Presidents 1945 - 1969

Harry S Truman (1884-1972)
- **Two Terms** (1945-1953) Democrat
- **Nickname** - Give 'Em Hell Harry

Oddly enough, Truman had no middle name. He used the middle initial "S," which represented the names of his grandfathers.

Dwight David Eisenhower (1890-1969)
- **Two Terms** (1953-1961) Republican
- **Nickname** - Ike

Oddly enough, he moved 27 times in his 38-year military career. He was Allied commander of the D-Day invasion.

John Fitzgerald Kennedy (1917-1963)
- **Term** (1961-1963) Democrat
- **Nicknames** - JFK and Jack

Oddly enough, he was the first president born in the 20th century and the youngest ever to be elected president. He received a Pulitzer Prize for his book Profiles in Courage. He started the Peace Corp.

Lyndon Baines Johnson (1908-1973)
- **One+ Terms** (1963-1969) Democrat
- **Nicknames** - LBJ, Landslide Lyndon and Light-Bulb Lyndon

Oddly enough, his college career was interrupted for a year so he could teach and serve as a principal for a Mexican-American school. His wife, Lady Bird was founder of the National Wildflower Research Center.

U.S. Presidents 1969 - 1989

Richard Milhous Nixon (1913-1994)
- **One+ Terms** (1969-1974) Republican
- **Nicknames** - Dick and Tricky Dick

Oddly enough, Nixon was an accomplished pianist and violinist. He was the first president to visit all 50 states and the first to resign from office.

Gerald Rudolph Ford (1913-2006)
- **Term** (1974-1977) Republican
- **Nicknames** - Jerry and Mr. Nice Guy

Oddly enough, Ford was the only president not elected by the people to become president. He was the only president who faced assassination attempts twice, and both times the attempts were by women. He was a former model. He was once locked out of White House, and the Secret Service let him in.

James Earl Carter, Jr. (1924-)
- **Term** (1977-1981) Democrat
- **Nicknames** - Jimmy and the Peanut Farmer

Oddly enough, he became involved in Habitat for Humanity in 1984 and won the Nobel Peace Prize nearly 20 years after his presidency.

Ronald Wilson Reagan (1911-2004)
- **Two Terms** (1981-1989) Republican
- **Nicknames** - The Gipper, Dutch, the Great Communicator and the Teflon President

Oddly enough, he was the oldest elected president at age 69. Reagan was an accomplished western-saddle equestrian and an actor. He survived an assassination attempt by John Hinkley, Jr.

U.S. Presidents 1989 - 2017

George Herbert Walker Bush (1924-)
- **Term** (1989-1993) Republican
- **Nicknames** - Poppy, 41 and Papa Bush

Oddly enough, at 18 years old, he was the youngest American Navy pilot in WWII.

William Jefferson Clinton (1946-)
- **Two Terms** (1993-2001) Democrat
- **Nicknames** - Bill, Slick Willie, Bubba, the Comeback Kid and the Big Dog

Oddly enough, he was the second president to be impeached, but the proceedings were overturned in the Senate. He was a talented saxophonist.

George Walker Bush (1946-)
- **Two Terms** (2001-2009) Republican
- **Nicknames** - 43, W and Dubya

Oddly enough, the election of 2000 was one of the most contentious in U.S. history; Bush lost the popular vote, but won the electoral vote. This was the second time in history that a son followed in his father's presidential footsteps.

Barack Obama (1961-)
- **Two Terms** (2009-) Democrat
- **Nickname** - No Drama Obama

Oddly enough, he was the first president born outside the contiguous U.S. He won the Nobel Peace Prize in 2009. He was nicknamed O'Bomber in high school because of his basketball skill.

WESTERN HEMISPHERE

Part 2
Canada,
Central America &
South America

Beginning - c. 8000 BCE

- First People in Canada
- Mesoamerican Chronology
- Paleo-Indian Period
- Archaic Era

Prehistoric Period

First people arrive in Canada (c. 30,000-c. 15,000 BCE) - These migrants were ancestors of the indigenous people living in Canada when European explorers arrived. Between 6000 BCE and 2000 BCE, the ancestors of the modern **Inuit** were one of the last groups to make the **Bering land bridge** migration to North America. More suitable southern land was already inhabited, and the Inuit settled in what is now the Canadian Arctic, Alaska, Greenland and Siberia, a frigid and extreme terrain.

Mesoamerican chronology - This was a method of defining time periods for civilizations of Mesoamerica, which included the region and cultural area from central Mexico down through Central America to the northern part of Costa Rica. It began with the **Paleo-Indian period**, which started with the first human habitation, and it extended through the **Postclassic** period, ending around 1700 CE.

Paleo-Indian period - This period began about 12,000 years ago and ended in about 8000 BCE. During this time, people practiced subsistence farming, hunting and gathering. Some pottery was made and small permanent settlements began to develop toward the end of the period. The **Amazon Basin** showed evidence of early cultures growing potatoes, chilies and beans. Domestication of llamas and alpacas began toward the end of this period.

Archaic Era - This era stretched from 8000 BCE to around 2000 BCE. Agriculture increased in scale, looms were used in weaving and settlements grew. Villages became populated with many non-related people living together. Cultures during this period grew many more crops, such as quinoa, corn, peanuts, manioc, sweet potatoes, squash and cotton. The latter was grown as the only major fiber crop. By this period, fishing had become a widespread practice. This period was followed by the **Pre-Classic** or **Formative Era**.

NOT ESKIMOS - The Inuit are spread across a large distance and often mistakenly referred to as Eskimos. However, the Inuit find this term, which purportedly translated as another tribe's word for eaters of raw flesh, offensive. The word Inuit *translates to the people.*

c. 8000 BCE - c. 1200 BCE

- Norte Chico civilization
- Valdivia Culture
- Preclassic/Formative Era
- Chavín Culture

Prehistoric Period

Norte Chico civilization - This was the oldest **pre-Columbian** society. A pre-Columbian society was any group that lived in the Western Hemisphere prior to Columbus' travel in the Americas. It has been dated to about 3500 BCE, more than a thousand years after **Sumer**. This was located along the coast of Peru. At the same time that this civilization was developing, the **Egyptians** were building their pyramids. This civilization predated the **Olmec culture** by nearly two thousand years.

Valdivia culture - While other great civilizations were growing elsewhere in the world, the people of Latin America were also developing. Though little was known about the Valdivia culture of Ecuador, their cities were built between 3000 BCE and 1800 BCE. Archeological remains showed that their houses were built in a circle around a piazza, and the people lived by farming and fishing, plus some hunting.

Preclassic or Formative Era - During this period, which began around 1800 BCE, city-states with ceremonial centers developed. **Hieroglyphic writing** began, and maize farming started to dominate agriculture. Pyramids were built, and jaguar-worship had begun. The **Olmec** thrived, and the **Zapotec**, **Maya** and **Teotihuacan** civilizations began. This era ended around 200 CE and was followed by the **Classic Era**.

Chavín culture - The Chavín culture developed in Peru and laid a foundation on which other societies were built. This group flourished between 1200 BCE and 200 BCE. Their architecture was complex and included pyramids, which indicated a well-developed and organized society. The Chavín excelled in stone-carving, especially large building blocks with pictures depicting serpents, birds and jaguars.

HORNET BOMBERS - Mayan legends indicate that during battle, warriors would toss a hornet bomb, which was composed of either a hornet's nest or an object attached to a gourd filled with the hostile insects, into groups of enemy combatants. Understandably, these bombs caused panic and chaos. Other ancient cultures, including the Greek, also used bees and wasps as weaponry.

c. 1200 BCE   c. 100 BCE

- Olmec Culture
- Zapotec Civilization

Early Civilizations

Olmec culture - This group began around 1200 BCE and lasted some 800 years. They were the first great civilization of Mesoamerica. They lived in what have become the present-day Veracruz and Tabasco states along the Gulf Coast of Mexico, and their two greatest cities were **San Lorenzo** and **La Venta**.

The **Olmec** were most famous for the colossal heads they carved of stone, which reached heights of more than nine feet. They also carved intricate designs in both ceramic and jade and created a writing system based on symbols.

Though the cause of Olmec decline was unknown, the culture was influential and considered the "mother culture" of later Latin American societies, such as the Veracruz, Maya, **Toltec** and Aztec. The Feathered Serpent, Maize God and Water God were worshipped by the Olmec, and these were present in later cultures. The influence of certain Olmec artistic styles on later Mayan and Aztec works were obvious to even the untrained eye.

Zapotec civilization - The **Zapotec** were a sedentary people who lived in the central part of the **Valley of Oaxaca** in present-day southern Mexico. Their civilization began around 700 BCE and their influence gradually spread. They traded with the **Aztec** of **Tenochtitlan**. **Monte Albán** was their greatest city. Archeologists have found evidence of buildings, ball courts, magnificent tombs and gold jewelry at that site.

They cultivated maize, developed irrigation systems and created a **logo syllabic writing system** in which each glyph, or picture, represented a syllable. The Zapotec were defeated by the Spaniards in 1563 and, though the civilization fell apart, a large number of ethnic Zapotec have remained in Oaxaca in Mexico to current times.

· ·

CROSS CULTURES - Some speculate that there was some cultural exchange between the ancient people of Valdivia and Japan based on their similar pottery styles. Though not confirmed by archeology, geneticists have found a link between the two peoples.

c. 100 BCE - c. 200 CE

- Teotihuacan
- Nazca Culture
- Classic Era

Early Civilizations

Teotihuacan in Valley of Mexico - Teotihuacan was built near present-day **Mexico City**. It peaked between 100 BCE and 650 CE and possibly supported a population in the hundred-thousands. Archaeologists have found evidence of **Maya**, **Mixtec** and Zapotec cultures, but none appeared dominant. A wide, mile-long road called the **Avenue of the Dead** connected the most prominent buildings, the **Pyramid of the Sun** and **Pyramid of the Moon**. Teotihuacan was abandoned by its original inhabitants around 750 CE.

Many Mesoamerican city-states collapsed suddenly after a period of decline with no obvious explanation. The same happened later to the Maya. The **Aztec** moved into the region around 1325, and it was they who named the city **Teotihuacan**, meaning *City of the Gods*. Murals found in the city have been compared to those created by painters of the European Renaissance.

Nazca culture - The Nazca culture flourished on the southern coast of Peru between around 100 BCE and 750 CE. They developed underground aqueducts called *puquios*, which have remained in use, to water their small farms. The **Three Sisters**, considered to be squash, beans and maize, formed their main diet. The Nazca had well-developed ceramic and textile skills but were most famous for their **geoglyphs**, the **Nazca lines**. Some were geometric shapes while others, some as large as a football field, represented animals.

The decline of the Nazca culture may have resulted from their own farming practices. Deforestation of the slopes to add farmland increased flooding and erosion and would have damaged irrigation systems. The weather extremes associated with the **El Niño** phenomena also likely contributed to the decline.

Classic Era - Beginning around 200 CE and lasting about 800 years, this period saw development of more distinct cultures throughout Mesoamerica, both socially and artistically. Widespread growth of city-states occurred as farming increased. This period was followed by the **Postclassic Era.**

• •

SPIDERWOMAN - The primary deity of Teotihuacan was a female. She was the Great Goddess or the Teotihuacan Spider Woman. She did not appear in other Mesoamerican cultures, but is present in Pueblo and Navajo cultures.

c. 200 CE - c. 800 CE

- Tiwanaku Civilization
- Mayan Period

- Arawak and Carib Cultures

Early Civilizations

Tiwanaku civilization - This culture dominated the **Titicaca Basin** and the region around the present-day borders of Chile, Bolivia and Peru between 200 CE and 1000 CE. **Lake Titicaca** was believed by this group to be the center of the world. The city of Tiwanaku was built on a grid system. Their open ceremonial spaces with precise stonework were hallmarks of the culture. Some sacred imagery carved into monoliths revealed an influence from the Chavín culture. The civilization collapsed after attacks from the **Ayamara** and droughts. This culture influenced the Inca architecturally and administratively.

Mayan Period - Maya, or Mayans, occupied southern Mexico and the **Yucatán Peninsula**. They spread to present-day Guatemala, El Salvador and most of Honduras. They reached their height between 300 CE and 900 CE. **Tikal** in Guatemala was their first major city with around 500,000 people. **Chichen Itza** in Yucatan was also a major center. They practiced terraced farming, built canals and used selective pollination to grow maize. Cities were laid out with specific buildings for government and apartments for the elite.

The Maya never united under one ruler. Specialized city-states remained common. They used **hieroglyphic writing**, and advanced mathematics was applied in astronomy, enabling them to calculate the solar year, lunar month and eclipses. The Mayan calendar was extremely accurate. Reasons for the collapse between 800 CE and 900 CE were unknown, but the Mayan people have remained a strong presence in Guatemala and southern Mexico today.

Arawak and Carib cultures - These related cultures developed along the **Orinoco River** in Venezuela and spoke an Arawakan language, the most widely used dialect encountered by early Europeans. These people were skilled boat builders and traveled to the islands which came to be known as the **Caribbean Islands**, but it has not been determined when this occurred.

. . . .

EL NIÑO - This warm current of water known as El Niño occurs in the eastern Pacific Ocean and has a great effect on weather conditions in the hemisphere. It was named as reference to the Christ child because periodic warming in the Pacific near South America was often noticed around Christmas. The actual translation is the male child.

- Toltec Civilization
- Postclassic Period
- Aztec Empire

Early Civilizations

Toltec civilization - Some scholars believe the **Toltec** were expelled from Teotihuacan in the late 400s CE. However, it was certain that by the 800s CE they had established a thriving city-state at **Tula**, or **Tollán**, near present-day Mexico City. The militaristic Toltec conquered several other communities and established an extensive trade network. They influenced the Mayan city of Chichen Itza. The Toltec were regarded as great artisans, metallurgists, farmers, sculptors and herbalists, and they had a mythical status among the Aztec. By 1022, the Toltec society collapsed, perhaps due to extensive drought or an internal power struggle. Remnants of the Toltec relocated to **Chapultepec**, near **Lake Texcoco**.

Postclassic Period - This era began around 1000 CE. Most earlier civilizations had collapsed, and the Toltec, **Mixtec** and **Aztec** had risen in their wake. The **Mayan** of present-day **Yucatan** and southern **Guatemala** experienced a brief renaissance in art, pottery and gold-work. Metallurgy continued to be refined for making jewelry and tools. A merchant class of people evolved. Priests and shamans increasingly shared leadership with civilian or military rulers. This period ended when the Spanish forces defeated the natives in 1697.

Aztec Empire - According to legend, one of the early people saw a vision that a city was to be built where they found an eagle eating a snake while sitting on a cactus. This was supposedly seen on an island in **Lake Texcoco** in the **Valley of Mexico** in the early 1300s. The city of **Tenochtitlan** was founded on this lake island. The Aztec gradually built an empire centered here.

When Spaniards arrived, it was estimated that the city had a population of around 250,000 people, which was comparable only to Paris, Venice and Constantinople. The city served as capital for about five million people in central and southern Mexico. These people called themselves the **Mexica**, though history has termed them the Aztec. They spoke a **Nahuatl** language and had a well-developed writing system. The image of the eagle, snake and cactus was used on the Mexican flag of today.

• •

EXCUSES FOR EATING CHOCOLATE - *In Oaxaca, Mexico, healers called* curanderos *use chocolate to treat illnesses, such as bronchitis.*

- Rise of Inca Empire
- Treaty of Tordesillas
- Slaves in Haiti

Early Civilizations

Rise of the Inca Empire - Around 1000 CE, **Cuzco** in present-day Peru became important and later served as capital of the **Inca Empire**. **Pachacuti** came to power in the 1400s and expanded the empire in all directions through a long period of conquest. It eventually stretched from **Quito** in present-day Ecuador to **Santiago** in the **Andes Mountains** of present-day Chile.

The Inca considered themselves *children of the sun*, and Tiwanaku and Lake Titicaca were significant in their religion. They constructed a road system that connected all regions to Cuzco. They used a series of knots and strings called a **quipu** to keep track of harvests, laborers, taxes and other statistics. Their most famous city, **Machu Picchu**, was built in 1450 CE. Located in the Andes Mountains, it was impressively built into the cliffs.

Treaty of Tordesillas - This agreement between Portugal and Spain divided the **New World** in 1494. Portugal kept everything east of the meridian 970 miles west of the **Cape Verde Islands**, and Spain controlled everything to the west. This set the stage for modern demographics in the area. They did not include others in this division, such as the French, British, Italians or Dutch.

Slaves in Haiti - Between 1492 and 1494, more than two million **Taino** people, who were natives of Haiti, died of disease brought by the Spanish and of enslavement. With the local population so decimated, the Spanish needed an additional workforce for mines and plantations. King **Ferdinand** of Spain approved a transfer of slaves from Africa to work in **Hispaniola** gold mines.

The slave trade had existed for years prior to this but bringing slaves from Africa paved the way for the huge transatlantic **slave trade**. The capture and enslavement of millions of Africans continued through the 19th century. Much later, **Bartolomé de las Casas**, a Spanish missionary, campaigned against enslaving the Taino people of Hispaniola. The Spanish did cease enslaving the Haitian natives by around 1542, but this did not apply to African slaves.

. . . .

QUETZALCOATL - This was one of the main Teotihuacan gods. He was regularly offered human sacrifices. The name of this god meant feathered serpent. *A feathered serpent appeared in the Aztec pantheon as this same god and as the Mayan god Kukulcan.*

1500 - 1540

- Conquistadors
- End of Aztec Empire
- End of Inca Empire
- Council of the Indies
- Congo Slave Trade

Colonization

Conquistadors - Beginning in 1499, Spanish and later Portuguese conquistadors arrived with steel weaponry. They competed for land and resources while searching for riches. They stole native treasures and religious artifacts that were gold and melted them down to ship to Europe. Europeans brought livestock, and this became important to their economies and has remained so. They also brought influenza, measles, smallpox and typhus, which decimated the populations. The Europeans conquered and destroyed existing empires. Missionaries arrived to convert the natives to **Christianity**. Many groups blended with the native population, creating a **mestizo** class.

End of Aztec Empire - The ninth Aztec emperor of Mexico was **Moctezuma**. The empire was at its height when the Spaniards arrived. Moctezuma unsuccessfully attempted to appease the Spaniards with gifts. **Hernán Cortés** allied himself with an enemy tribe, the **Tlaxcalan**, and marched on Tenochtitlan. Moctezuma was taken captive and used to control the empire until he was killed in 1520.

End of Inca Empire - In 1533, **Francisco Pizarro** defeated the Inca. **Atahualpa**, a new and inexperienced leader, was captured by the Spaniards. They used him to control the empire and eventually executed him. The Inca were decimated by smallpox brought by the Spanish conquistadors. Their language was **Quechua**, which has been spoken continually in this area until present times.

Council of the Indies - This council of six to ten people appointed by the king was the governing body for Spanish colonies from 1524 to 1834.

Congo slave trade - In 1530, **Juan de la Barrera** of **Seville** in Spain altered the structure of slave trade by taking slaves from Africa and transporting them directly to the New World, bypassing Europe.

. . . .

SUSPENDED IN TIME - The Inca-built suspension bridge, Qeswachaka, is rebuilt annually, as it has been for the past 1,500 years, back into Inca times. All the women weave grass ropes. All the men construct the rope bridge. Women may not be present during construction as this is considered bad luck!

91

1540 - 1790

- Amazon River Exploration
- Founding of Manaus
- Treaty of Ryswick
- Canadian Development
- Rebellion in Peru

Colonization

Amazon River exploration - In 1541, **Francisco de Orellana** left **Quito**, in what is now **Ecuador**, with an expedition headed by **Francisco Pizarro**, a Spanish conquistador, to locate the *Land of the Cinnamon* where trees grew that produced the valuable cinnamon spice. The two explorers became separated, and Orellana continued to the headwaters of the Amazon to search for gold. From the headwaters, his group traveled to the mouth of the Amazon in 1542.

Founding of Manaus - Around 1669, Manaus began as a fort. It became a city in 1848, and was the rubber capital of South America. Located in the middle of the Amazon rainforest, it was primarily accessed by boat. Later, it could be reached by plane. Many native tribes near Manaus have preserved their ancient cultures, primarily because of its isolation.

Treaty of Ryswick - To settle colonial differences, this treaty in 1697 split the island of Hispaniola into a Spanish side, which was **Santo Domingo**, and a French side, which was **Saint-Domingue**. The latter became **Haiti.**

Canadian development - During **Queen Anne's War**, which lasted from 1702 to 1713, the British won control of the French Acadian colonies. This included parts of present-day Quebec and Maine. Britain and France conflicted again in the **French and Indian War**, resulting in mass expulsion of French **Acadians** and in France's ceding its Canadian claims to the British.

Rebellion in Peru - **Túpac Amaru II** was one of the last of the Incan royal family. He was a mestizo and had received his education through Jesuit missions. He led a rebellion of native people in Peru against Spanish rule in 1780 and 1781. Although unsuccessful, the revolt influenced native populations in other areas and triggered their revolts. This instilled a nationalistic spirit that has continued to present times.

• •

PLAY BALL - An ancient ball game was played by many Mesoamerican cultures. The game used a rubber ball and dated to about 3000 BCE. Cortés sent ballplayers back to Spain in 1528 to perform for Charles V. The Spaniards were amazed by the skill of the players, but were more fascinated by the bouncing rubber balls. Europeans were unfamiliar with rubber, while South Americans had used rubber for 4,000 years.

1790 - 1810

- Haitian Revolution
- Venezuelan Independence
- Argentine Independence
- Mexican Independence

Independence

Haitian Revolution - The French slavery system was brutal. Haiti had more slaves than free people. This, combined with the influence of the French Revolution, resulted in a successful slave revolt that began in 1791. Haiti became the first free African-led nation in 1804 during the post-colonial period.

Venezuelan independence - In 1811, **Francisco de Miranda** led a group that created a constitution and declared Venezuela independent, but this movement failed. After unsuccessful revolts against the Spanish government, commander **Simón Bolívar** led his *Campana Admirable*, or Admirable Campaign, to free Venezuela from Spain. Independence was finally gained in 1821. Bolívar followed his work in Venezuela by helping to free Colombia, Ecuador, Peru and Bolivia. He was given the nickname *El Libertador,* or **The Liberator**.

Argentine independence - **José de San Martín**, born in what is now Argentina and educated in Spain, returned to his native country to fight for independence. Upon freeing his country, he made **Buenos Aires** the capital. This city dated to around 1580 as a port city that depended on trade. He then fought in Chile for independence along with **Bernardo O'Higgins**. He fought in Peru and Ecuador with Bolívar for freedom.

Mexican independence - Uttered from the small town of Dolores in 1810, the *Grito de Dolores*, which meant the *Cry of Dolores,* was an appeal to natives and *mestizos* to rise up in revolution against Spaniards. **Miguel Hidalgo y Costilla**, a Catholic priest, issued the call to action against the oppression of Spain. A bloody class struggle ensued as the **Mexican War of Independence** began, and it culminated in Mexico's gaining independence from Spain by 1821. During this same period, many Latin American countries were fighting for independence from European nations.

GIANT ANACONDA - Early explorers in South America reported seeing anacondas that were more than 150 feet long. The longest reputably-measured and confirmed anacondas are about 25 feet long and 44 inches in girth and weigh several hundred pounds.

1810 - 1820

• Independence in Latin American Countries

Independence

Independence in Latin America - During the late 1700s and early 1800s, most of Latin America gained independence from European nations.

Country	Gained Independence in ...	Independence from...
Mexico	1810	Spain
Venezuela	1811; 1821	Spain; Spain
Argentina	1816	Spain
Chile	1810	Spain
Colombia	1810	Spain
Paraguay	1811	Spain
Peru	1821	Spain
Costa Rica	1821	Spain
El Salvador	1821	Spain
Guatemala	1821	Spain
Honduras	1821	Spain
Nicaragua	1821	Spain
Brazil	1822	Portugal
Ecuador	1822	Spain
Bolivia	1825	Spain
Uruguay	1825	Brazil
Dominican Republic	1844	Haiti
Cuba	1898; 1905	Spain; U.S.
Panama	1821; 1903	Spain; Colombia
Guyana	1905	UK
Suriname	1975	The Netherlands
Belize	1981	UK
Puerto Rico	No Date	U.S. commonwealth; gained from Spain
Falkland Islands	No Date	UK - British Overseas Territory
French Guiana	No Date	French Overseas Department

. . . .

LITTLE VENICE - In 1499, Amerigo Vespucci, a navigator, landed in what is now Venezuela. Vespucci thought that it looked like Venice in Italy because of the houses on stilts around the lake. He named it Veneziola, *meaning* Little Venice. *The Spanish later colonized and modified the spelling.*

1820 - 1848

- Plan of Iguala
- Monroe Doctrine
- Rise of Caudillos
- Mexican-American War

Independence

Plan of Iguala - During the Mexican War, **Agustin de Iturbide**, a general, and **Vincente Guerroro**, a rebel leader, signed this plan. It dictated that Mexico was to become a constitutional monarchy whose only official religion was to be Roman Catholicism. After the war, Iturbide was proclaimed president of the provisional government. He designed the first Mexican flag. He was exiled in 1823 and later executed. A period of turmoil followed.

Monroe Doctrine - An 1823 congressional address by **James Monroe**, then president of the U.S., defined U.S. foreign policy of the time. This statement, which came to be known as the Monroe Doctrine, was based on three concepts, which included separate spheres of influence for the Americas and Europe, non-colonization and non-intervention. Monroe's address warned Europe not to interfere in freshly independent Latin American countries.

Rise of caudillos - Instability created in the wake of Latin American independence left room for the rise of *caudillos*, which meant *generals on horseback* or military men with sizable followings. Many assumed power and led revolutions during the 19th century, establishing revolving military dictatorships.

Mexican-American War - The U.S. and Mexico fought this war between 1846 and 1848. Mexico was against American expansionism and the idea of **Manifest Destiny**, which was a widely held belief in the U.S. that American settlers were destined to expand throughout the continent. **James K. Polk**, the U.S. President, attempted to buy land from Mexico, but his offer was rejected. He initiated military conflict. American troops were victorious and Mexico City fell in 1847.

. . . .

SANTA ANNA'S INFAMOUS LEG - Antonio López de Santa Anna's leg was damaged by cannon fire in a battle in Mexico and amputated. In the Mexican-American War, he used a cork prosthesis. The artificial leg was captured by American troops. It is on display at the Illinois State Military Museum. The Museum has not returned it to Mexico. You might want to read more about Santa Anna's real and artificial leg episodes.

1848 - 1870

- Treaty of Guadalupe Hidalgo
- War of Triple Alliance
- Cuban Uprising

Independence

Treaty of Guadalupe Hidalgo - This treaty ended the Mexican-American War in 1848. The U.S. was the decisive victor of this conflict and this treaty established the boundaries of the Mexico-U.S. border. Mexico also recognized U.S. annexation of Texas. The U.S. acquired over 500,000 square miles, which amounted to more than half of Mexico's territory, for $15 million dollars. The U.S. rose to become a world power, and Mexico was destined to remain a third world country for a time. U.S.-Mexico relations have remained complicated throughout history.

War of the Triple Alliance - This conflict, also known as the **Paraguayan War**, was fought between Paraguay and the allied countries of Argentina, Brazil and Uruguay. There had been boundary disputes between Paraguay and its neighbors for years. When Brazil helped a Uruguayan leader oust his opponent, the Paraguayan President **Francisco Solano López** retaliated by declaring war on Brazil. Argentina and Uruguay allied with Brazil as the **Triple Alliance**, and López found his country at war with three nations.

Paraguay was defeated. The Paraguayan population was more than cut in half by what was termed Latin American's bloodiest clash. The victors demanded money, and annexed and divvied up much Paraguayan land at the end of the war in 1870.

Cuban uprising - In 1868, a nationalist uprising began against Spanish rule. It culminated in the unsuccessful **Ten Years' War**. This began when sugarcane grower, **Carlos Manuel de Céspedes**, led a revolt and proclaimed Cuba's independence from Spain. The war continued for ten years, but independence was not gained during this period.

· ·

HEMINGWAY IN CUBA - "Let him think that I am more man than I am and I will be so." ~ Ernest Hemingway from The Old Man and the Sea (Hemingway moved to Cuba when he was 40, and he spent most of the following 20 years of his life there. He received the Nobel Prize for literature shortly after publishing this book.)

1870 - 1890

- North-West Mounted Police
- End of Slavery in Brazil
- War of the Pacific
- Last Emperor
- Pan-American Union

Independence

North-West Mounted Police - In 1873, Canada established a mounted police force to enforce Canadian authority in the Northwest Territories. They later merged with the **Dominion Police** and changed the name in 1904 to the **Royal Canadian Mounted Police**, also called the **Mounties**.

End of slavery in Brazil - For centuries, slavery was a significant part of Brazilian culture. This was the last country in the Western Hemisphere to abolish slavery, which occurred in 1888. Racial tension has remained there since.

War of the Pacific - Between 1879 and 1883, Chile and Bolivia fought over disputed, mineral laden territory located in the **Atacama Desert**, a strip of land west of the Andes Mountains along the Pacific coast. It was an access point to the Pacific Ocean for otherwise landlocked Bolivia. Rivalry with Chile prompted Peru to join the conflict, allying with Bolivia. Bolivia and Peru were defeated, and Chile won much of the disputed territory. Bolivia remained landlocked. Thousands perished, and significant amounts of property were destroyed during the course of this conflict.

Last emperor in South America - Brazil was led by **Dom Pedro II** for 58 years, beginning in 1831. His reign was considered one of the strongest periods in Brazil's history. He created an emerging power from a failing nation. His reign ended when the military elite and a few wealthy individuals overthrew him in 1889, and they abolished the monarchy. It was replaced with the **First Brazilian Republic**. From this point, Brazil suffered a continual decline.

Pan-American Union - This organization was created in 1890 at the initial **Pan-American Conference** and served to promote Latin American-U.S. relations. In 1948, this became the **Organization of American States (OAS)**.

. . . .

BUTCH & SUNDANCE - In the late 1890s, Butch Cassidy and the Sundance Kid were busy robbing banks and trains in the Western U.S. The law was on their trail, and they fled to Bolivia. The popular movie with Paul Newman and Robert Redford portrayed their escape and turned them into folk heroes in the 1969 movie, Butch Cassidy and the Sundance Kid.

1890 - 1910

- Klondike Gold Rush
- Platt Amendment
- Valparaiso Earthquake
- North Pole Expedition

Turmoil & Conflict

Klondike Gold Rush - This was also called the **Yukon Gold Rush**. It began in 1896 when gold was found in a Canadian creek in the Klondike region. **Dawson City** was established in 1896, and the **Yukon Territory** was established in 1898. The end of the gold rush was 1899, but an estimated 100,000 prospectors had stampeded to the territory during that rush. Due to the gold rush, this area was developed and attained a romanticized legacy in popular literature.

Platt Amendment - This agreement in 1901 listed conditions under which the U.S. would leave Cuba at the close of the **Spanish-American War**. Two provisions allowed the U.S. to unilaterally intervene in Cuban affairs and to lease land in Cuba for U.S. naval bases. This was the basis of the long-term lease of **Guantanamo Bay Naval Base** that has remained in use until present times.

Great Valparaiso earthquake - This Chilean earthquake in 1906 measured 8.2 on a magnitude scale. It caused severe damage and a tsunami; 3,886 people were killed. It was predicted a week before it occurred.

North Pole expedition - In 1909, American explorer **Robert Peary** claimed to have reached the geographic North Pole. A competing claim by **Frederick Cook**, another American, insisted that he had reached the North Pole in 1908, but a commission of the University of Copenhagen ruled that he had not proven that he reached the pole. Both claims were questioned. The first undisputed expedition was led by British explorer **Wally Herbert** in 1969.

. . . .

"THE SPELL OF THE YUKON" - *"There's gold, and it's haunting and haunting; / It's luring me on as of old; / Yet it isn't the gold that I'm wanting / So much as just finding the gold. / It's the great, big, broad land 'way up yonder, / It's the forests where silence has lease; / It's the beauty that thrills me with wonder, / It's the stillness that fills me with peace." ~ Robert Service (Service participated in the Yukon Gold Rush, and wrote many poems about the area.)*

1910 - 1931

- South Pole Exploration
- Mexican Revolution
- Lost Inca City
- Oil in Venezuela
- Christ the Redeemer Statue

Turmoil & Conflict

South Pole exploration - A Norwegian explorer by the name of **Roald Amundsen** led the first successful expedition to reach the South Pole in 1910 and 1911.

Mexican Revolution (1910-1920) - **Francisco I. Madero** led an uprising against Mexico's autocratic ruler, **Porfirio Díaz**. Rebellion became a full-fledged civil war between multiple opposing groups. The dictatorship was replaced with a constitutional republic and violence continued to break out after its establishment. About one million people were killed during this conflict.

Lost Inca city - In 1911, Yale anthropology professor **Harry Bingham** stumbled upon the lost city of **Machu Picchu** during a Peruvian expedition. Machu Picchu, which means *old peak* in the **Quechuan** language, was an Incan city constructed in the 15th century. This mountainous city was possibly a royal retreat for the Inca. It was deserted in the 16th century for unknown reasons.

Oil found in Venezuela - First used by pre-Columbian era people for medicinal purposes, oil was rediscovered and foreigners drilled for it in 1912. **Royal Dutch Shell** and **Standard Oil** participated. Venezuela became a top oil producer. Workers left farms for lucrative jobs in oil fields. The movement toward developing natural resources at the expense of agriculture and manufacturing was widespread and became known as the *Dutch disease*. This focus on oil and drop in agricultural production resulted in a failure of the country to industrialize.

Christ the Redeemer Statue - This Art Deco statue was constructed between 1922 and 1931 atop the mountain of **Corcovado** overlooking the city of **Rio de Janeiro**. The height of the statue was 98 feet, and it stands on a 26-foot pedestal. It was funded primarily by Brazilian Catholic donations and was designed as a monument to Christianity and as a symbol of peace.

PANCHO VILLA - José Doroteo Arango Arámbula became a folk hero when fighting for Mexico's independence from Spain. A colorful character, according to Villa's last surviving widow, he officially married 25 times, but only had 25 children. In fact, he married twice a year between 1910 and 1923. He also had a movie contract with a Hollywood producer to film his battles.

1931 - 1962

- Statue of Westminster
- Chaco War
- Exile of Perón
- Cuban Revolution

Turmoil & Conflict

Statute of Westminster - Britain granted Canada and its other dominions legislative independence in many things with this statute in 1931. Canada became a British Commonwealth realm with a parliamentary democracy and constitutional monarchy linked to the British Crown.

Chaco War - Loss of coastal territory in the **War of the Pacific** left **Bolivia** landlocked. In an attempt to gain **Chaco Boreal**, which would give access to the **River Paraguay** and, thus, the **Atlantic Ocean**, Bolivia fought Paraguay. Both countries sustained heavy casualties. In 1935, Paraguay rose victorious. The **Chaco Peace Conference** settled the dispute with Paraguay's gaining the majority of the disputed area and Bolivia's gaining access to the Atlantic.

Exile of Perón - **Juan Perón**, the president of Argentina, was forced to resign after a period of discontent. The military took action against him. This occurred shortly after the death of his wife, **Evita**, who was popular with the people. He was exiled but came back to Argentina in 1972 and was re-elected by a landslide vote. Perón died in 1974.

Cuban Revolution - A combination of internal problems and the **26th of July Movement** of guerrilla warfare led by **Fidel Castro** resulted in the overthrow of Cuban dictator **Fulgencio Batista**. He was forced to flee Cuba in 1959 after a defeat by **Che Guevara**, who was an Argentine Marxist revolutionary.

Guevara played a key role in Castro's revolution, as did **Raul Castro**, Fidel's brother. The power vacuum was filled by the Communist Party. This government aligned with the Soviet Union, and Castro's extremely brutal dictatorship was established. Thus, the stage was set for the **Cuban Missile Crisis**. Fidel Castro remained dictator for 50 years.

"DON'T CRY FOR ME, ARGENTINA" - *This was the epitaph on a plaque on Evita Perón's grave that was presented by the taxi drivers' union of Buenos Aires. It became the title of a song and a musical. It was later popularized by the pop singer Madonna. Evita was beloved by the people for her work aiding the poor.*

1962 - 1973

- Cuban Missile Crisis
- Falkland War
- Dirty War
- Civilian Rule in Chile

Turmoil & Conflict

Cuban Missile Crisis - This was a conflict between the U.S. and Soviets on Cuban soil in 1962. Russia promised to help protect Cuba, and they armed them with nuclear missiles. This was perceived as a threat to the southeastern U.S. President **John F. Kennedy** ordered the U.S. to blockade Cuba to prevent the arrival of further armaments. He and Soviet leader **Nikita Khrushchev** negotiated. The Soviets withdrew missiles from Cuba, and the U.S. withdrew missiles from Turkey. This **Cold War** conflict almost culminated in nuclear war.

Falkland War - This military dispute between Argentina and Britain in 1982 was an unsuccessful attempt by Argentina to retake the islands. Argentine Lieutenant General **Leopoldo Galtieri** invaded, hoping a victory would strengthen the position of his government. Britain's Prime Minister **Margaret Thatcher** then declared the area a war zone. About 655 Argentines and 255 British died during the conflict.

Dirty War - Between 1976 and 1983, a statewide campaign to eliminate anyone opposing Argentina's government caused between 15,000 and 30,000 people to "disappear." After the Falkland War, details of the brutal purge emerged to a shocked world. Argentina has remained unstable to current times and has never acknowledged what happened to the missing populace.

Civilian rule in Chile - In a 1973 military coup, **Augusto Pinochet** took control of Chile. An economic recession and his violent response to dissent from his opposition and the Catholic Church led to the end of his rule. In 1987, the law allowed non-Marxist political parties, and a decisive election overturned Pinochet and installed **Patricio Aylwin Azocar** in his stead in 1990. Pinochet remained commander-in-chief of the army until 1998. He was arrested in England for human rights violations and died in Chile while under house arrest. There were more than 300 pending charges against him.

• •

EULOGY FOR CHE GUEVARA - Fidel Castro closed his impassioned eulogy after Guevara's death in 1967 thus: "If we wish to express what we want the men of future generations to be, we must say: 'Let them be like Che!' ... If we want the model of a man, who does not belong to our times but to the future, I say from the depths of my heart that such a model...is Che!"

1973 - Present

- Drug Cartels in Colombia
- Amazon Rainforest
- Territory of Nunavut

Modern Era

Drug cartels in Colombia - Marijuana traffickers began to move cocaine to the U.S. in suitcases in the mid-1970s. U.S. demand for the illegal substance grew quickly, and Columbian drug cartels grew with it. Two infamous cartels were the **Medellin** and **Cali**. These cartels were eventually disassembled, but the drug business has remained, though it has been fragmented.

Territory of Nunavut - The territory of Nunavut was carved from Canada's **Northwest Territory** in 1999. Nunavut encompassed most of the **Canadian Artic** and was created for the **Inuit**, people indigenous to Canada. It included their traditional lands and was organized to be largely self-governed.

Amazon rainforest - The Amazon rainforest was home to more than 2½ million different species of insects, more than 40,000 varieties of plants, 1,500 bird species and more than 2,000 fish species. About 25% of all medicinal drugs were derived from rainforest ingredients. However, it was estimated that scientists have only tested 1% of tropical plants for medicinal uses.

The rainforest was so large that it spanned nine countries: Bolivia, Brazil, Colombia, Ecuador, French Guiana, Guyana, Peru, Suriname and Venezuela. Over 7,000 square miles of the rainforest have been deforested annually while being cleared by logging, slash-and-burn agricultural techniques, cattle ranches and mining and subsistence agriculture, among other things.

The Amazon River was named by **Francisco de Orellana** in 1541. He was exploring the river and encountered and battled against female warriors. They reminded him of the Amazon women of Greek mythology, and he named the river after them.

· ·

SLOW RAIN - Very little sunlight makes it through the dense canopy of trees and foliage covering the Amazon rainforest. On the ground, it is nearly completely dark. In fact, when it starts raining, it takes about ten minutes before rain hits the ground!

EASTERN HEMISPHERE

Part 3
Europe

- Paleolithic Period
- Neolithic Period
- Minoan Civilization

Prehistoric Europe

Paleolithic Period - Part of the **Stone Age**, this period started about 1½ million years ago and ended around 10,000 BCE. During this time, people were using tools and began using fire and creating art. The paintings in **Lascaux Cave** in France and in the **Cave of Altamira** in Spain were some of the oldest examples of Paleolithic art ever found. These depicted animals, such as horses and bison, and they were probably painted around 15,000 BCE, about 5,000 years before the end of the period.

Neolithic Period (c. 10,000 BCE-2900 BCE) - Still part of the **Stone Age**, this period saw the rise of agriculture and domestication of animals. Most consider this to be about 10,000 BCE in the Near East. Farming reached Britain around 5000 BCE, and the cultivation of maize began in Mexico and South America about 500 years later.

Megaliths were large stone monuments found along the coast of Spain and France and up to Scotland and Norway. Many were associated with solar or lunar cycles. The oldest were in the **Orkney Isles** off Scotland. The most famous were at **Stonehenge**, built in England over a period of 1500 years. Most were built during the Stone Age, but some were constructed later.

Minoan Civilization - The early **Aegean** people of **Crete** were **Minoans** who produced the first great civilization of Europe. This culture developed during the **Bronze Age** around 2000 BCE. Crete has shown evidence of habitation since roughly 7000 BCE. Minoans developed naval skills that enabled them to become a central power. As an island, it was not subjected to regular hostilities suffered by settlements on the mainland of either Greece or Turkey. They became traders with a vast reach, traveling across most of the Mediterranean. They populated other Aegean islands, and adapted some of the ways of the people with whom they traded to create a unique culture.

• •

BELOW STONEHENGE - Sophisticated techniques in recent years have enabled scientists to see underground, and they have found an amazing complex of ancient monuments and buildings beneath the Stonehenge area. These dated to a much earlier period. Among the discoveries were ritual monuments, burial mounds and evidence of a possible processional route.

c. 1450 BCE - c. 700 BCE

- Knossos
- Mycenaean Civilization
- Phoenician Alphabet
- Trojan War

Early Civilizations

Knossos - This was the greatest Minoan city. This civilization ended abruptly around 1450 BCE. Nearby volcanic activity on the island of Thera had serious repercussions on the Minoans, making them vulnerable to attack, probably by the **Mycenaeans**. This site has been excavated slowly over a period of time and has long been considered the oldest city of Europe.

Mycenaean civilization - Beginning in the **Bronze Age** around 1550 BCE, this group evolved about the time the Minoan civilization ended. These people initially occupied the northern Aegean Islands and parts of the Greek mainland. Unlike Minoans, this was a warring society that built fortresses, such as **Corinth**, **Olympia**, **Sparta** and **Mycenae**. Like Minoans, they traveled the Mediterranean. Their civilization lasted about 300 years before falling to **Dorian** invaders, who had iron rather than bronze weapons. These **Hellenes**, or **Greeks**, came from the mainland and were centered in Corinth.

Phoenician alphabet - This alphabet was produced around 1400 BCE separately from the **cuneiform** writing of the time that was common in **Mesopotamia**. The Phoenicians, because they were traders, needed a better way to keep track of records and developed an alphabet with no vowels. Because of their travels, many cultures were exposed to this script.

Trojan War - Around 1200 BCE after a ten-year war, the Greeks destroyed the city of **Troy**, which was in present-day Turkey. Described by **Homer** in *The Iliad* and by **Virgil** in *The Aeneid*, the wars pitted **Trojans** against the **Spartan** and **Achaean** warriors of Greece. The war was not started by the beauty of Helen, as legends popularized, but by commercial rivalry and a desire to control the **Dardanelles Straits** and the **Black Sea** trade. It was believed that Troy was first built around 3000 BCE and survived well into the Ottoman era.

• •

NOT ALL BULL - The original labyrinth was supposedly built on Crete, possibly at Knossos, but archeological evidence has not been found. It was designed to hold the Minotaur, a creature of Greek mythology that was part man and part bull, to whom sacrifices were made.

c. 700 BCE - c. 600 BCE

- Roman Kingdom
- Roman Republic
- First Olympics
- Greek Writers

Ancient Rome & Greece

Roman Kingdom - **Romulus** was the first king of the Roman Kingdom. He was reputed to have founded **Rome** about 753 BCE on seven hills along the **Tiber River** at the beginning of the **Classical Age** in Europe. This period followed the **Iron Age** and lasted until the **Middle Ages**, or **Medieval period**. Rome's location was favorable to trade both with the **Greeks** to their east, who introduced literacy, religion and architectural styles, and with **Etruscans** to their north, who taught them skills as merchants. The kingdom grew rapidly, but the last of the seven kings of Rome, **Tarquin**, was overthrown in 509 BCE.

Roman Republic - **Lucius Junius Brutus**, a leader of the revolt against Tarquin, introduced a new type of government, the **Republic**, and he became the first consul. It was common to have more than one consul. This republic lasted some 500 years. Rome expanded, but did not become the **Roman Empire** until 27 BCE. **Gaius Julius Caesar** was the most famous leader of the Republic.

First Olympics - This competition began about 776 BCE. It was held every four years at **Olympia** in Greece. It was initially a 210-yard race. Gradually, other contests were added. Women were not participants, but often owned the horses used in chariot races. As the **Roman Empire** expanded, Romans adopted celebrations of other nations, and so the games arrived in Rome. By around 375 CE, Emperor **Theodosius** had made Christianity the official religion of the Roman Empire. He considered the games to be part of a pagan cult, and he disbanded them. Modern Olympics date to the 17th century.

Greek writers - One of the oldest storytellers whose stories still abound was **Aesop**, a slave. His tales were passed down through ages and eventually collected as *Aesop's Fables*. His actual existence was uncertain, but scattered details of his life were found in writings of **Aristotle**, **Herodotus** and **Plutarch**.

. . . .

TALK OF TROY - It is debated whether or not the poet Homer wrote the epic poems, The Iliad *and* The Odyssey. *They were written around 725 BCE, and they have had a profound influence on later writers of Western literature.*

- Greeks of Math & Science
- Birth of Democracy
- Battle of Marathon
- Roman Law

Ancient Rome & Greece

Greeks of math and science - The period between 570 BCE and 212 BCE saw great contributions to math and science by the Greeks. **Pythagoras** officially documented what would become known as the **Pythagorean Theorem**, $a^2+b^2=c^2$. **Hippocrates** has been considered father of Western medicine and probably created the **Hippocratic Oath** of ethical standards still, in part, used by doctors today. **Euclid** has been considered father of geometry, and **Archimedes** was one of the greatest mathematicians of all time. He was an engineer and inventor who developed the **Archimedes' screw**, which was key to the development of larger ships and is still in use today.

Birth of democracy - An **Athenian** statesman, lawmaker and poet, **Solon** laid the foundations for democracy around 505 BCE. He was followed by **Cleisthenes**, who reformed the constitution and set Athens on a democratic footing.

Battle of Marathon - Part of the **Greco-Persian Wars**, this battle was between the **Athenians** of Greece and the invading **Persian** forces on the **Plain of Marathon** in 490 BCE. The Greeks were victorious. The battle proved that the Greek long spear, sword and armor were more effective than the Persian weapons. This was considered a pivotal battle in European history. It encouraged the Greeks to realize that the Persians could be beaten, though they had the reputation of never having been defeated.

Roman law - The **Twelve Tables** were written in 450 BCE to establish a set of laws that would be binding on both **patricians**, who were the nobility, and **plebeians**, who were commoners. The laws were to be enforced equally. Each of the tables had several laws. Each table covered a specific topic, such as courts and trials, parental and guardianship rights, public laws and sacred laws and other things.

• •

*RUNNING THROUGH TIME - The **Battle of Marathon** is now more famous as the inspiration for the marathon race in the Olympics. Although thought to be historically inaccurate, the legend of the Greek messenger Pheidippides running to Athens with news of the victory became the inspiration for this athletic event. This event was introduced at the 1896 Athens Olympics, and it was originally run between Marathon and Athens.*

• Greek Philosophers • Macedonia

Ancient Rome & Greece

Ancient Greek philosophers - Greece began a new period in philosophy with **Socrates** of Athens. He developed a style of cross-examining people to determine if they really understood their own beliefs. He was charismatic and gathered many followers, which led authorities to accuse him of corrupting youth and to execute him in 399 BCE.

Socrates' student **Plato** carried on his tradition and founded a school of philosophy called the **Academy**. **Aristotle**, Plato's student, was considered the greatest philosopher of antiquity. Aristotle's thoughts differed from Plato's, and he opened his own school, the **Lyceum**. Ideas of these three ancient Greeks dominated philosophy for 2,000 years.

Though he lived much later than these philosophers did, **Plutarch** was an historian and writer who lived during the 1st and early 2nd centuries. He was a Greek who became a Roman citizen and studied at the Academy. His most famous works were biographies of people, such as **Alexander** and **Caesar**.

Macedonia - Though this kingdom dates to 800 BCE, it had become chaotic and was on the verge of collapse when **Philip II** ascended to the throne in 359 BCE. Philip was 21 years old. He used diplomacy to remove threats of being overthrown and armed his soldiers with 18-foot spears. He developed new fighting techniques, drove out invaders and reconquered former territories.

The **Battle of Chaeronea** was successfully fought by the Macedonians against the Greeks. Greece was then occupied by these foreigners until the early 19th century. Philip's son, **Alexander III**, also called **Alexander the Great**, inherited a large country with a large experienced army.

· ·

PICK YOUR POISON - *When Socrates was found guilty of corrupting youth and for refusing to recognize the gods of the state, he was given the choice to publicly deny his ideas or die -- Socrates chose death. Death by poison was a legal sentence for offenders who were found guilty under Athenian law, and, at 70 years old, Socrates died from drinking poisonous hemlock.*

- Empire of Alexander
- End of Roman Republic
- Assassination of Caesar

Ancient Rome & Greece

Empire of Alexander - Alexander periodically ran the country during his father's absences, but his ascent to the throne triggered internal strife and some conquered peoples, such as the Greeks, rebelled. He executed his enemies quickly, and put down revolts in a 'surrender or be wiped out' mode.

Within two years, Alexander and his army moved east to conquer **Asia Minor**, **Persia**, **Egypt** and part of **India**, building the largest empire of the ancient world. Around 330 BCE, he looted the city of **Persepolis** and burned the palace. This officially ended the **Persian Empire**. He died without designating an heir. Eventually, four generals divided much of the empire. Two of these created their own dynasties: **Seleucus** in Asia and **Ptolemy** in Egypt.

End of the Roman Republic - The Roman Republic was a network of towns that ruled themselves with different degrees of independence. **Gaius Julius Caesar** was a consul who was born to a wealthy family who favored more rights for the lower class. After holding various positions, Caesar became *Dictator Perpetuus*, meaning *dictator for life*, in 44 BCE, about a month before his death. Most of his time was spent as a soldier, expanding the Roman Empire into Gaul and Britain. He reformed the existing calendar, which became the **Julian calendar**. It was used until 1582 when the **Gregorian calendar** mostly replaced it. He eliminated the tax system. He seldom conferred with the senate, which unnerved many politicians.

Assassination of Caesar - In 44 BCE, on the **Ides of March**, or March 15, Caesar was killed by senators led by **Brutus** and **Cassius**. This ended the **Roman Republic** era. **Octavian**, the adopted son of Caesar, was named heir. The senator-assassins had not planned for 'what next,' which allowed **Mark Antony**, **Octavian** and **Marcus Lepidus** to rule as the **Second Triumvirate**.

ET TU, BRUTE - Shakespeare's play, Julius Caesar, written around 1600, depicted this heroic period and the assassination of Caesar. In the play, Caesar's last words were "Et tu, Brute!" The meaning is "And you, Brutus!" It is now widely used to signify the utmost betrayal by a trusted friend, as Brutus was to Caesar. In the play, Antony calls it the "unkindest cut of all."

- Egypt & Rome
- Roman Empire
- Invasion of Britain

Roman Empire

Egypt and Rome - Egypt was a very rich and powerful country. Both Caesar and Antony allied with **Cleopatra**. Antony's alliance caused conflict between him and Octavian, and the Triumvirate was torn apart by civil war. Upon Antony's death in 30 BCE, Octavian took the name **Augustus Caesar**, becoming emperor, beginning the **Roman Empire** and conquering Egypt.

Roman Empire - From 27 BCE until 476 CE, this empire was a significant force in Europe. Around 100 CE, the Empire was at its peak and covered both sides of the Mediterranean. It went as far north as **Poland** and the **Ukraine**, as far east as **Mesopotamia**, as far northwest as **Britain** and as far southeast as **Egypt**. It was the largest empire of the **Classical Era** and one of the largest in world history.

The military was a powerful force during the Empire. As territories were conquered, they became **Romanized**. Roman culture was assimilated into existing cultures. Languages were mixed, and public buildings were built for baths and games. Roads and **aqueducts** were constructed. Architecture and art were changed based on Roman standards. This was a slave society with a small, voting upper class. Women were citizens and independent of husbands, but not of their fathers. Roman law was spread throughout the empire.

Invasion of Britain - **Claudius** was uncle of the Roman emperor **Caligula**. Part of Claudius' strategy for staying alive in the world of Roman politics was playing a fool. When the emperor Caligula and his family were murdered in 41 CE by the **Praetorian Guard**, who served as bodyguards for the emperor, Claudius was brought before the senate and confirmed as emperor. He was paranoid and ruthless, but astute and spent money to keep his citizens fed, even through a period of drought. He led the successful invasion of Britain and expanded Roman rule in Africa.

. . . .

CELTIC HEROINE - Queen Boudicca, of the Celtic Iceni, led the last large revolt against Roman occupation in Britain in 60 CE. Over 80,000 Romans were killed in the struggle before her defeat at the Battle of Watling Street. She became a national heroine who is still recognized today.

- Burning of Rome
- Mt. Vesuvius
- Five Good Emperors of Rome

Roman Empire

Burning of Rome - **Nero** was a conniving and ruthless ruler who was emperor at the time of a six-day fire that destroyed much of Rome in 64 CE. He took full advantage of the destruction to rebuild Rome with many improvements, such as a better residential district, wider streets, colonnades, brick buildings rather than wood and, of course, a golden palace, called **Domus Aurea**, with a gold-plated ceiling for himself.

Mt. Vesuvius - This volcano exploded in 79 CE and destroyed numerous communities southeast of present-day Naples. **Pompeii** was entirely covered by volcanic ash, and nearby **Herculaneum** was preserved under a coating of pyroclastic flow. Poisonous gasses killed those who survived the ash and pumice. Further eruptions buried the cities with as much as 50 feet of ash. Both cities were exceedingly well preserved for 1500 to 2000 years, and when excavated, they provided an incredible glimpse into ancient Roman life.

Five Good Emperors of Rome (96 CE-180 CE) - The **Roman Empire** had many disastrous rulers; some were unremarkable, but they had five men who ruled in what is considered the **Golden Period** of the Roman Empire. Though he only ruled for two years, **Nerva** brought stability to an empire badly shaken by cruel, self-absorbed leaders. He had no children and so adopted **Trajan**, the governor of Upper Germany, to be his successor.

Trajan was a successful general and governor, and he ruled for nearly 20 years. He adopted his cousin **Hadrian**, a Spanish general in his army, to be his successor. Hadrian was considered a brilliant administrator and governor. He was best known for **Hadrian's Wall**, built across Scotland to keep the barbarians from the north out of the Roman-held area. He also rebuilt the **Pantheon**, which still stands, as well as numerous cities throughout the Balkans. **Antonius Pius** was adopted by Hadrian at age 51.

. . . .

FANNING THE FLAMES - There is no proof that Nero set the great fire of Rome, but he had such a poor reputation, no one would have put it past him. He was said to have been playing the fiddle while Rome was burning. He was actually a talented lyre player; however, he was 35 miles away from Rome when the fire broke out.

- Last Good Emperors
- Division of Roman Empire
- Christianity in Rome
- Nicene Creed

Roman Empire

Last Good Emperors - **Antonius** had a surprisingly long reign of relative peace. He adopted 16-year-old **Marcus Aurelius**, as Hadrian had wished. Marcus Aurelius was the last of the five emperors and he ruled until 180 CE, putting needs of his people ahead of his own glory. A philosopher, he wrote *The Meditations*, though he never intended them to be published. He was succeeded by his self-indulgent son, **Commodus**, who had no work ethic. The decline of Rome began.

Division of the Roman Empire (285 CE) - When **Diocletian** came to power, the *Pax Romana*, which was a period of Roman peace, had been gone for more than a century. The empire was in chaos, and Diocletian split it into the Eastern Roman Empire, or **Byzantine Empire**, and the **Western Roman Empire** with two emperors and two sub-rulers. He created a tetrarchy, a rule of four. Unfortunately, the East thrived and the West continued its fall. Rome later fell in 476 CE to **Odoacer**, a soldier, who became the first King of Italy.

Christianity in Rome - The Christian religion spread through the Mediterranean area, but the Roman government persecuted those adhering to this religion for about three centuries. Under the rule of the Emperor **Constantine**, it became the dominant religion. He was baptized shortly before his death. The **Edict of Milan** in 313 CE was an agreement that granted religious freedom to Christians as well as other religions. Vandals from southern Scandinavia were allowed to settle in some remote western areas of the empire.

Adoption of Nicene Creed (325 CE) - The first **Ecumenical Council** of the **Catholic Church** was called by Constantine, the first Christian to lead the Roman Empire. In **Nicea**, near Constantinople, the council established religious and civil order by creating a consistent doctrine for the religious movement. All bishops were invited; the result was the **Nicene Creed**, which forms the basis of beliefs of the **Catholic Apostolic Church**. It established a date for the Easter celebration, which had been timed to occur with the Jewish Passover.

. . . .

RAISED BY WOLVES - According to legend, two twin brothers named Romulus and Remus were abandoned by their mother and left in a basket in the river. It was said a wolf found and raised the babies. One of the brothers, Romulus, was said to have founded Rome.

- Romans Leave Britain
- Invasion by Visigoths
- Arrival of St. Patrick
- End of Western Roman Empire

Roman Empire

Romans leave Britain - Although there was no official decolonization order by the late 300s, Roman rule of northern and western Britain was ending. In 393, ten-year-old **Honorius** was the Western Roman emperor, but power was in the hands of his father-in-law **Stilicho**. Troops were needed to combat the **Visigoths**, who were invading Rome, and troops were withdrawn from the area near **Hadrian's Wall** to defend Rome. The British appealed for help from Honorius in 410 CE, and he sent his **Rescript of Honorius**, which told them to tend to their own defense. Some think this decree was intended for a group in Italy, not the British. The **Huns** were invading from Central Asia and pushing the Vandals toward Spain during this same period.

Invasion of Rome by Visigoths - The **Visigoths** were a branch of the Germanic **Goth** tribe. They were led by **Alaric I** in the sacking of Rome in 410 CE. At this time, the capital had been moved from Rome to **Ravenna** for strategic reasons, but Rome was still an important city of the Roman Empire.

Arrival of St. Patrick in Ireland - Patrick was born in Scotland to Roman parents. He was captured at age 16 and taken to Northern Ireland, where he became a slave and a shepherd. He escaped, returned to his family and studied for the priesthood so he could return to Ireland. He spread Christianity throughout Ireland from 433 CE until his death in 461 CE. Ireland has remained one of the world's most devoutly Catholic countries.

End of Western Roman Empire - This empire was considered to have ended in 476 CE, when **Odoacer**, a German chieftain, deposed **Romulus Augustulus**, who had usurped the crown. Odoacer proclaimed himself ruler of Italy, and the reigning **Byzantine** emperor **Zeno**, who controlled what had been the Eastern Roman Empire, gave him the title of Duke of Italy. During this same time, **Herodotus** lived and compiled systematic histories of events of the ages before him. He is widely known as "**The Father of History**."

ROUND TABLE TALK - Though no evidence exists of a King Arthur in the 5th or 6th century in Britain, Arthurian legends abound that include such characters as Sir Lancelot and other knights of the Round Table, Guinevere and Merlin the wizard. Arthur's fabulous sword was named Excalibur!

- Middle Ages
- Reconquista

Middle Ages

Middle Ages - This era began with the collapse of the Western Roman Empire during the 5th century and lasted until the beginning of the **Renaissance** in the 15th century. The early part of this period was called the **Dark Ages**. The Middle Ages were a period of conflict in the Roman Empire with barbaric German invaders, who formed kingdoms in the western part of the Empire. The **Byzantine Empire** survived in the eastern part. Agriculture became important; trade increased; and the manor system emerged with a feudalistic format. The **Crusades** took place during the latter part of this period.

Reconquista - The traditional beginning of this period of history in Spain and Portugal was about 718 CE when the **Christian Asturians** tried to overthrow the **Muslim Moors** who occupied the Iberian Peninsula. However, it was not until the Moorish **caliphates** began facing disunity from within that the Christians of **Iberia** had an opportunity to regain the region from the Muslims. Wars began in earnest in the 11th century, and the majority of Iberia returned to Christian hands by the 13th century.

A great military leader, **Rodrigo Díaz de Vivar** was in service to the king of **Castile**, **Alfonso VI**. Díaz became known as **El Cid**, meaning *the lord*. He was undefeated in battles in the last part of the 11th century, whether he was fighting Christians or Moors. He expanded the territory under the control of Castile. His prowess was so great that he became a national hero; statues of him were erected, and plays, films and songs were written about him.

The city of **Granada** in **Andalusia** was the capital of the Moors of the **Naşrid dynasty**. The famed **Alhambra** palace was built here as a castle and refined under this dynasty. By 1492, internal strife within the Naşrid dynasty gave the kingdom of Castile the chance it needed to overrun Granada and retake the last Moorish stronghold on the Iberian Peninsula.

NO HORSE SENSE - According to legend, El Cid's godfather allowed him to pick a horse from an Andalusian herd. He supposedly made so poor a choice that his grandfather exclaimed "Babieca!" which meant stupid. Thus his beloved warhorse was named.

- Viking Age
- Holy Roman Empire

Middle Ages

Beginning of the Viking Age - The **Vikings** came from present-day Sweden, Denmark and Norway starting about 793 CE. The **Swedes** traveled along the Volga River into present-day **Russia** creating settlements. The **Danish** settled in England and in the Normandy area of France. They traveled into the **Mediterranean** and to the **Black Sea**. The **Norwegians** raided and settled in the **Orkney** and **Shetland Isles**, as well as **Ireland**. The Norwegians also created settlements in **Greenland, Iceland**, and even a short-lived settlement at **L'Anse aux Meadows** in Newfoundland, Canada. This latter settlement was founded by **Leif Erikson**, who was the son of **Erik the Red**.

Most historians consider the attack on the monastery at **Lindisfarne** in **Northumbria** in Britain the beginning of the Viking Age. Monasteries were a source of gold and silver and were repeatedly sacked along British and European coasts.

Not all Viking activity was destructive or barbaric. They were instrumental in founding **Dublin** and **Waterford** as trading centers. Vikings introduced various legal concepts that applied to everyone, not just the rich. A general assembly called the **Thing** or **Althing** was responsible for maintaining laws and enforcing equal punishments. Both sides of complicated cases were heard by a group of learned men, who then passed judgment on the case in question.

Holy Roman Empire - **Charles I** was the king of the **Franks** and later king of Italy. He came to be known as **Charles the Great** or **Charlemagne**. He created the **Carolingian Empire**, which ultimately encompassed much of Eastern Europe. Charles was a protector of the papacy. In 800 CE, Pope **Leo III** crowned Charles as emperor at **St. Peter's Basilica**. For the first time since the fall of the **Roman Empire**, most of Western Europe was united. The Holy Roman Empire ended in 1806 with the retirement of **Francis II** of the **House of Habsburg**.

* *

LAND HO! - *Leif Erikson Day is an annual American celebration on October 9. It marks the date that the first Europeans set foot on the North American continent. The Vikings were the first to reach American shores, and they came about 500 years before Christopher Columbus sailed this way.*

- Hero of Wessex
- First Scottish King
- Battle of Hastings

Middle Ages

Hero of Wessex - Alfred the Great was the first king of the Anglo-Saxons, ruling for 28 years beginning in 871 CE. A Christian king, he defeated the Vikings and kept control of southern England, including London. His designation of 'the Great' was added centuries later, and he has remained the only monarch with that title in Britain.

First Scottish king - Kenneth MacAlpin had claims to both the Gaelic **Dál Riata** throne of western Scotland and the **Pict** throne of eastern Scotland. He rose to take power and defend the land from **Norse** invaders. There were numerous myths associated with his kingship and rise to power, but he united the **Gaels** with the more dominant Picts into the **Kingdom of Alba**, which became **Scotland** around 839 CE.

Battle of Hastings - When **Edward the Confessor** died, there were three people who claimed the English throne: **Harald Hardrada**, King of Norway, **Harold Godwinson**, Earl of Wessex, and **William I**, Duke of Normandy. The **witan**, England's royal council, quickly crowned Godwinson as **Harold II**, King of England. Hardrada invaded England from the north with an army of 8,000, but he was defeated and killed at the **Battle of Stamford Bridge** by Harold.

By this time, **William of Normandy** and his forces had landed in southern England. Harold was forced to quickly turn his army and rush to meet William. The **Battle of Hastings** was fought in 1066, and Harold was defeated. William became king and was known as **William the Conqueror**. **Normans** subdued the **Saxon** peoples, although it took years to accomplish. The **Norman Conquest** of England was a major turning point in history. The combining of England and Normandy created a wealthy nation with a strong military and changed the face of Europe forever.

BEOWULF - Between the 8th and 11th centuries, this epic poem came into existence as an early example of Old English literature. It is Scandinavian in origin and depicts a hero of the 6th century who fought monsters, first in his youth and later at a final battle in his old age.

• Investiture Controversy   • Crusades

Middle Ages

Investiture Controversy - This was the most serious conflict between church and state in medieval Europe in the 11th and 12th centuries. It dealt with whether the pope or the monarch would name powerful church officials, such as bishops of cities and abbots of monasteries. The controversy began between Pope **Gregory VII** and **Henry IV**, the **Holy Roman Emperor**. It ended in 1122, when **Henry V** and Pope **Calixtus II** compromised in the **Concordat of Worms**. This agreement separated royal and spiritual powers and gave emperors a limited role in selecting bishops. It was mainly a victory for the pope.

Crusades (1095-1291) - The **Crusades** were military campaigns which began when Pope **Urban II** of the **Roman Catholic Church** decided that access to **Jerusalem** and other Christian holy sites needed to be restored to Christians. Some historians believed that the Crusades were defensive wars against **Islamic** conquests.

The **First Crusade** in 1095 created four small Latin kingdoms in the Eastern Mediterranean and the **Knights Hospitaller**, **Knights Templar** and the **Teutonic Knights** rose in power. Most historians consider that there were less than ten major crusades. Other minor crusades occurred as late as the 14th and 15th centuries primarily opposed the **Ottoman Empire**.

The **Third Crusade** was led by three rulers: **Frederick I** of Germany who was the Holy Roman Emperor known as **Barbarossa**, **Richard I** of England, who was called **Richard the Lionheart**, and **King Philip II** of France. Barbarossa drowned crossing a river in southern Turkey. Richard I eventually captured **Cyprus**, and negotiated a peace with **Saladin** to allow merchants and unarmed Christians access to Jerusalem. The **Fourth Crusade** resulted in a political power struggle and a siege of Christian **Constantinople**. The **Albigensian Crusade** in 1209 was launched by Pope **Honorius III** against the **Cathars** of France.

. . . .

PACKING LIGHT - *During the Crusades, transporting the dead from the battlefield for burial was a major problem. To solve this enigma, they brought a huge cauldron to boil the bodies down to the bones for easy transport.*

- Founding of Oxford
- House of Plantagenet
- *Magna Carta*
- *Travels of Marco Polo*

Middle Ages

Founding of Oxford - Students were being educated at the **University of Oxford** in England, as early as 1096, making it the oldest college for English-speakers in the world. The **University of Paris** was founded before **Oxford**, and the **University of Cambridge** was founded in 1209 after Oxford students and the townspeople conflicted, and riots and tension resulted.

House of Plantagenet - **Eleanor of Aquitaine** was considered the most influential woman of the 12ᵗʰ century. She was the wife of **Louis VII**, king of France, but after two daughters were born, their marriage was annulled. Eleanor then married **Henry II**, king of England, in 1152. Their union created the **Plantagenet dynasty** and the **Angevin Empire**. She was mother of two kings, **Richard the Lionheart**, and **John I**, who signed the *Magna Carta*. She was outspoken, involved in government and served as administrator when Richard was gone.

Magna Carta (1215) - King **John I** of England taxed the church and people heavily and limited the rights of his barons. A document called the *Article of the Barons* was presented to John by his barons, with the support of the **Archbishop of Canterbury**. It was accepted with some modifications a few days later. It applied to the church, landholders, tenants, townships and trades. Most importantly, it contained laws reforming the way royal officials could treat the people. The final clause ensured John's obedience by threatening a war by the barons should the *Magna Carta* not be followed.

Travels of Marco Polo - In the late 1200s, Marco Polo, a Venetian, joined his father and uncle on a 24-year journey throughout Asia. While there, he spent some time with **Kublai Khan**, a powerful leader of the **Mongol Empire**. He was not the first European to travel to Asia, but he was the first to write a detailed account. His book inspired many others, including **Christopher Columbus**.

. . . .

THE PERFECT MAN - The archetype of a Renaissance Man *or* Universal Man *was derived from the humanist philosophy to describe ideal, gifted men who excelled in many categories and embraced knowledge. Leon Battista Alberti, who coined the term, Leonardo da Vinci and Michelangelo Buonarroti are each described as Renaissance Men.*

- Reformation of English Common Law
- Renaissance

Rebirth & Exploration

Reformation of English common law - **Edward Longshanks** became king as **Edward I** in 1272. He enacted numerous laws and statutes aimed at consolidating and reforming the legal system. He actively used his parliament, which he turned into a permanent part of government, to modify laws and ensure compliance among the population. The end of his reign was strained by wars, especially those with Scotland.

Renaissance (c. 1300-c. 1500) - This was a period of rebirth of culture, art, philosophy and classical antiquity that marked the emergence of Europe from the **Middle Ages**. As Italy's trade developed, wealth increased. People had time and money to pursue other interests, such as the arts and philosophy. When **Constantinople** fell in 1453, numerous scholars fled to Italy, bringing books, manuscripts and traditional Greek scholarship.

The **humanism movement** in philosophy began as part of the beginning of the **Italian Renaissance**. Its peak occurred in the mid-16th century as foreign invasions brought turmoil of the **Italian Wars**. However, the ideas and ideals of the **Renaissance** endured and spread to the rest of Europe, starting the **Northern Renaissance** and the **English Renaissance**. This period paved the way for the **Reformation**, the **Scientific Revolution** and the **Enlightenment**.

Three of Italy's greatest poet-scholars wrote in both Latin and Italian as it was spoken by the local people. **Dante Alighieri** wrote the *Divine Comedy* and other classics, and he was sometimes called the **Father of the Italian Language**. He began the *Dolce Stil Novo* literary movement. **Francesco Petrarch** was sometimes considered **Father of Humanism** and an initiator of the **Italian Renaissance**. **Giovanni Boccaccio** wrote *On Famous Women*, a book of biographies of women, but his best-known work was the *Decameron*.

. . . .

BUBONIC NURSERY RHYME - "Ring around the rosie, / Pocket full of posy, / Ashes, ashes, / We all fall down" ~ Anonymous (This childhood rhyme originated around 1350. Red rings around a rosy bump was the first sign of infection. A stench was associated with the infection, and people carried flowers to mask the odor.)

- Renaissance Man
- Hundred Years' War

Rebirth & Exploration

Renaissance Man - An archetype of this period was **Leonardo da Vinci**, who was from Florence. Most saw him as the painter of *Mona Lisa* and *The Last Supper* and the person who drew the *Vitruvian Man*. Yet none of these reflected the extent of his genius. His notebooks showed concepts in designs for double hull ships, musical instruments, hydraulic pumps and flying machines. He was a military engineer and worked for the son of Pope **Alexander VI** of the **House of Borgia**. There was little da Vinci could not do.

Another archetype of the Renaissance Man, **Michelangelo Buonarroti** was a sculptor, painter, architect, poet and engineer who exerted an enormous influence on Western art. He was best known for his sculpture of *David* and painting of the ceiling of the **Sistine Chapel**, which took four years. He was also the primary architect of the rebuilding of **St. Peter's Basilica**.

Hundred Years' War (1337-1453) - **Edward III**, a **Plantagenet** in England, refused to pay homage for lands he owned in France to **Philip VI** of France, who was of the **House of Valois**. These lands were part of an inheritance through **William the Conqueror** and also through **Eleanor of Aquitaine**. Philip took the French lands, Edward decided to claim the French crown, and war ensued.

The **Battle of Agincourt** in 1415 was a significant battle won by England's **Henry V**. The defeat brought France to a low point, and Henry married **Catherine of Valois**, the daughter of the French king, **Charles VI**. Henry nearly conquered France but died unexpectedly. **William Shakespeare**'s play *Henry V* used this battle as the focal point.

In the final **Lancastrian** phase of war, **Joan of Arc** fought for France, was captured by the English, was tried, was found guilty of 70 charges and was burned at the stake. Her death energized morale. She became a martyr and national heroine. The war ended in 1475 with the **Treaty of Picquigny**. The English received payments; **Louis XI** retained the French throne.

· ·

NO COLLEGE FOR CUPID - At one point, Oxford had a specific rule that prohibited students from bringing bows and arrows to class with them.

- Black Death
- Unification of Scandinavia
- *Canterbury Tales*
- Great Schism in the West

Rebirth & Exploration

Black Death - Also called the **bubonic plague**, this pandemic began in 1348 in the arid plains of Central Asia. It altered history as it spread along the **Silk Road** and then on ships from the Far East to Europe. An estimated 25 million Asians died before the plague ever reached Europe. Rats carried the fleas that transported the virus. It was one of the worst pandemics in human history and ultimately killed 30-60% of the population in Europe. This signaled the end of the Middle Ages and a transition to the beginning of the Renaissance.

Unification of Scandinavia - The **Kalmar Agreement** in 1397 united Denmark, Norway and Sweden, which then included the area of present-day Finland. It also included Norway's territories of Iceland, Greenland and the Faroe Islands. These nations were trying to prevent Germany's northern expansion. Sweden left the group in 1523, but Norway and Denmark remained together under the **Oldenburg dynasty** until the early 1800s.

Canterbury Tales - This was a collection of over 20 stories written in English by **Geoffrey Chaucer** in the late 14th century, during the period of the **Hundred Years' War**. The tales were primarily written in verse, with some in prose.

Great Schism in the West - A great split opened in the papacy in the late 14th century, when several claimed to be the pope. The split was driven by politics, not theology, and it was resolved by the **Council of Constance**. John XXIII of Pisa and Benedict XIII of Aragon were deposed. Pope Gregory XII chose to abdicate. Martin V was elected to the papacy in 1417 and the schism drew to an end.

. . . .

A GIRL LIKE NO OTHER - Joan of Arc claimed to be God's messenger. Although she changed the course of the Hundred Years' War and the course of history, she was burned at the stake for not renouncing the voices she heard as deviltry. Twenty-four years after her death, Joan of Arc's case was reopened by the French and Joan was acquitted. The Catholic Church accepted this claim and canonized her 490 years later as St. Joan.

1400 - 1460

- Portuguese Empire
- House of Habsburg
- War of the Roses
- House of Tudor

Rebirth & Exploration

Portuguese Empire - In 1415, **Henry the Navigator** financed expeditions to Africa. Sailors used innovations in navigation and maritime technology, as well as improved cartography. They sought a route to Asia to participate in the lucrative spice trade. In 1488, **Bartolomeu Dias** rounded the **Cape of Good Hope**, and ten years later **Vasco da Gama** reached India. **Pedro Álvares Cabral** landed on the coast of **Brazil**, beginning the exploration and colonization in South America.

House of Habsburg - Though this dynasty began in **Switzerland** around 1020, it gradually grew in power. They relocated to **Austria** and occupied the throne of the **Holy Roman Empire** between 1438 and 1740. The rule of the Habsburg spread across Europe through strategic marriages. At their peak, the Habsburg held 16 European thrones, including Spain and part of France. Empress **Maria Theresa** ruled Austria, Hungary, Bohemia and Croatia for 40 years and had 16 children. She was Empress of the Holy Roman Empire for 20 years during this period with her marriage to **Charles VI**. She was the only female Habsburg ruler. The Habsburg dynasty ended after World War I with the dissolution of the **Austro-Hungarian Empire**.

War of the Roses - This English conflict began in 1455 between rival branches of the **House of Plantagenet**: the **House of Lancaster**, whose heraldic symbol was a white rose, and the **House of York**, whose heraldic symbol was a red rose. It was a series of sporadic battles over 30+ years. **Henry Tudor** of the House of Lancaster was the final winner. He defeated the Yorkist king, **Richard III** at the **Battle of Bosworth Field** in 1485 and became **Henry VII**.

House of Tudor - Originally **Welsh**, the Tudors became rulers of England with **Henry VII**, thus founding the **Tudor dynasty** in 1457. **Henry VIII**, who had six wives, was a Tudor as well as **Mary I**, called **Bloody Mary**, and **Elizabeth I**.

TEA & CRUMPETS? - *People of Britain consume more tea per capita than any other people in the world, which amounts to 2.5 times more than the Japanese and 22 times more than the Americans or the French. Crumpets date back to Anglo-Saxon days and were first mentioned in 1382 in John Wycliffe's Bible translation.*

- Spanish Inquisition
- European Colonialism

Rebirth & Exploration

Spanish Inquisition - This tribunal punished heretics. It was not the first Inquisition, but it was the most famous. It was originally started in 1478 by **Ferdinand II** of Aragon and **Isabella I** of Castile, who were Catholic, to help people convert from Judaism and Islam to become proper Catholics. Two decrees that forced Jews and Muslins to convert or leave Spain led to the Inquisition's increased power.

The most famous inquisitor of the time was **Tomás de Torquemada**, who obtained many confessions by using torture. It is believed that nearly 5,000 people were actually burned as heretics, and these included Protestants, Jews, Muslims, Freemasons and those thought to be witches or blasphemers. Less than 100,000 were actually expelled from Spain.

European colonialism - During the 15th and 16th centuries, there was an expansion of European colonialism pioneered first by Portugal and, later, by Spain. Portugal developed trade outposts in India, Africa and eastern Brazil under Bartolomeu Dias and Vasco da Gama.

Spain sought to build an empire in the Americas. This started with the travels of **Christopher Columbus** in 1492. Each time he reached land, he thought he had reached Asia. Columbus continued to believe he had found Asia, though mounting evidence showed he had landed on a new continent.

The first colony in the New World, **St. Augustine**, was founded by Spanish explorer **Don Pedro Menéndez** in 1565, 55 years prior to the founding of **Plymouth**. Not only was it the central seat of Spanish power in Florida through the 18th century, it has remained the oldest continually occupied town colonized by Europeans in the continental U.S.

NO PARKING ZONE - The skeleton of King Richard III was discovered in 2012 beneath a parking lot in central England. The excavation confirmed that the king did indeed have severe spinal curvature, confirming Shakespeare's description in his play, King Richard III. *Richard ruled between 1483-1485. He was the last English king to die in battle.*

- Treaty of Tordesillas
- Medici Family
- House of Borgia

Rebirth & Exploration

Treaty of Tordesillas - In 1494, Portugal and Spain decided to divide the New World between them along a meridian 370 leagues west of the **Cape Verde Islands**. The treaty gave Portugal everything to the east of the line, including **Brazil**. Thus, Spain was kept out of Africa and the Middle East. Spain kept all of South and Central America, except Brazil. They did not consult with England, France or the Netherlands, who soon staked their own claims.

Medici family (c. 1400-1737) - The Medici family established rule through bribery funded by proceeds of prosperous commerce and banking. They maintained a firm reign over the **Florentine** government during the 15th to 18th centuries and were grand patrons of the artists of the **Renaissance**, including **da Vinci**, **Michelangelo** and others.

The Medici family was exiled for a time and returned to Florence in 1512 and resumed ruling. Many Medicis married into royal families, but the last ruler died heirless in 1737, ending their three-century reign. During this period, conflict was common with the **Borgia** family.

House of Borgia - The ruthless, corrupt **Borgia** family was of Spanish descent, but played a large role in the Italian church and in politics during the 15th and 16th centuries. **Cesare Borgia**, the illegitimate son of Pope **Alexander VI**, was made Archbishop of Valencia and a cardinal. He was a notorious symbol of papal corruption, debauchery and murder.

Three marriages were arranged for **Lucrezia**, Cesare's sister, to further the political standing of the family. Cesare denounced his church responsibility, became a military leader, and is sometimes credited with helping to unite Italy for his own selfish motives. All three died between 1503 and 1529.

. . . .

PURE GENIUS - Leonardo da Vinci was the stereotypical Renaissance Man, *a concept often applied to gifted individuals who are highly intelligent and limitless in what they can do. His notebooks show that he drew plans for a tank, a helicopter and scuba equipment hundreds of years before they were invented. He also discovered arteriosclerosis, which is plaque build up in the arteries that can trigger a heart attack.*

- Machiavellianism
- New St. Peter's Basilica
- Little Ice Age

Rebirth & Exploration

Machiavellianism - Around 1513, **Niccolò Machiavelli** published *The Prince*, which described guidelines that German princes later used to consolidate power. It was the basis of Machiavellianism, which is synonymous with unscrupulous politics, and it was probably based on Cesare Borgia.

New St. Peter's Basilica - Pope **Julius II** was considered the most significant papal art patron, supporting artists like **Michelangelo**, **Bramante** and **Raphael**. In 1506, he began the process of rebuilding St. Peter's Basilica, which had fallen into poor repair over time, but it was not completed until around 1620. All three artists participated in the design for the new structure, and **Michelangelo** served as the chief architect.

Little Ice Age - This was not really a period of ice, but it was a period of cooler temperatures that had a big impact on civilization. The warming trend, which had preceded it, encouraged settlements and farming in northern latitudes, including **Iceland** and **Greenland**. The cold period began around 1350 and the most severe period was during the early 1600s to late 1700s. Longer winters and shorter summers reduced crop yields, causing shortages and famines.

The **Thames River** froze solidly enough for ice-skating, and it was possible to walk across **New York Harbor**. **Greenland** was abandoned and the population of **Iceland** dropped by half. Alpine glaciers grew and swallowed towns and fields. The **Niger River** flooded **Timbuktu** an unprecedented 13 times. Typhoon strikes increased in Guangdong Province, and oranges were abandoned as a crop in Jiangxi Province of China. In North America, many Native Americans joined leagues and confederations to combat food shortages. The cause for the cooling trend was unclear, but temperatures had returned to normal by 1850.

. . . .

HOLY GROUND - Emperor Constantine built the first St. Peter's Basilica where he did because this was the location of where St. Peter's bones were said to lie. Today the altar is directly over the same spot at the second St. Peter's Basilica.

- **Protestant Reformation**
- **Act of Supremacy**

Rebirth & Exploration

Protestant Reformation - A reaction to questioning traditional thought that was a part of the Renaissance led to the Reformation. **Martin Luther** had become dissatisfied with corruption in the **Catholic Church**. Based on the **Bible**, he developed the theory that faith guaranteed salvation. He favored reform of the Catholic Church, and he did not advocate a break with the church.

He tacked the famous *Ninety-Five Theses* on the door of **Wittenburg Cathedral** in 1517, decrying the **Roman Catholic Church** and the practices of Pope **Leo X**, which included the selling of indulgences. The Church named him a heretic and excommunicated him. He continued to criticize the church. Development of the printing press by **Johannes Gutenberg** in 1450 enabled his *Theses* to reach many people.

Luther refused to recant to the German parliament, thus influencing a social revolution and upsetting the Church's thousand-year reign. Reform swept through Germany, Switzerland and Holland. There, **John Calvin** and **John Knox** derived other branches of Luther's theory. In England, it ignited a civil war. **Pilgrims** brought it the New World, building a nation on Protestant beliefs.

Act of Supremacy - **Catherine of Aragon**, first wife of **Henry VIII**, bore a daughter but no sons. Seeking a male heir, Henry unsuccessfully worked to persuade the pope to grant him a marriage annulment. Thus, in 1534, Parliament passed this Act, which named the king as head of the **Church of England** and **Defender of the Faith**, thus breaking from the **Roman Catholic Church**. It enabled him to annul his marriage. Later wives included **Jane Seymour**, **Anne of Cleves**, **Catherine Howard** and **Catherine Parr**.

Parliament also passed the **Act of Succession**, which created a precarious English line of succession to the throne.

. . . .

RELIEF FOR WRITER'S CRAMP - The Gutenberg Bible was the first major book printed with movable type. Before this time, books were copied by hand. Only 48 copies exist in the world today with nine of these on display in the U.S. Each book has an estimated worth of $25-$35 million, and just a single page has been sold for as much as $100,000.

- Irish Uprising
- Scientific Revolution

Rebirth & Exploration

Irish Uprising - Receiving false information that his father was executed in London, deputy governor of Ireland, **Thomas FitzGerald**, renounced his office and took over **Dublin**. This, combined with unrest resulting from the breach between **Henry VIII** and the papacy, culminated in a revolt in 1534 called the **Geraldine Rebellion**. The revolt failed, a permanent English military presence was established in the country, and FitzGerald was executed.

Scientific Revolution (c. 1550-c. 1700) - The new ability to think 'outside the box' that developed during the Renaissance laid the groundwork that enabled changes in science. Great minds challenged traditional thoughts and beliefs. The **scientific method** was devised. It began when **Nicolaus Copernicus** proposed that the sun was the center of the universe with planets, including Earth, orbiting around it. Thus, Copernicus inspired a new era of modern thought.

Johannes Kepler proved the earth was mobile and proposed elliptical orbits. **Galileo** devised a telescope that proved Copernican theory. The Catholic Church brought Galileo before an inquisition in the 1600s, which found him guilty of heresy and placed him under house arrest for the duration of his life.

After 100 years of changes in science, **Robert Boyle**, along with some associates, researched and documented what became known as **Boyle's Law**. This defined that the pressure of a gas decreased as the volume of the gas increased. He came to be known as the **First Chemist**. With 11 others, he founded the **Royal Society of London**, a forum for scientific discussions.

During this same period, Sir **Isaac Newton** made discoveries in mathematics and physics, devised calculus, conceptualized gravity, theorized the laws of motion and ultimately came to be known as the **Father of Physical Science**. This led into the **Industrial Revolution**, which was a period of advancement in thinking and innovation and part of the **Age of Reason**.

WHAT'S UP? - Sir Isaac Newton was the first to describe gravity in a mathematical way. One of his greatest inventions was calculus because math and algebra were not enough to explain ideas that were in his head.

- Marian Persecution
- Last of the Tudors
- Defeat of Spanish Armada

Rebirth & Exploration

Marian Persecution - After **Henry VIII**, **Edward VI** ruled. When he died, **Lady Jane Grey** was named his heir. Her reign lasted nine days. Questions arose about succession, and **Mary I** became the first queen regent of England and Ireland in 1553. She was the daughter of **King Henry VIII** and **Catherine of Aragon**, whose marriage had been annulled. Mary tried to restore the nation to Catholicism, wed Spanish Catholic **Philip II** and viciously persecuted Protestants. This earned her the nickname, **Bloody Mary**.

Last of the Tudors - When Queen **Mary** died in 1558, **Elizabeth**, daughter of **Anne Boleyn** and **Henry VIII**, ascended the throne. Anne had been tried, convicted and beheaded under Henry VIII when he was unable to annul their marriage. In the wake of Mary's bloody reign, **Elizabeth I** was popular with her people and characterized as a strong, shrewd ruler. She did not marry, despite a barrage of suitors who were seeking her hand and the power that went with it. She reinstalled **Protestantism** in England, and Parliament passed another **Act of Supremacy** and **Act of Uniformity**.

She reluctantly executed **Mary**, Queen of Scots, her first cousin, to retain her throne when plots against her life were discovered. The largest military threat that England faced during her reign was the **Spanish Armada**, but England prevailed. She died in 1603, and the Tudor dynasty ended. The reign of the **Virgin Queen** was characterized as that of a woman married to her kingdom.

Defeat of the Spanish Armada - In 1588, 130 Spanish ships began their voyage to invade England for **Philip II**. The Armada encountered a storm that damaged many of its ships, forcing their return for repairs and losing the element of surprise. The Armada's failure kept England and the Netherlands safe from becoming part of the Spanish empire.

. . . .

RIP - *"Good friend, for Jesus' sake forbeare, / To dig the dust enclosed here. Blessed be the man that spares these stones, / And cursed be he that moves my bones." ~ Shakespeare (The Bard wrote this for own epitaph. He intended it to thwart grave robbers who plundered England's cemeteries. It worked; his grave has remained undisturbed.)*

- Elizabethan Era
- Gregorian Calendar
- Thirty Years' War

Rebirth & Exploration

Elizabethan Era (1558-1603) - This period encompassed the reign of Queen Elizabeth and was a golden age in English history. **William Shakespeare** was considered one of the world's most renowned and prolific playwrights. Some of his most famous works include sonnets and plays. He wrote *A Midsummer Night's Dream*, *Henry IV*, *Romeo and Juliet*, *Macbeth* and *Hamlet*. In later times, he gained the title of **Bard of Avon** or just the **Bard**.

Gregorian calendar - To combat inaccuracies, Pope **Gregory XIII** ordered the deletion of ten days from the month of October and the creation of leap years. Thus, the new calendar was born in 1582. It was a controversial concept, but Catholic states adopted it, and other countries followed.

Thirty Years' War (1618-1648) - This was a series of destructive wars fought in central Europe between Protestant states and Roman Catholic states. It became an attempt to control the provincial princes of German states. The **Defenestration of Prague** precipitated this war, which was an incident in which two Imperial officials were tried, convicted, and thrown from a 3rd floor window. They miraculously survived, and Catholics contended it was divine intervention. Protestants disagreed, and conflict ensued.

Albrecht von Wallenstein served as general of the armies of **Ferdinand II**, the Holy Roman Emperor until he was defeated by **Gustavus Adolphus**, the Swedish king, at the **Battle of Lützen**. The **Peace of Westphalia** in 1648 was the concluding conference that acknowledged the independence of **Switzerland** and the **Netherlands**. This also marked the recognition of Switzerland as a neutral state by most nations. The German states were granted autonomy with religious toleration. The French acquired **Alsace-Lorraine**. The permanence of the Protestant religion in Europe was ensured, and the Holy Roman Empire entered a period of decline.

· ·

THE TRUTH HURTS - *"It is dangerous to be right in matters on which the established authorities are wrong."* He also observed, *"There are truths which are not for all men, nor for all times."*
~ *Voltaire, (He was an Enlightenment thinker and satirist.)*

1625 - 1650

- Consolidation of France
- English Civil War

Rebirth & Exploration

Consolidation of France - During the reign of **Louis XIII**, Cardinal **Richelieu** served as the king's chief minister beginning in 1624, and he became powerful both in the Catholic Church and in politics. He pushed for centralization of power in France and opposition to the **Habsburg dynasty** in both Austria and Spain. He attacked the **Huguenots**, who were French Protestants. He limited the power of the nobility, promoted royal absolutism, raised money, and created a powerful, centralized France. He also served during the **Thirty Years' War**, and he was considered one of the best politicians in French history.

English Civil War - When the last **Tudor**, **Elizabeth I**, died, **James VI** of Scotland, a member of the **House of Stuart**, became **James I** of England, ruler of three inherently different kingdoms: Scotland, Ireland and England. Scotland was **Calvinist;** England, Protestant; and Ireland, Catholic. All had minority factions. The king's handling of Catholics in England resulted in the planning of the **Gunpowder Plot**, a foiled plan to plant explosives in Parliament.

He was succeeded in 1625 by his son, **Charles I**. Tension mounted due to his religious policies and refusal to cooperate with Parliament and, by 1642, civil war broke out. The **Royalist** camp was primarily situated in the north and west, while the **Parliament** group was based in the south and east. It looked as if the tide was in Charles' favor until Parliament forged an alliance with the Scots, and Charles' forces were foiled at **Marston Moor** and **Naseby**. Charles surrendered and was beheaded for high treason in 1649. A republican regime was established and, in 1653, **Oliver Cromwell** became **Lord Protector** of the **Commonwealth of England, Scotland and Ireland**. In 1660, **Charles II**, the exiled Stuart heir, was restored to the throne.

. . . .

SOLAR POWERED MONARCHY - Louis XIV ruled for 72 years and 110 days, the longest of any European ruler. He shocked his court by choosing to rule without a chief minister, and he claimed he didn't need one because he was the direct minister of God. With this belief, he called himself Roi Soleil, *meaning the* Sun King, *which implied that the world revolved around him. He ruled as an absolute monarch. The grand palace of Versailles was one of the king's greatest accomplishments. Today, the palace is located in Paris and is a popular tourist attraction.*

- Baroque Style
- Age of Enlightenment

Rebirth & Exploration

Baroque style - This was a reaction to the **Reformation** that spanned from about 1600 to 1750. The music of this period was typified by elaborate ornamentation. **G. F. Handel**, though born in Germany, was an English composer during the Baroque era. While he composed a variety of works, he was most famous for his operas and oratorios, including the most famous oratorio, **Messiah**. German composer, **Johann Sebastian Bach**, was known for his **Brandenburg Concertos**. Italian composer **Antonio Vivaldi** created a set of four violin concerti, entitled **The Four Seasons**, which contained musical interpretations of each season and were accompanied by a set of poems.

Age of Enlightenment - Also called an **Age of Reason**, this intellectual movement spread over the globe beginning in the late 1600s through the 1700s. It signaled a shift from the dark, superstitious beliefs of the **Middle Ages** to a focus on rationality, reason and challenging traditional institutions and morals.

One of many key contributors, **Francis Bacon** was considered an early developer of the scientific method. **Thomas Hobbes** viewed human nature negatively and thought an absolute monarch was necessary to maintain order. **John Locke** believed in a representational government with a social contract with the citizens. **Montesquieu** pioneered the idea of a balance of power.

Voltaire advocated separation of church and state. He wrote **Candide** as a satire of the condition of Catholicism. **Jean Jacques Rousseau** advocated private ownership of property as a pillar of a civil society. **Immanuel Kant**, a central figure of modern philosophy, believed that constitutional monarchies were the best plan for ruling. All these ideas were reflected in writings of America's founding fathers and in the *Constitution of the United States*.

. . . .

BLIND TRUST - Both Bach and Handel, who lived at the same time, went blind in their old age and died following an eye surgery. At the time, there was no concept of bacteria or anesthesia so doctors had to work as quickly as possible. To make matters worse, they both used the same doctor, who was known as a 'quack.' Their 'oculist' rode a coach decorated with eyeballs and the saying, "He who gives sight, gives life."

- **Hudson Bay Company**
- **League of Augsburg**
- **Cape of Good Hope**
- **Colonization of India**

Expansion & Colonization

Hudson Bay Company - Frenchmen **Médard des Groseilliers** and **Pierre-Esprit Radisson** discovered that **Canada's Hudson Bay** was a bountiful source for fur and worked to get a **Royal Charter** from the English monarchy. This joint stock company was formed in 1670. When fur lost popularity at the end of the 19th century, they began to sell a broader variety of goods. It remained in operation to become North America's longest continually operated company.

League of Augsburg - In an attempt to curb the expansion of **Louis XIV**, the French king, a coalition of European rulers was formed in 1686. It was formed by **Leopold I**, emperor of the Holy Roman Empire, as well as rulers of many other countries surrounding France, but it was unsuccessful. Later, England and France entered the alliance in 1689 and, henceforth, it was referred to as the **Grand Alliance**.

Colonization of Cape of Good Hope - The **Huguenots** were 16th and 17th century French Protestants influenced by **John Calvin**. They were heavily persecuted for their religious beliefs, and many were forced to flee and relocate. The Dutch government sent some to colonize the Cape of Good Hope in South Africa in 1687 as farmers for the **Dutch East India Company**. This company was active in trading in the **Moluccas**, known as the **Spice Islands**, which had been a Portuguese stronghold in trade.

Colonization of India - The **British East India Company** was originally formed to trade with the East Indies. It founded the port of **Calcutta** in 1690 as a trading post, and this later became the capital of colonial British India. There was conflict with the **Dutch East India Company**, and the British company maintained a presence in India while the Dutch company remained active in the Moluccas.

SALT OF THE EARTH - Initially set up to trade spices, the Dutch East India Company was created in 1602 and lasted until about 1800. It is considered to be one of the first and most successful international corporations and was the first company to issue stock. The trade company also had government-like powers in which they could mint coins, establish colonies, build forts, imprison people and even have their own army and navy.

- Battle of the Boyne
- War of Spanish Succession
- Act of Union
- *Robinson Crusoe*

Expansion & Colonization

Battle of the Boyne - In 1690, **James II** was forced to abdicate the English throne in what was called the **Glorious Revolution**. After creating an alliance with the French and Irish, James tried unsuccessfully to win the kingdom back from **King William III** at this battle. William was victorious and retained the throne. This conflict proved especially crucial to Catholic Ireland, who saw their chances fade for their own sovereignty, Irish land ownership and religious freedom with the defeat of James II.

War of Spanish Succession (1701-1714) - Austria, Britain, Prussia and the Netherlands united in an unsuccessful effort to curb the power of **Louis XIV**, the French king, and prevent a French, Spanish and Bavarian alliance. A power vacuum was created when Spanish Habsburg ruler, **Charles II**, died heirless. Though several treaties had been created to determine the heir prior to Charles' death, he willed the throne to Louis XIV's grandson, **Philip V**, hoping that a **Bourbon** could keep the Spanish realm together. Philip kept the throne, but this marked the beginning of the rise of the British Empire.

Act of Union - Via this act, Scotland and England united to become **Great Britain** in 1707. This treaty was made because the Scots wanted economic security and materials, and England wanted a guaranteed buffer zone to protect its flanks from French attacks. Protestant succession was guaranteed, and trade was declared to be free and equal throughout Britain.

Robinson Crusoe - This English novel was published in 1719 and was written by **Daniel Defoe** about a character named Robinson Crusoe and his shipwreck experiences. He survived alone on a remote island for 28 years, before saving a native and finding a way to return home. It is believed to have been based on the story of a castaway, **Alexander Selkirk**.

. . . .

NO LOSS FOR WORDS - The original title of the book Robinson Crusoe *was the following:* The Life and Strange Surprizing Adventures of Robinson Crusoe, Of York, Mariner: Who Lived Eight and Twenty Years, All Alone in an Un-inhabited Island on the Coast of America, Near the Mouth of the Great River of Oroonoque; Having Been Cast on Shore by Shipwreck, Wherein All the Men Perished but Himself. With An Account how he was at last as Strangely Deliver'd by Pyrates...*what a mouthful!*

- Austrian Succession War
- Seven Years' War
- House of Hanover

Expansion & Colonization

War of Austrian Succession (1740-1748) - After the death of **Charles VI**, an Austrian Habsburg and ruler of the **Holy Roman Empire**, Austria, Britain and the Netherlands fought Prussia, France and Spain to determine who would assume the Austrian throne.

The oldest daughter of Charles, **Maria Theresa**, was victorious despite protests that she could not inherit rule since she was a woman. She became **Archduchess of Austria**, **Queen of Hungary and Bohemia**, and **Holy Roman Empress** when her husband became Holy Roman Emperor. She was mother to French queen, **Marie Antoinette**. An enlightened absolutist, she abolished serfdom and instituted universal education during her 40-year reign.

Seven Years' War - This war began in 1756 with a switch of long standing European alliances called the **Diplomatic Revolution**. Thus, France, Austria, Saxony, Sweden and Russia were pitted against Prussia, Hanover and Great Britain in a conflict initiated by the Austrian Habsburg. They wanted to regain control of Silesia, but were unsuccessful. The conflict ended with the **1763 Treaty of Paris**, which gave North America and India to Britain, and the **Treaty of Hubertusburg**, which gave Silesia to **Frederick the Great** of Prussia.

House of Hanover - This German dynasty followed the **Stuarts** as rulers of Britain. **George III** was king of England from 1760 until 1820. He was the third Hanoverian king but was the first born in England and spoke English as his predominant language. During his reign, the **Seven Years' War**, **American Revolution**, **French Revolution** and **Napoleonic era** occurred. In essence, he presided over the country during a time when it won an empire, lost the American colonies but then became a leading European power. A patron of the arts, he founded the **Royal Academy of Arts**. After suffering from illness, he went mad, and his son, **George IV**, reigned as regent then king until 1830.

· ·

POTATO PEDDLER - Europeans disdained potatoes as fit for human consumption. Frederick the Great introduced potatoes and made a spectacle while eating potatoes by smacking his lips enthusiastically. This didn't make them more popular, so he planted a field and had it guarded. Soon people began stealing the 'valuable' roots.

- Industrial Revolution
- Russia's Golden Age
- Classical Period

Expansion & Colonization

Industrial Revolution (c. 1760-c. 1840) - This was a period of British industrial development and the birth of the **factory system**. Revolutionary innovations, such as machines and mechanisms, allowed for the replacement of manual labor. The **spinning jenny** was a mechanized spinning wheel that revolutionized the textile industry. The **steam engine** and improvements that made it much more powerful enabled the change from using wood to coal for a source of energy along with using water to power tools used in factories.

Russia's Golden Age (1762-1796) - **Catherine**, the daughter of a Prussian prince, married the heir to the Russian throne, **Peter**, the grandson of **Peter the Great**. When Peter's mother, Empress **Elizabeth**, died in 1792, Peter ascended to the throne. He was unfit, unpopular, and eventually abdicated and assassinated. Catherine assumed the title of Empress and worked to restore the empire and instituted many reforms, becoming known as **Catherine the Great**. She was an enlightened ruler who felt serfdom was wrong, but strengthened it to maintain control of her empire. She was a patron of education, art and culture, and her reign has been termed the **Golden Age**.

Classical Period - After the **Baroque period** came the **Classical period** (c. 1730-c. 1820). This period signaled a move from heavily ornamented musical compositions to classical, Grecian-inspired styles.

Joseph Haydn (Austria) - *The Creation*, *Seasons* - He was Mozart's friend and Beethoven's teacher, and known as Father of the Symphony.

Wolfgang Amadeus Mozart (Austria) - *The Marriage of Figaro*, *The Magic Flute*, *Requiem* - A child prodigy, Mozart was described by Haydn as "the greatest composer known to me in person or by name."

WISE BEYOND HER YEARS - Catherine the Great challenged social norms and set the precedent for women in powerful positions. During her rule, which occurred after her husband was assassinated, she directed two successful wars and founded academies and libraries.

1790 - 1800

EUROPE

• French Revolution   • Reign of Napoleon

Turmoil & Conflict

French Revolution (1787-1799) - In France, discontent was broiling due to resentment of the privileges of nobility and clergy, crop failures, expensive wars, aid given to the American colonies, peasant awareness of their condition and the feudal system. A **National Assembly** was ultimately formed, and the powers were committed to forming a constitution. Their demands were not met, and this unrest culminated in a Parisian uprising and the **Storming of the Bastille**, a prison symbolic of the abuses of the monarchy. This revolt spelled an end for France's *ancien régime*.

France became a constitutional monarchy but, when **Louis XVI** and his wife **Marie Antoinette** attempted to escape the country, they were beheaded via the **guillotine**. Radical **Maximilien Robespierre** and the **Jacobins** took over, marking the beginning of the bloody **Reign of Terror**. Thousands of nobles and anyone considered an enemy of the Revolution were sent to the guillotine, which was supposedly a humane device for killing the accused. It ended with the beheading of Robespierre himself, and the **Directory** took power. It was corrupt and incapable, and **Napoleon Bonaparte** overthrew it and became dictator, thus ending the French Revolution.

The revolution saw the rise of ideas, such as popular sovereignty and inalienable rights. It also ended the French monarchy and feudal system.

Reign of Napoleon - Napoleon Bonaparte was also called the **Corsican**. He was a French general who became first consul of France in 1799 and later its emperor. He overturned the ruling **Directory** in a *coup d'état* that ended the Revolution and formed the **Consulate** in its stead. He focused on expansion until a disastrous campaign in Russia and foreign intervention forced him to abdicate in 1814. The **Treaty of Fontainebleau** was an agreement between Napoleon and representatives of Austria, Russia and Prussia that ended Napoleon's rule and exiled him to the island of Elba.

. . . .

STORMING THE BASTILLE - There were only seven inmates in the prison when the revolutionaries stormed it. The prisoners were mainly of high rank, but the edifice represented royal authority in central Paris. Bastille Day is a national holiday on July 14.

136

- Battle of Trafalgar
- Move to Romantic Period

Turmoil & Conflict

Battle of Trafalgar - During the **Napoleonic War**, this was a naval battle in 1805 that ensured that Napoleon would not invade England. Thirty-three Spanish and French ships were pitted against 27 British ships under Admiral **Horatio Nelson**. Nelson intercepted them *en route* to Naples off Cape Trafalgar. While Nelson died of wounds sustained during the battle, the British were victorious, and 14,000 French and Spanish were captured.

Move to Romantic Period - Bridging the **Classical** and **Romantic** eras were works of the following composers, and this was by no means a comprehensive list. This period permeated art, music and literature. It was a revolt against the social and political format of the Age of Enlightenment and scientific rationalization and was a drive to showing feeling and emotion.

Ludwig van Beethoven (German) - *Für Elise*, *Sonata No. 14* (known as *Moonlight Sonata*), *Fifth Symphony* - A bridge between eras, he studied under Haydn and was a gifted pianist and then a great composer.

Frédéric Chopin (Polish) - *Minute Waltz, Revolutionary Etude* - A child prodigy on piano, he produced expressive music. He was often ill and died young.

Franz Liszt (German) - *Faust Symphony, Liebestraum* - The first pianist to hold concerts as the only performer, Liszt composed over 1,000 piano pieces.

Richard Wagner (German) - *The Valkyrie, Tristan and Isolde* - A political activist, his operas were a total fusion of music, poetry, art and drama.

Johannes Brahms (German) - *Brahms' Lullaby* - He conformed to the Classical Era format and rigidity and most admired Beethoven. There was a strong rivalry with both Liszt and Wagner.

. . . .

VERTICALLY CHALLENGED - There is debate that Napoleon was sensitive about his height. He is rumored to have measured 5'2". Other sources claim that he was actually 5'7". The colloquial term, 'Napoleon Complex,' still refers to a false machismo personality that makes up for feelings of inferiority based on short stature.

1810 - 1815

- Holy Roman Empire's End
- Austro-Hungarian Empire
- Romantic Period

Turmoil & Conflict

End of Holy Roman Empire - During his conquests, Napoleon wanted to create a coalition loyal to him, not a unified German state. He created the **Confederation of the Rhine** in 1806, and each state separated from the Holy Roman Empire. **Francis II** of Austria abdicated after receiving a Napoleonic ultimatum, and he effectively then dissolved the empire. It was during this period that **Johann Wolfgang von Goethe** wrote *Faust*. This topic was later revised by **Christopher Marlowe** into a play.

Romantic Period (c. 1815-c. 1910) - Strong emotion was expressed by the writers and musicians of this period. Some showed a strongly nationalistic direction. Writers included **William Wordsworth**, **Samuel Coleridge**, **John Keats**, **Lord Byron**, **Charlotte Brontë**, **Emily Brontë**, **Mary Shelley** and more. The **Brothers Grimm** also wrote during the period, publishing German folklore, such as *Cinderella*, *Hansel and Gretel*, *Snow White* and others. In Denmark, **Hans Christian Andersen** published fairy tales and folk tales of his culture, such as *The Ugly Duckling*, *Thumbelina* and *The Little Mermaid*.

Peter Ilyich Tchaikovsky (Russian) - *1812 Overture, The Nutcracker, Sleeping Beauty* - His enormous musical talent was rooted in his unhappy and depression-prone life, and his compositions are highly emotional.

Sergei Rachmaninoff (Russian) - Equally well known as a pianist and a composer, Rachmaninoff produced passionate, complex, mysterious and sometimes gloomy music. He fled Russia after the 1917 Revolution and lived in America the rest of his life.

Austro-Hungarian Empire - Forged in 1867 through compromise and alliance, this was a **Dual Monarchy**. Hungary was autonomous and the empire formed solely for war and foreign affair purposes. The empire collapsed in 1918.

• •

LOST OR LEFT? - In the original version of the fairy tale, Hansel and Gretel, *the woodcutter and his wife abandoned the children. The story may have originated during the Great Famine of the medieval period when some abandoned their children and resorted to cannibalism out of desperate starvation.*

- **Bourbon Restoration**
- **Congress of Vienna**
- **Last French Monarchs**
- **Works of Karl Marx**

Turmoil & Conflict

Bourbon Restoration - After Napoleon's defeat, the Bourbons were restored, and **Louis XVIII** assumed the French throne. However, Napoleon escaped exile in Elba, returned to France in 1815 and ruled for a **Hundred Days**. His reign came to a final end with the **Battle of Waterloo**, where Napoleon was defeated by allied British and Prussian armies. This defeat was the end of the 23-year period of war in France that began with the French Revolution.

Congress of Vienna (1814-1815) - The French Revolution, Napoleonic War and dissolution of the Holy Roman Empire made it necessary for European nations to converge and redraw the continental political map. This conference was an inspiration for the formation of the **League of Nations** and later the **United Nations** (**UN**) and was marked by the creation of a period of relative stability and peace.

Last French monarchs - Following Louis XVIII, **Charles X** became king of France. After six years, he was forced to abdicate during the 1830 **July Revolution**. Though he had been exiled for much of the French Revolution and during Napoleon's rule, **Louis Philippe** of the **House of Orléans** became king, ending the Bourbon dynasty. Louis Philippe's reign, known as the **July Monarchy**, ended with his 1848 abdication. This was also called the **February Revolution**. The **Second French Republic** was created in the monarchy's stead.

Works of Karl Marx - Marx was a German who coauthored the famous *Communist Manifesto*, which was published in 1848. He was a sociologist, historian, economist, communist and revolutionary. **Marxian theory** is centered around the idea that people are divided into classes, including the workers, which is the largest class, and the ruling, or **capitalist** class. Marx believed the ruling class exploited workers, which resulted in **class struggles** and that people would naturally progress toward socialism, a system in which everything is owned in common. This controversial theory was revolutionary.

. . . .

UNKEMPT KARL - Karl Marx had a PhD, but never held a job. Three of his six children died from malnutrition or neglect. The book, Karl Marx: An Intimate Biography, *by Saul K. Padover, describes Marx as highly disorderly, cynical and a poor host with a nomadic existence. He noted that he rarely washed, was often drunk and loafed daily.*

- Victorian Age
- Potato Famine in Ireland
- Second French Empire

Victorian Era

Victorian Age - The last monarch of the **House of Hanover** line was **Victoria**, and she reigned as queen of the United Kingdom of Great Britain and Ireland from 1837 to 1901 and as empress of India during the last half of that period. She ushered in the Victorian Age as a period of peace, prosperity, refined sensibilities and nationalism. It was during her 63-year reign that the English monarchy became ceremonial.

During this period, the writings of **Charles Dickens** critiqued English society. His best-known works are *A Christmas Carol*, *A Tale of Two Cities* and *Great Expectations*.

Potato famine in Ireland - In 1845, blight destroyed most of Ireland's potato crop. This continued for three years and resulted in widespread famine, as potatoes made up most of the Irish diet. The English government exported available food products and crops, while more than one million Irish people starved. Around two million chose to emigrate, drastically decreasing the Irish population and increasing the British rule's unpopularity with the Irish people.

Second French Empire (1852-1870) - After instigating several unsuccessful Bonapartist uprisings, **Napoleon III**, who was Napoleon's nephew, exploited the Napoleonic myth to oppose **Louis Philippe** and was elected president of France's Second Republic in 1848. Following in his uncle's footsteps, he proclaimed himself emperor of the **Second French Empire** in 1852. He imposed reforms, rebuilt the city of Paris and worked to expand the empire. An imperialist attempt in Mexico and the **Franco-Prussian War** resulted in his deposition. The **Third Republic** was established in 1870. France is now on its **Fifth Republic**.

· ·

TWIST OF FATE - Charles Dickens was a prolific author who produced numerous classics, but success was never handed to him. Dickens had to quit school to go to work when he was 12 because his father went to jail for an unpaid debt. Hardship opened opportunity when at 16 he was hired as a freelance reporter. He eventually became publisher of a magazine and began his first novel, Oliver Twist, *which reflected his feelings of living impoverished and having to survive as child.*

- German Unification
- Psychoanalysis
- Theory of Evolution
- Works of Tolstoy

Victorian Era

German Unification - **Otto Von Bismarck** was an authoritarian ruler credited with accomplishing the Herculean task of creating a unified **German Empire** between 1850 and 1871 through a series of short, but highly successful, wars. He became its first chancellor after unification and served until 1890. He was appointed to serve as Prussian Prime Minister by King **Wilhelm I** during much of that period.

Founding of psychoanalysis - During this same time in Austria, **Sigmund Freud**, a neurologist, developed a clinical method to treat patients with mental problems by probing their unconscious thoughts and dreams. His ideas revolutionized the study of psychology and psychiatry in the early 20th century.

Theory of evolution - **Charles Darwin** was a British scientist credited with the formulation of the theory of evolution. Influenced by *Principles of Geology* written by **Charles Lysell**, Darwin found it interesting that individual islands of the **Galapagos Islands** each had a different type of finch. This was learned on a trip around the world on the **HMS *Beagle***. He worked to refine a theory on species evolvement. In 1859, he published ***On the Origin of Species by Means of Natural Selection***, which was a highly controversial book. He was attacked by Victorian society, particularly the Catholic Church, but his theories eventually became accepted.

Works of Tolstoy - One of the most noted authors of all time, **Leo Tolstoy**, an aristocratic Russian, lived from 1828 to 1910 and is best known for his books, ***War and Peace*** and ***Anna Karenina*** and for his short story, ***The Death of Ivan Ilych***. His writings on nonviolent resistance had a profound impact on Mahatma **Mohandas Gandhi** and **Martin Luther King, Jr.**

. . . .

BLOOD AND IRON - In what is now called the "Blood and Iron" speech, Otto von Bismarck, German chancellor, plainly stated his willingness to use force to expand the nation. He sought funding to increase the strength of the Prussian borders and stated that "the future of the nation did not rest on words, but iron and blood." His diplomacy and powerful rulership earned him the nickname of the "Iron Chancellor."

- *Kulturkampf*
- Impressionism

- Beginning of WWI

World War I

Kulturkampf - By 1871, **Otto von Bismarck** had created a unified German empire and styled himself as **Chancellor**. Determined to keep a unified state, he was concerned with the Catholic Church's concept of papal infallibility. Thus, he began the *kulturkampf* or *culture struggle*, attempting to place state controls on the church. The Catholic Church fought against his policies through an increase of their representatives in Parliament and that, combined with a new pope, helped convince Bismarck to repeal some legislation deemed offensive. Pope **Leo XIII** officially declared the conflict's end in 1887.

Impressionism - Begun in the late 1800s, this movement in French painting flourished. It later spread to music. Impressionist artists sought to capture the *impression* of their subject rather than its details. Key artists of the movement included **Claude Monet**, **Pierre Renoir**, **Edgar Degas**, **Paul Cézanne** and others.

Beginning of WWI - Between 1914 and 1918, **World War I** began, pitting the **Central Powers**, Germany, Austria-Hungary and Russia, against the **Allies**, France, Great Britain, Russia, Italy, Japan and, in 1917, the U.S. Known as the **Great War**, this was fought in the Atlantic Ocean and on three primary fronts: the western front in France, the eastern front in Russia and the southern front in Serbia. The trigger that started the war was the assassination of Archduke **Franz Ferdinand**, heir to the **Austro-Hungarian** throne. Thus, Austria then declared war on Serbia.

The British blockaded Germany, and Germans used submarines called *U-boats* to blockade Britain to cut off the supply lines from North America. They sank the passenger ship **RMS *Lusitania*** in 1915. This turned into unrestricted submarine warfare. The British interception of the **Zimmerman Telegram** prompted the U.S. to abandon its isolationist policy and join the war efforts. This turned the tide against the Central Powers.

AN ALMOST ALLIANCE - The Zimmerman Telegram was a coded message from Germany to Mexico that proposed an alliance between the two countries against the U.S. if the U.S. entered the war. In exchange, Mexico would regain territory of Texas, Arizona and New Mexico they had previously held. The U.S. was outraged and thus entered the fray.

1915 - 1918

- WWI Fighting
- Easter Rebellion
- Spanish Flu

World War I

WWI fighting - England had launched the **HMS *Dreadnought*** battleship in 1906, and its name was associated with a generation of fast and superior battleships with improved artillery and steam turbines. The design and short construction time made it clear that Britain's lead on the oceans was unassailable. On land, troops used trench warfare and machine guns. The Germans instituted **stormtroopers** to infiltrate weak points in infantry attacks with speed and surprise. Chemical warfare was used, including chlorine, mustard gas and phosgene. Fixed-wing airplanes, including the effective British **Sopwith Camel**, were used to drop bombs and combat enemy aircraft.

The last major Allied movement was the **Hundred Offensive**, which forced the Germans back to the **Hindenburg Line**, and then the final assault brought the end of the war. In 1919, the **Treaty of Versailles** closed the war and set the stage for the next one. The **League of Nations** was created, in part to keep the defeated nations from rising again, but it initiated further hostility and was unsuccessful. The German, Russian, Ottoman and Austro-Hungarian empires disappeared. Germany was severely punished. More than ten million soldiers and six million civilians died worldwide.

Easter Rebellion in Dublin - In 1916, in the midst of the war, an uprising against the British government was led by members of the nationalist **Irish Republican Brotherhood** during Easter week. Though the British caught wind of their plans, they went ahead with them and the British put down the insurrection quickly. While the movement had been unpopular with the Irish, the execution of 15 rebellion leaders transformed them into martyrs and lit the beginning of the **Irish Republican Revolution**.

Spanish flu - This pandemic killed 50 to 100 million people worldwide between 1918 and 1920. Massive troop movements in WWI spread the disease.

__A HARD PILL TO SWALLOW__ - A Siberian peasant and mystic with a history of debauchery, Grigori Rasputin was an advisor to Tsar Nicolas II and the Romanov family. Rasputin helped treat the Tsar's hemophiliac son who was heir to the throne. He likely prevented the boy's death by halting the use of aspirin, which was commonly used for pain, but is also a blood-thinner.

1918 - 1919

| • Bolshevik Revolution | • Weimar Republic |

World War I

Bolshevik Revolution (1917-1918) - This revolt was composed of two parts. First, the **February Revolution** was precipitated by corruption and inefficiency of the government, food shortages and the country's disastrous participation in WWI. Moderates joined radicals and deposed the Russian imperial government of Tsar **Nicholas II**. The tsar was forced to abdicate and, later, he and his family were executed, ending the **Romanov dynasty**.

The second part of the revolt saw the overthrow of the **Provisional Government**, which had also proved to be inadequate. This bloodless coup in Petrograd was called the **October Revolution** and was led by **Vladimir Lenin** and **Leon Trotsky**, who were advocates of **Marxism**.

The **Russian Social Democratic Worker's Party** split into two groups, the **Bolsheviks** and **Mensheviks**. The revolutionary leader of the Bolsheviks, who were **Russian Communists**, was Lenin. The overthrow of the Provisional Government led to a three-year period of civil war. The Bolsheviks were victorious and founded the **Soviet Republic** in 1917. Lenin acted as leader of this Republic and then of the **Union of Soviet Socialist Republics (USSR)**, which was formed in 1922. Lenin died in 1924.

Weimar Republic - After WWI, a constitutional assembly met in Weimar. Germany's imperial government was destroyed and the state became a parliamentary republic from 1919 to 1933. The official name of the state was the **German Reich**. This short-lived republic was plagued with problems due to the oppressive requirements of the WWI victors and the **Treaty of Versailles**. Hyperinflation and other political and social conditions were problematic.

POTATO PRESERVATION - Like most nations, Russia introduced food rationing and price controls during WWI. One unpopular item was the tsarist government's banning of the production of vodka in a supposed attempt to conserve potato crops for food. The ban, however, was likely intended to reduce drinking of vodka because the Russians at that time were known to consume it in large quantities.

- League of Nations
- Irish Free State

World War I Aftermath

League of Nations - At WWI's close, the Allies created this entity during the **Paris Peace Conference** in 1919. They hoped to preserve peace through a body of representatives that arbitrated disputes and cut down on arms. It was to be headquartered in neutral Geneva in Switzerland.

However, it did not have a military force, and three powerful nations did not join. Despite President Woodrow Wilson's wishes, Congress did not ratify the agreement. Germany and Russia were not permitted to participate. Thus, it began to collapse in the 1930s, unable to back its threats, and **World War II (WWII)** began. The League was dissolved and later replaced by the **United Nations** in 1945.

Irish Free State - England had presided over Ireland since the 1100s, but, by the early 1900s, a nationalist movement culminated in the anti-British **Easter Uprising**. Though this uprising was quelled, the movement continued. In 1919, the **Irish Republican Army (IRA)** was formed, led by **Michael Collins**, and it employed armed force and guerrilla tactics as means to achieve its goals of Irish independence and unity. A cease-fire was called in 1921, followed by a treaty that divided Ireland into the Irish Free State in the south with the United Kingdom still controlling the northern part.

Unrest followed, and Ireland was reunified, but contention continued. In 1937, the unified southern counties were renamed **Éire** and adopted a constitution that declared their sovereignty and independence. Northern Ireland remained a part of the British Empire, leaving room for IRA and the British and Protestant-Catholic religious conflict.

· ·

PHONY BALONEY - Anastasia, youngest daughter of the last Russian emperor, was executed by Bolsheviks during the October Revolution. However, multiple women later stepped forward claiming her identity and claiming to have escaped execution. Their motivation? The inheritance of the Romanov fortune. Genetic testing later revealed that none was Anastasia. The myth became the subject of a play and film.

- USSR
- Stalinism
- Black Shirts

World War I Aftermath

Union of Soviet Socialist Republics (USSR) - Vladimir Lenin retained control of the Soviet Republic from 1917 until the USSR was formed in 1922. He continued as head of the government until his death in 1924. The government under Lenin nationalized all industry, land and business. At his death, a power struggle ensued between Leon Trotsky and **Joseph Stalin**. Eventually, Stalin gained power. Lenin had distrusted him. Lenin's rule had been based on social justice, equality and the rights and welfare of the working people. With Stalin in power, **Trotsky**, a **Leninist**, was exiled and later assassinated.

Stalinism - In 1922, Joseph Stalin acted as the secretary-general of the **Communist Party of the Soviet Union** under Lenin. After Lenin's death, Stalin consolidated power by suppressing Lenin's criticisms and eliminating opposition. He became a brutal dictator whose reign was characterized by forced collectivization of agriculture and industrialization. He was responsible for the **Great Purge** that eliminated the Communist Party and government officials as well as peasants and anyone suspected of sabotage. His rule was ensured by a violent police force, which became the **KGB**. This group was charged with security, secret police work and intelligence. Stalin remained in control until his death in 1953.

Black Shirts - A nationalist, anti-Bolshevist, **Benito Mussolini** served as Italian Prime Minister from 1922 to 1943 and then as a dictator. A talented agitator, he formed the **Fascist Party** after breaking with the socialists. Those who followed him wore black shirts. These followers acted as a military unit and helped him to assume power in the chaos that was Italian politics at the time. He ruled through brute police force. Mussolini, with visions of an empire, successfully invaded and occupied Ethiopia in 1935. He allied with **Adolf Hitler** during WWII in the **Pact of Steel**. This alliance ensured his demise. Mussolini was deposed in 1943 by discontented members of his own group and the Italian king, **Emmanuel III**. He was executed in 1945.

. . . .

COLD AS STEEL - The name Stalin translates to man of steel, and the name was not his given name; he chose it. He was responsible for an estimated 20 million deaths in WWII and once coldly stated, "One death is a tragedy, one million is a statistic."

- Rise of Hitler
- Spanish Civil War
- Beginning of WWII

World War II

Rise of Hitler - After WWI, **Paul von Hindenburg** became president of Germany. He pushed for a policy of *Lebensraum*, which was intended to gain territory for Germans to have better living space. Hitler led the **National Socialist German Workers Party (Nazi Party)** that had gained a great deal of power due to his charismatic speaking ability, and Hindenburg ultimately appointed **Hitler** as Chancellor to gain support from the Nazi Party. Hitler ultimately gained sole control, became **Führer** in 1934, and instilled German nationalism in the people. His was a brutal fascist regime called the **Third Reich** which initiated the next world war.

Spanish Civil War (1936-1939) - Antagonism against the Spanish Republican government boiled into a violent civil war inflamed by foreign intervention. **Nationalist** rebels, led by General **Francisco Franco**, were supported by both fascist Italy and Nazi Germany. The Republic received aid from the USSR and volunteers of the **International Brigades**. Franco was victorious and established a fascist dictatorship that lasted from 1939 to 1975.

Beginning of World War II - The rise of fascist states and discontent lingering from WWI set the stage for this **Second World War**. The **Axis** powers were composed of Italy, Germany and Japan. All three were brutal, propaganda-fueled, ultra-nationalist military regimes, and the problems started as they began to expand outward, specifically when Germany invaded **Poland** in 1939. The war lasted until 1945. Japan was already at war with China with further expansions planned. The **Allied** powers were led by Britain, the USSR, France, Poland and later the U.S. Hitler continued his rampage, attacking and conquering Denmark, Norway, the Netherlands and France.

POP QUIZ - During WWII, American Military Police (MPs) grilled troops at checkpoints on things every American was expected to know, like the name of Mickey Mouse's girlfriend, baseball scores or the capital of a state. General Omar Bradley was briefly detained when he correctly identified Springfield as the capital of Illinois because the American MP who questioned him mistakenly believed the capital was Chicago.

- WWII and the U.S.
- Battle of Stalingrad
- Operation Overlord
- Battle of the Bulge

World War II

WWII and the U.S. - Germany's first setback occurred in late 1940, when their air force, the **Luftwaffe**, was defeated by the **British Royal Air Force** in the **Battle of Britain**. Meantime, Italy invaded Greece and North Africa. This was a disastrous campaign, and **Nazi Germany** was forced to bail them out in 1941. The war in the Pacific theatre began for the U.S. and European nations when Japan bombed the U.S. Navy base at **Pearl Harbor** in Hawaii in 1941. This brought the U.S. into the fray.

Battle of Stalingrad - Germany turned north to invade Russia. The campaign initially seemed to be a success, but the Russian winter and resistance turned it into a disaster. The Battle of Stalingrad in 1942 was a major turning point of the war. Casualties included 850,000 of the more than a million German soldiers in the lengthy battle and more than a million of the USSR forces. By 1944, all German forces were driven from Soviet lands.

Operation Overlord - Also called **D-Day**, this operation by the Allies was led by **Dwight D. Eisenhower**, a U.S. general. It was the largest amphibious invasion in history, and it was coupled with an airborne assault against a greatly weakened Germany. The Allies landed over 150,000 troops on the beaches of **Normandy** in **France**. They pushed the Germans back through France, liberating that country as they went.

Battle of the Bulge - This next serious encounter was in the dense forests of the **Ardennes** region in Belgium, France and Luxembourg. It was a surprise offensive by the Germans. The successful Allies then forged northward into Germany. The Soviet forces meantime were advancing from the north toward Berlin in 1945. Soviets reached Berlin. This marked the end of the **Third Reich** and the German surrender. Hitler and many of his leaders committed suicide.

. . . .

PUSHING BOUNDARIES - The name of the Battle of the Bulge was coined by articles that described the Allied line that 'bulged' inward on wartime maps printed in newspapers. Remember, there were no TVs, cell phones or computers. Communication was by letter, telegraph, newspaper or radio.

- Concentration Camps
- Yalta Conference

World War II

Concentration camps - Hitler and the Nazi regime believed the white German race was superior and worked to create an **Aryan Germany** populated with a '**pure race**' of German people. In a chilling series of escalating events, later termed the **Holocaust**, they sent millions to concentration camps and carried out horrific abuses and the systematic execution of those they deemed inferior. This included Romani, Jews, Poles, Slavs, plus the physically and mentally disabled and those with differing ideological, religious and political beliefs. **Dachau** was the first concentration camp, and it was opened in 1933. Other camps were **Auschwitz**, **Buchenwald** and **Bergen-Belsen**, but there were many, many more. The camps were liberated as Allied forces occupied Germany.

A life of hiding in attics and concealed rooms was written about in *The Diary of Anne Frank*. This young girl kept a diary that was discovered after her death in the Bergen-Belsen concentration camp. Her father was the only member of the family to survive and was responsible for seeing her diaries published. Also, **Elie Wiesel** wrote about experiences at Auschwitz, **Buna** and Buchenwald in his book, *Night*. He earned the **Nobel Peace Prize** for his delivery of a message of peace, atonement and human dignity in his works for the cause of peace.

Yalta Conference - The U.S. president, **Franklin D. Roosevelt**, along with **Winston Churchill**, the British Prime Minister, and Joseph Stalin, the Soviet Premier, met at **Yalta** in February of 1945. They discussed final plans to defeat the Nazis and end the war in the Pacific theatre, as well as potential postwar negotiations. It was at this conference that it was decided to divide Germany into occupied zones, and Stalin agreed to fight Japan and to allow Eastern Europe to hold free elections, among other things.

NAZIS & SWASTIKAS - The Nazis rarely referred to themselves by that name. It was coined by the German press. Hitler intensely disliked it. Before the advent of the Nazis in Europe, the swastika was a common symbol in churches, and it signified good luck. Hitler had seen swastikas on walls of his cathedral as a youth and adopted it.

- **Potsdam Conference**
- **Francoist Spain**

World War II

Potsdam Conference - Held in 1945, this was a continuation of the Yalta Conference. The goal was not to create a treaty, but to establish post-war peace procedures. Germany had fallen, Roosevelt had died, and a new British Prime Minister was elected during this conference, all of which caused problems. The leaders of this July conference included Joseph Stalin, Soviet Premier, **Harry S Truman**, a new U.S. president, and **Clement Attlee**, a new British Prime Minister. New leadership and Allied concern about communism's growth resulted in contention centered on how to deal with defeated Germany's occupation, reparations and elections, all of which were complex issues. The Allies demanded unconditional surrender by Japan, but the Japanese ignored this demand.

Knowing a continuation of the war on the Pacific front would have a high cost in American lives, Truman decided to use nuclear weapons. In August, 1945, the U.S. aircraft *Enola Gay* dropped the first **atomic bomb** on **Hiroshima**, and later, a bomb was dropped on **Nagasaki**. Japan quickly surrendered. As a result of this war, European colonialism ceased and the U.S. and USSR became world powers and entered the **Cold War** period, which continued until 1991, when the USSR disbanded.

Francoist Spain - During these WWII years, Nationalist **Francisco Franco**, also known as **El Caudillo** or *the leader*, served as Spain's absolute dictator and remained in that position until his death in 1975. He distanced Spain from the conflict, persecuted all who were not Catholic or who were thought to be political or ideological enemies. He created a spy network to control the people and did not allow free speech. As he aged, he allowed his authoritarian reign to slip and, at his death, Spain moved to become a democracy in the form of a constitutional monarchy. His successor **Juan Carlos** led the transition toward democracy.

FIRST NUCLEAR DISASTER - *The uranium bomb dropped on Hiroshima was named* Little Boy *and weighed about 9,000 pounds. It destroyed around five square miles. The second target, Nagasaki, was hit by a plutonium bomb called,* Fat Man, *which weighed over 10,000 pounds. It destroyed 2½ square miles; the mountainous region reduced its effect.*

- Aftermath of WWII
- Division of Yugoslavia
- Division of Germany
- United Nations

World War II Aftermath

Aftermath of WWII - England was one of the 'big three' powers leading the effort to tie up post-war affairs. They had suffered nearly 450,000 deaths during the war and were weakened economically. The end of WWII signaled the beginning of the end for Britain's colonial empire. By 1947, **India** gained independence, and most other British colonies followed suit by 1960 and joined the **British Commonwealth of Nations**. The British monarch remained the official Head of State for these nations in a symbolic role.

France was also weakened, having lost over 550,000 people. At the war's close, a long, violent conflict with resistant colonies seeking independence began. Over time, all French colonies won their independence, and the French empire ceased. One of these colonies was **Vietnam**.

Division of Yugoslavia - This country was freed of German control. The former kingdom was recreated into the **Federal People's Republic of Yugoslavia** and contained the six **Socialist Republics** of **Croatia**, **Bosnia and Herzegovina**, **Montenegro**, **Slovenia**, **Serbia** and **Macedonia**. Thus, the second Yugoslavia was established, and the communist regime of **Josip Tito** was formed. He ruled until his death in 1980 as a benevolent dictator.

Division of Germany - This country was broken into four zones occupied by the French, British, U.S. and Soviets. Cold War tension between communist Soviets and non-communist powers turned this division from temporary to long-standing. In 1949, zones occupied by the British, U.S. and French were combined to create the **Federal Republic of Germany**, or **West Germany** as it came to be called. The Russian held territory became known as **East Germany**. Thus divided, hope for reunification of Germany was dashed.

United Nations (UN) - During the last days of the war in Europe, representatives of 50 countries drafted a new charter for an organization to replace the **League of Nations**, and it became this entity.

. . . .

__UNITED NATIONS__ - During the war, the United Nations became the official term for the Allies. To join, countries had to sign a declaration and declare war on the Axis powers. Iraq was an original member in 1945.

- Conclusion of WWII
- *Sputnik*
- De-Stalinization of USSR
- Berlin Wall
- Stagnation Era in USSR

World War II Aftermath

Conclusion of WWII - Approximately 70 million people, including civilians and military personnel, died during WWII. Over 30 countries were involved. It was the deadliest conflict in human history.

Sputnik - The Soviet Union launched a series of man-made satellites, the first being *Sputnik I* in 1957. This was the first man-made satellite ever launched to orbit Earth. It ignited the **Space Age** and **Space Race**.

De-Stalinization of the USSR - Joseph Stalin died in 1953. **Nikita Khrushchev**, a rising star in the Communist Party, soon became the USSR Premier. He deviated from Stalin's direction and delivered a secret speech denouncing Stalin and his policies. The speech was published, and word spread quickly, inflicting harm to the Soviet Union's image and inciting rebellions in Poland and Hungary that were violently stopped. Khrushchev promoted a return to traditional **Leninism**.

Berlin Wall - In 1961, a heavily guarded, concrete wall was built to encompass **West Berlin**. It divided that area from communist **East Berlin** and the rest of **East Germany**. It was built by the Soviets to prevent East Germans from escaping, though many desperately made the dangerous attempt. The wall served as a symbol of Soviet oppression and Cold War division. It was torn down in 1989, when Berlin was finally reunited.

Era of stagnation in USSR - In 1964, Khrushchev was unseated and shortly after, **Leonid Brezhnev** rose to power. At the beginning of the Brezhnev era, the weakened USSR was prosperous and had a growing economy. By the end of his reign, it had entered a period of social, political and economic stagnation. This continued until **Mikhail Gorbachev** came into power and ultimately ended with the dissolution of the Soviet Union.

. . . .

"ICH BIN EIN BERLINER" - In 1963, President John F. Kennedy gave a speech to an audience of 450,000 people in West Berlin to express support for West Germany. This occurred less than a year after the Soviets had erected the Berlin Wall. Twice in the speech, he used these German words to say, "I am a Berliner." His words were the following: "Today, in the world of freedom, the proudest boast is 'Ich bin ein Berliner!'"

- British Invasion
- Prague Spring
- Thatcherism
- *Tear Down this Wall!*

Globalization

British Invasion - In the 1960s, the **Beatles**, a British music group, started their climb to international acclaim with a new kind of music. Experimenting with a variety of genres and messages, the group led a youth cultural movement for a short period of time that came to be known as the British Invasion. This group, at one time, held the top five positions on the Billboard Hot 100 Singles chart. Other groups followed, including the **Rolling Stones** and **The Who**, and pop music was forever changed.

Prague Spring (1968) - **Alexander Dubček** led a short period of liberalization in **Czechoslovakia**, which included the Prague Spring reforms. The intent was to decentralize the economy and promote democracy. Reforms loosened restrictions of free speech, the media and travel. Slovakian autonomy was encouraged as well as democratization and de-Stalinization. The Soviets and other members of the **Warsaw Pact** invaded the country to halt the reforms and deposed Dubček. The Warsaw Pact was a collective defense treaty between the USSR and eight other communist European countries. It was intended to protect and safeguard the existence of communism in Europe.

Thatcherism - In 1979, **Margaret Thatcher**, representing Britain's Conservative Party, became the first female Prime Minister. Those that promoted her conservative policies of monetarism, privatization and self-help followed a political philosophy that has come to be called Thatcherism. She became known as the **Iron Lady** for her uncompromising politics and leadership. She remained in office until 1990.

"Tear down this wall!" - This dictate by **Ronald Reagan**, U.S. president, challenged Mikhail Gorbachev to tear down the Berlin Wall as a symbol of the USSR's moving in the direction of increased freedom in the Eastern Bloc through *glasnost* and *perestroika*. This speech was delivered in front of **Brandenburg Gate** in West Berlin at the 750th anniversary of the city of Berlin.

- -

SLIPPERY SITUATION - The Sea Gem was the first British offshore oil rig. When the rig's legs collapsed in 1965, 13 crew members died. Since that time, procedures have been put in place to ensure safety on oil rigs, including always having a boat on stand-by.

- **Beginning of Solidarity**
- **Chernobyl Disaster**
- **Velvet Revolution**
- **Lockerbie Bombing**

Globalization

Beginning of Solidarity - Founded in 1980, this was a **Polish** trade union federation. It was organized by **Lech Wałęsa** as the first independent trade union federation in a Soviet bloc country. It quickly became a social movement that deeply worried Soviets. In 1981, the Polish government declared martial law and proclaimed the union illegal. This union was eventually recognized and became a rival of the **Polish Communist Party**. In essence, this group was a step toward capitalism for Poland.

Chernobyl disaster - A catastrophic **nuclear** accident occurred at a power station located in Chernobyl in the **Ukraine** in 1986. This resulted in explosions, an exposed reactor and the widespread release of high levels of radiation. The reactor was encased in a makeshift 'sarcophagus' of steel and concrete. This disaster resulted in mass displacement of surrounding populations, in the deaths of around 30 staff and emergency workers and in a high incidence of cancer and deformities. An enormous portion of land surrounding the reactor has remained unstable and been abandoned.

Velvet Revolution - A series of protests, initially led by the student community, were held in 1989 in **Czechoslovakia**. After a peaceful revolution, the communist government chose to step down, and the country transitioned from communism to democracy. The first elections were held in 1990. Three years later, Czechoslovakia split into the **Czech Republic** and **Slovakia**.

Lockerbie bombing - In 1988, **Pan American Flight 103** was destroyed by a terrorist bomb, killing 259 people on board and 11 people on the ground. The flight was downed near **Lockerbie** in **Scotland**. Two **Libyan** nationals were blamed. Ultimately, it was the leader of Libya, **Muammar Gaddafi**, who took responsibility for the attack and paid compensation to families of the victims.

. . . .

RADIOACTIVE FISHING - A thousand square mile Exclusion Zone was set up in the Ukraine around the Chernobyl site to protect the public from increased radioactivity from nuclear fallout. However, some people within the zone chose not to leave their homes and still live there today. A recent episode of River Monsters *featured the TV show's host fishing in the cooling channels of the Chernobyl reactor.*

- **Dissolution of USSR**
- **Persian Gulf War**

Globalization

Dissolution of USSR (1989) - This began in the 1980s, after Mikhail Gorbachev came to power. He instituted radical reforms that upset the USSR's precarious balance, and the Soviets began to move toward democratization.

Perestroika was a political movement to restructure economic and political policy, and this lent to the instability of the government. **Glasnost** was the beginning of a Soviet policy of transparency. It encouraged a policy of free speech that allowed discontent to become a movement toward independence. Both were met with resistance by officials who were reluctant to cede any measure of power, and these policies weakened the USSR.

Realizing that the nation was falling apart and attempting to resuscitate it, a Soviet group kidnapped Gorbachev and staged an unsuccessful coup. However, by 1991, Gorbachev's resignation and the dissolution of the USSR were announced. Fifteen independent states were born in its place. Twelve have associated as the **Commonwealth of Independent States** (**CIS**). The Baltic states have not joined a post-Soviet organization, as of 2014.

Persian Gulf War - Often termed **Operation Desert Shield**, this conflict included a coalition force from 34 nations, led by the U.S., in response to Iraq's invasion and attempted annexation of **Kuwait** in 1990. The **UN** imposed economic sanctions against Iraq. Iraqi troops were forced out of Kuwait in 1991, after setting fire to 700 oil wells. Fires raged for ten months and caused widespread pollution. **George H. W. Bush**, U.S. president, was criticized for not enabling the military force to continue into Baghdad and overthrow the government of **Saddam Hussein**, who remained in power.

. . . .

LET ME ENTERTAIN YOU - Gorbachev had a long and successful political career. It was not always work, however; he appeared as himself in a movie in 1993, and he and his granddaughter Anastasia were in a Pizza Hut commercial in 1997. He recorded an album of old Russian love ballads that was entitled "Songs for Raisa." Raisa was his wife and mother of his daughter, Irina Mikhailovna Virganskaya.

- Splintering of Yugoslavia
- European Union
- Iraq War
- London Suicide Bombings
- Treaty of Lisbon
- Eurozone Crisis

Globalization

Splintering of Yugoslavia - A series of political conflicts during the 1980s culminated in wars between ethnic groups from 1991 to 1999. This resulted in creation of seven new nations and elimination of Yugoslavia.

European Union - The **European Economic Community** (**EEC**) was an organization of countries to consolidate economic integration, including a common market among its members. In 1993, with the **Maastricht Treaty**, the group became the **European Union** (**EU**). With this treaty, the group adopted a new institutional structure and made possible a changeover to the **Euro**, which was to become a common currency in many of the member countries.

Iraq War - This **Second Persian Gulf War** was an armed conflict that began in 2003 with an invasion force led by the U.S., United Kingdom, Australia and Poland. Iraq was suspected of possessing weapons of mass destruction and would not allow UN weapon inspectors to completely verify their weapon situation. After the initial invasion, Saddam Hussein was captured and turned over to Iraqi authorities to stand trial and was executed. U.S. troops remained as a peace keeping force until 2011.

London suicide bombings - In 2005, three separate suicide bombers detonated explosives on three different **London Underground** trains in a 50-second time span. Some 52 people were killed and almost 800 injured. The terrorist attack was confirmed to be the work of Muslim extremists.

Treaty of Lisbon - New global challenges of the 21st century and increased membership in the **EU** resulted in the group reworking its rules and organization with the 2007 treaty. The intent was to create a more democratic organization and reform internal and external policies.

Eurozone crisis - In 2009, ten banks in central and Eastern Europe failed and requested bailouts. This resulted in an ongoing financial debt crisis in Eurozone countries, including Greece, Italy, Spain and 15 more.

EASTERN HEMISPHERE

Part 4
Asia

c. 9000 BCE - c. 5000 BCE

- Settlement of Jericho
- Anatolia
- Early Chinese Cultures
- Beginning of Hinduism

Prehistoric Period

Settlement of Jericho - Originally begun around 9000 BCE, this **Neolithic** settlement was located north of the **Dead Sea** in the **West Bank** on the **Jordan River**. It was probably the first city established on Earth and was the first walled city. It was significant because Jericho was the first place where families lived together in a permanent community with other families. The main trade commodity was salt.

Anatolia - By around 7000 BCE, **Çatalhöyük**, located in the Anatolian highlands of present-day **Turkey**, was a Neolithic settlement. Excavations at this site revealed signs of agriculture, including wheat and barley, as well as domestication of cattle and the creation of pottery and textiles. Homes had small ovens for baking. **Obsidian** was the trade commodity that supported the community.

Early Chinese cultures - Beginning around 6500 BCE and lasting 1,500 years, the Chinese cultivated rice in terraces on hillsides of the **Yangtze** and **Yellow River** valleys. **Stone Age** tools and pottery found by archeologists indicated that the society was more advanced than previously thought for this period in China. The Yellow River area was sometimes called **China's Cradle of Civilization**.

Beginning of Hinduism - Hinduism has been practiced as a religion longer than any other religion. It began between 5000-4000 BCE and grew to become the globe's third largest religion. It did not begin as a religion, but rather as a way of living. The term **Hindu** was used by Greeks and Arabs to describe the actions of the people they encountered in present-day India. The religion established the **caste system**, which has been part of the culture in India since this period. The cow was considered a sacred animal. Primary deities included **Brahma**, **Vishnu** and **Shiva**. Belief in **karma**, the idea that how you act in this life will be reflected in your next life, was an integral part of this religion.

. . . .

DEAD LAKE? - *The Dead Sea is really not a sea at all, but a lake. Its very high salt content makes it difficult to sustain life, hence the name. It is over 1,200 feet lower than the nearby Mediterranean Sea and is the lowest point on Earth's surface.*

- Early Oceania
- Cradle of Civilization
- Domestication of Horses
- Beginning of Bronze Age

Prehistoric Period

Early Oceania - Except for Australia, the Torres Strait, New Guinea and the Solomon Islands, Oceania was uninhabited for a long time. The original people of this region arrived around 30,000 BCE. It was thought that they traveled through the **Malay Peninsula**, then island-hopped through **Malaysia** and **Indonesia** to reach their destination. As sea levels rose, the distances between islands became greater and these cultures developed in isolation for roughly 30,000 years. Much of Oceania has remained virtually unpopulated for most of known history, but began developing around 4000 BCE.

Cradle of Civilization - Considered the *land between rivers*, **Mesopotamia** was a region in what is now Iraq. It included the lands around the **Tigris** and **Euphrates Rivers**. These rivers originated in Turkey and emptied into the Persian Gulf. During the Stone Age, this region was fertile, easily traveled and easily farmed. Numerous small towns were built there around 3500 BCE, thus earning the description of *Cradle of Civilization*.

Domestication of horses - Around 3500 BCE, Asians began domesticating horses. This produced a revolutionary change in lifestyle for humans. Previously, horses were hunted for meat, but, with their domestication, people had a source of milk and milk products. Of the highest importance, horses provided mobility. Horses were first used as pack animals, then to pull carts and travois and finally as mounts. The people of the **steppes** in what is now **Kazakhstan**, **Russia** and the **Ukraine** developed a nomadic culture built around the horse. Around 2500 BCE, domesticated horses reached the **Sumerians**.

Beginning of Bronze Age - Due to geography, early people of China developed with little outside influence. The **Yellow** and **Yangtze Rivers** saw the first population centers grow around farming. Silk and bronze were produced around 2700 BCE.

. . . .

MINI-HORSES - Emerging 60 million years ago, the first horse was called Eohippus, *which meant* the dawn horse. *It was very small at just over a foot tall and weighed only 12 pounds. Unlike the horses of today with hooves, the tiny, ancient horse had four toes on its front feet and three on its hind feet.*

- Indus River Civilization
- Rise of Sumer
- Sumerian Writings
- Minoans

Early Civilizations

Indus River civilization - The people of the Indus River Valley began farming and domesticating animals some 8,000 years ago. Small settlements slowly grew in the region. This area was located in what is now **Pakistan** and **India**. The use of cattle to pull farm implements increased production in the region. Indus Valley people were also the first people in southern Asia to work in metal. By 2500 BCE, the city of **Harappa** grew to dominate the region and lent its name to the culture, although the city of **Mohenjo-Daro** was likely larger. The **Harappan culture** was built around and thrived on trade, manufacturing and farming for 700 years.

Rise of Sumer - The first of the great world civilizations to develop was **Sumer** beginning around 2300 BCE. It occupied the lower Mesopotamian valley. Sumerians had great success as farmers and produced a surplus of food. Initially, there were many conflicts between the cities of the region. King **Sargon** united the cities, and ideas and concepts developed by the Sumerians began to spread along trade networks far beyond the region.

As the culture became agrarian, rather than a hunter-gatherer culture, people had time to develop a formal religion and religious elite. Artisans developed greater skills and taught them to others. The Sumerians were among the first people to work in metallurgy and the first to develop a writing system.

Sumerian writings - The *Epic of Gilgamesh* was written around 1900 BCE. This Sumerian epic poem was probably the first great work of literature. There are parallels and common themes between this epic poem and the **Bible**, including a story of a **Great Flood**. The oldest known cookbook was inscribed on clay tablets in Mesopotamia around 1700 BCE.

Minoans - The Minoan civilization was founded more than 7,000 years ago. It was considered the first European civilization, and it extended into the eastern Mediterranean's **Levant region** and into **Egypt** in northern Africa.

. . . .

GOOD DRAGONS - Chinese dragons are considered to be beautiful, friendly and wise. China, Korea and Japan often depict dragons in their art. Interestingly enough, Chinese dragons have five toes; Korean dragons, four toes; and Japanese dragons, three toes.

- Code of Hammurabi
- Vedic Period of India
- Beginning of Judaism

Early Civilizations

Code of Hammurabi - Sumer's success created envy among other peoples, and attacks upon cities of the region increased. Eventually, these outsiders were organized by a man called **Hammurabi** of **Babylon**. The Babylonians were successful in astronomy, literature, mathematics and, perhaps most important, law. This set of laws was developed around 1792 BCE as a collection of ethical principles designed to protect the weak from the strong in everything from property disputes to medical treatment. The most famous of these laws was "an eye for an eye, a tooth for a tooth." The Babylonian culture was so well-established and often mimicked that, even after it was overrun by others, the culture and way of life continued.

Vedic period of India - The **Vedas**, which were the oldest scriptures in Hinduism, were composed at this time. This period between 1750 BCE and 500 BCE saw a rise in urban states centered on agriculture at the foot of the **Himalaya Mountains**. It spread to the **Ganges Plain**. A strict social hierarchy and the **Classical Sanskrit** language were developed by the end of the period.

Beginning of Judaism - Developed around 1800 BCE, Judaism was the first of the three **Abrahamic** faiths, and followers were known as **Jews**. **Christianity** and **Islam** are the other two Abrahamic religions. Judaism was a monotheistic religion, a belief in a single god. This religion provided guidance on all aspects of life. It was based on the **b'rit**, a covenant between the people and God with obligations on both sides. The founders were **Abraham of Ur** in **Babylonia**, his son **Isaac**, Isaac's son **Jacob**, who was also called **Israel**, and Jacob's sons.

Abraham was called to worship one god and to take his followers from Mesopotamia to **Palestine**. Eventually, they went to **Egypt**, and they were later enslaved. The Jews were called to leave Egypt and fled in the **Exodus** to what is now Lebanon, Israel, Palestine and Syria after years of wandering. They were led by **Moses**, who was said to have received the **Ten Commandments** from God on **Mount Sinai**. These commandments have been sacred in many faiths, and have formed the basis of law in many cultures.

• •

SAILING ALONG - Skill in navigation dates to a period over 6,000 years ago. The very word navigation *is derived from a Sanskrit word meaning* ship.

c. 1450 BCE - c. 1000 BCE

- Torah
- Settling of Fiji and Samoa
- Trojan War
- Zhou Dynasty in China

Early Civilizations

Torah - The Jewish holy book is the Torah, which was written between the 16th and 5th century BCE. It is part of the **Old Testament** in the **Bible.**

Settling of Fiji and Samoa - Around 1300 BCE, people first arrived in Fiji and Samoa. Archaeological evidence of pottery from the **Lapita** culture supported a date around 1500 BCE, while oral traditions have supported a date closer to 1000 BCE. Samoa, Fiji and **Tonga** have had a close relationship from the beginning, and intermarriage among rulers was common. Most Pacific nations had an oral tradition designating Samoa as their place of origin. The Samoans, however, have also designated Samoa as their place of origin. At some time after 1000 BCE, **Lapita pottery** disappeared, and oral traditions of Samoa and Fiji did not account for this.

Trojan War - This ended around 1200 BCE when the Greeks destroyed Troy after a ten-year war. The war was described by **Homer** in *The Iliad* and by **Virgil** in *The Aeneid*. It was believed the city was first built around 3000 BCE and survived far into the **Ottoman** era, which was around the beginning of the **Iron Age** in Asia. Troy was designated a heritage site by the **United Nations Educational, Scientific and Cultural Organization** (**UNESCO**).

Zhou Dynasty in China (c. 1046 BCE-256 BCE) - The **Mandate of Heaven** came into being during this period of the **Iron Age**. It dictated that only one person could lead China and leadership could only be passed to an honorable person. It required the leader to be a good steward of the land and people. This Mandate was often cited as the reason a ruler was overthrown in order to legitimize the position of the rebels. The Zhou limited large public works and reduced taxes, and the region stabilized. The Zhou culture spread. Their writing was codified, and iron metallurgy advanced.

• •

TRICK PONY - *Legend has it that the Greeks, after ten years besieging Troy, built a huge wooden horse. One man took this Trojan Horse into Troy as the remaining forces sailed off. The Trojans thought it a peace offering. During the night, the 30 soldiers who were inside the horse crept out, opened the gates and the Greeks fought and defeated the Trojans.*

- Israel and Judah Kingdoms
- Neo-Babylonian Empire
- Assyrian Empire
- Schools of Thought

Empires & Dynasties

Kingdom of Israel and Judah - This kingdom existed between 1020 BCE and 931 BCE as the **United Monarchy**. It contained the Kingdom of Israel in the north and of Judah in the south. The kingdom covered the territory of present-day Israel, Jordan, Syria, Lebanon and Egypt. The capital moved several times before finally being established at **Jerusalem**. Upon the death of King **Solomon**, the nation again split. The Kingdom of Israel remained an independent nation until it was conquered by the **Assyrian Empire** in 722 BCE and the Kingdom of Judah fell to the **Babylonian Empire** about 150 years later.

Assyrian Empire - The reign of **Tiglath-Pileser III** of the 1000-year-old Assyrian Empire began around 745 BCE. At this time, the region covered parts of Mesopotamia, Turkey, Syria and extended southward toward Egypt. Pileser introduced **Aramaic script**, replacing the complicated **Akkadian script** used at the time. All documents were translated into Aramaic. Aramaic spread from Israel to Greece and has survived as a written language, enabling scholars to translate Akkadian and Sumerian writings. The Assyrian Empire fell with the resurgence of the **Babylonians** around 727 BCE.

Neo-Babylonian Empire (626 BCE-539 BCE) - A combined force of Babylonians and **Medes** sacked **Nineveh** and overthrew the Assyrians. In 605 BCE, **Nebuchadnezzar II** became Babylon's greatest king. He captured Jerusalem and exiled the Jews to Babylonia. The walls he built around Babylon encompassed 200 square miles and were wide enough across the top to conduct chariot races. During his reign, tolerance was encouraged, education was encouraged, and craftsmanship reached new heights. He died in 562 BCE.

Hundred Schools of Thought - Under Zhou rule, philosophers, including **Confucius**, **Mozi** and **Laozi**, flourished from the 6th century BCE to the 4th century BCE. During this period, *The Art of War* was written by **Sun Tzu**, a **Taoist** philosopher and master of military strategy. The book changed warfare in China and has been studied in China since that time.

. . . .

RIDE 'EM - Alexander the Great had a horse named Bucephalus. As a ten-year-old prince, he trained the horse. Alexander taught the great horse to kneel so that he could mount him wearing full armor. When Bucephalus died, Alexander named a city for him.

- First Persian Empire
- Taoism
- Confucianism

Empires & Dynasties

First Persian Empire - From 550 BCE to 334 BCE, Persians conquered local tribes. Led by **Cyrus the Great** of the **Achaemenid family**, this was also called the **Achaemenid Empire**. Cyrus restored the gods of the local people and encouraged tolerance but was ruthless when challenged. **Darius I** built upon the original holdings and established a common currency. Eventually a **Royal Road**, which was 1,600 miles long, crossed the empire. It became part of the **Silk Road**.

Zoroastrianism, a religion founded in Persia, taught obedience to one deity. The empire eventually dominated present-day Turkey, northern Egypt and northern Saudi Arabia to Pakistan. In 333 BCE, **Alexander the Great** defeated Darius at the **Battle of Issus**, ending the Persian Empire.

Taoism - Also called **Daoism**, this was a philosophical, religious and ethical tradition in China. **Laozi** wrote *Tao Te Ching*, which means *the virtuous way*, between the 6th and 4th centuries BCE. It defined the fundamentals of this tradition of living in harmony with the universe. He was probably not the only author and, in fact, his name translated as *the Master*. He was a great philosopher, and, by writing the book, he helped to spread this 1,000 year-old Chinese philosophy. From Taoism came **yin** and **yang**, **Tai Chi** and the **Three Treasures**, which are compassion, moderation and humility.

Confucianism - This philosophical and ethical system was sometimes considered a type of religion. It was begun in China around 575 BCE by Confucius, who was called **Master Kong**. He sought knowledge and was a teacher who encouraged others to seek self-improvement. His basic philosophy suggested that knowledge created honest thinking, which promoted appropriate action. An individual who lived right created a family who lived right, which in turn affected the community, the nation and, eventually, promoted world peace.

. . . .

WORDS FROM THE WISE - *"Do the difficult things while they are easy and do the great things while they are small. A journey of a thousand miles must begin with a single step."* ~ *Lao Tzu*
"When it is obvious that the goals cannot be reached, don't adjust the goals, adjust the action steps." ~ *Confucius*

• Buddhism   • Maurya Empire

Empires & Dynasties

Buddhism - A religious system begun in northern India between 500 BCE and 400 BCE, this was based on the teachings of Prince **Siddhartha Gautama**. At some point in this period, Gautama saw the suffering of the common people and decided to leave his life of privilege. He began to meditate. It was said that one day he achieved enlightenment.

Buddhism was not based on a belief in a god or gods. A person who had achieved enlightenment was termed a ***Buddha***, meaning *the awakened one*. Buddhism acknowledged that there was suffering in the world, and there was a way to relieve this suffering after studying the situation and taking action. A form of Buddhism called **Zen** has been greatly influenced by the concepts of **Taoism**. All three philosophies, Taoism, Confucianism and Buddhism, had a great effect on Asian cultures and an impact on Western philosophy in the 20th century.

Maurya Empire - This was one of the largest empires of ancient times, territorially and population-wise. **Chandragupta Maurya** led a revolt that overthrew the remnants of Alexander the Great's army in India in 322 BCE. This started the Empire, which flourished near the end of the **Iron Age**. The emperor embraced **Jainism**, which was one of the oldest religions of the world. It emphasized nonviolence and equality of all forms of life.

This period was an era of social harmony, religious transformation and expansion of the sciences and of knowledge. The empire's influence in the East was as great as the Hellenic, or Greek, influence was in the West. The Sanskrit language was established, literature flourished, and sculpture of the time had a lasting impact on Indian art. **Hinduism** replaced Buddhism in dominance, and the ***Dharmaśāstra***, which were law books, were written during this period.

• •

KARMA - Hinduism is not an organized religion and has no single set of rules, but rather adheres to certain concepts such as truth, dharma and karma. One Hindu belief is that the physical body inhabited by the soul is determined by actions in other lives. The goal of the soul is moksha, the path of duty, knowledge and unconditional surrender to God.

- Decline of Maurya Empire
- Qin Dynasty
- Han Dynasty
- Silk Road

Empires & Dynasties

Decline of Maurya Empire - Chandragupta's grandson, **Ashoka the Great**, adhered to **Buddhism**, renouncing war and violence. Emperors who followed were weaker and the empire declined. The last leader of the dynasty was **Brihadratha**, who was assassinated.

Qin dynasty - In 246 BCE, **Qin Shi Huang** became the First Emperor of unified China (sounds like *chin*). He was an autocrat who abandoned the Confucian philosophy of kindness and compassion. He extended many public works, including canals and roads throughout China. Qin was also responsible for building the first **Great Wall** and a massive army of terracotta, or clay, warriors with horses, chariots and weapons to protect his tomb. This dynasty was overthrown in 206 BCE by the **Han dynasty**, ushering out the **Iron Age**.

Han dynasty - This dynasty began in 206 BCE and lasted approximately 400 years. Its greatest leader was **Wu-ti**, also called **Han Wu the Great**. Under his rule, China expanded culturally and began looking toward the west. Tolerance of other cultures resumed and Confucian principles guided the government. China expanded its control into Central Asia. Under the Han dynasty, ship rudders were advanced, mapmaking techniques were improved, papermaking was developed, and the year was set to 365¼ days.

Silk Road - This trade route officially opened in 130 BCE. This was the trade route begun by the Chinese that eventually encompassed more than 4,000 miles. Silk, porcelain, spices, tools and metals were all traded, as well as food and agricultural products. There was also an exchange of religion. Buddhism and **Islam** were spread along the route; unfortunately, so was the **bubonic plague**.

. . . .

UNDERGROUND ARMY - Emperor Qin Shi Huang had some 700,000 artisans begin their 36-year feat of building his tomb with over 6,000 life-sized, terracotta soldiers and some 40,000 bronze weapons. Upon completion, he executed the laborers to keep the location secret and to protect the treasures against looters.

- Beginning of Christianity
- Settlement of Eastern Polynesia

Empires & Dynasties

Beginning of Christianity - The group who became **Christians** believed that **Jesus of Nazareth** was their Messiah. He was born between 6 BCE and 2 BCE and died between 30 and 33 CE. He was a **Galilean Jew** who traveled in **Judea**, then part of the Roman Empire, conducting his ministry when he was about 30 years old. Much of his teaching was told in parables. Originally, Jesus was to be tried for blasphemy by the **Sanhedrin**, a Jewish judicial body, but he was turned over to **Pontius Pilate**, the Roman governor, instead. Jesus was condemned to death by crucifixion.

Close followers of Jesus, the **apostles**, continued to spread his teachings. All followers of Christ were thus called **Christians**. All Christians were called Catholics until the schism of the 11th century between the Roman Catholic and Greek Orthodox groups. The Christian holy book was the **Holy Bible**. Parts were written as far back as the 16th to the 12th centuries BCE.

The historical significance of Christianity was so great that most calendar dates were later changed to reflect the approximate time of his birth. The abbreviation *BC* indicated time *before Christ*, and *AD* stood for *anno domini*, which meant *in the year of our Lord*, that is *after his birth*. These were replaced by *BCE*, *before common era*, and *CE*, *common era*.

Settlement of eastern Polynesia - Emigration of Polynesian peoples across the Pacific began around 300 CE. This required great navigational skills, such as using the stars and the ability to read the tides. Polynesians began building double-hulled ships, the forerunner of catamarans, to carry all their supplies, including domesticated plants and animals. The settlement of the region of **Oceania**, **Hawaii**, **Easter Island** and **New Zealand**, was completed around 1000 CE.

. . . .

ZERO

NOTHING - *The idea of using zero was thought to be developed in India, and may date back to the Khmer Empire. It came to medieval Europe from the Arabs. Europeans were confused because they had no concept of zero. The Arab word was pronounced as* cipher. *Cipher has come to mean* a baffling message.

- Gupta Dynasty
- Invasion by the Huns

Empires & Dynasties

Gupta dynasty - The **Classical Age** of northern India began with the rise of the **Gupta Empire** around 320 CE and lasted more than 200 years. During this period, peace was widespread, culture flourished and great **Sanskrit epics** were written. **Kālidāsa** wrote during this period and was regarded as the greatest poet of the Sanskrit language. **Vishnu Sharma** was author of the *Panchatantra* fables, which used animals to teach moral lessons. These spread across Europe before 1600.

During this period of stability, **Aryabhata**, an astronomer and mathematician, suggested that the world was not flat. The game of chess was originated, and the **Hindu culture** was more or less defined. The dynasty ended around 550 CE after invasions by **Hephthalites**, also called the **White Huns**, from the mountains. Little was known about these people.

Invasion by the Huns - The origin of the Huns was defined as *beyond the Sea of Azov near the frozen ocean*. Their origin and the origin of the language they spoke were unknown. **Attila the Hun** was thought to have been raised by an uncle. He learned both **Latin** and **Gothic** in order to trade with the **Romans** and **Goths**. He rose to power in 434 CE.

Attila and his army were masterful horsemen who eventually used present-day Hungary as a staging area for attacks against Rome and the Roman Empire. Huns pushed the Vandals farther into the southwest and what is now Spain. He was an excellent strategist and used his fierce reputation to overrun cities. He moved across northern Europe to present-day Denmark. Attila's sole loss was his attempt in 452 CE to conquer **Gaul**, in what is now France. Attila died in 453 CE, and his sons were unable to hold on to his empire.

. . . .

HUNNIC WISDOM - *"It is unfortunate when final decisions are made by chieftains headquartered miles away from the front, where they can only guess at conditions and potentialities known only to the captain of the battlefield."*
~ Attila the Hun

- Byzantine Empire
- Silla Dynasty
- Beginning of Islam

Empires & Dynasties

Byzantine Empire - This empire was the outgrowth of the **Eastern Roman Empire** and began around 470 CE. The empire was named after a Greek colony on the **Bosporus**. It was noted for its laws and for its promotion and preservation of learning and art. In the 6th century, **Justinian I** reorganized the imperial government and wrote the **Codex Justinianus**, or Code of Justinian. It was a formal documentation of Roman law that served as the basis for Western law. During his reign, the silkworm was introduced, which gave Byzantium an independent supply of silk. His greatest architectural legacy was the **Hagia Sophia**, originally a **Greek Orthodox** basilica in **Constantinople**.

In the 7th century, **Heraclius** reformed the government. He introduced the concept of themes, or districts, and he used the local free peasants for defense, rather than using mercenary armies. The use of the self-supporting district system kept the empire strong until it was abandoned in the 11th century. He also centered the empire in **Anatolia**, which was in central Turkey. The empire fell to the **Ottoman Turks** in 1453.

Silla dynasty - This dynasty began in 57 BCE in the south-central region of the **Korean Peninsula**. It became the largest sector of the **Three Kingdoms of Korea** and reached its peak around 600 CE. It was one of the world's longest sustained dynasties when it fell to the **Goryeo**, or **Koryŏ**, for whom the peninsula was named. The Silla dynasty stayed in power until 935 CE.

Beginning of Islam - The prophet **Muhammad** founded the monotheistic religion of **Islam** around 622 CE. Islam stressed a relationship with God and a total surrender to His will. Muhammad was considered by adherents to this religion, known as **Muslims**, to be the last in a line of prophets, which included **Abraham**, **Moses** and **Jesus**. He received visions and God's word, which he passed on. He gained a following in much the same way that Jesus of Nazareth had. Islam also provided rules for human relationships.

. . . .

FORK IT OVER - The Romans learned about using a fork to eat from the Byzantine wife of the Holy Roman Emperor Otto II when she nonchalantly used one at an imperial banquet in 972 CE. All were amazed, and it became popular in Italy in the 11th century.

- **Rules and Laws of Islam**
- **Publication of the Quran**
- **Umayyad Caliphate**
- **Khmer Empire**

Empires & Dynasties

Rules and laws of Islam - Not just a religion, Islam was built as a way of life governed by a set of laws called **Sharia**. The cities of Mecca, Medina and Jerusalem were considered holy sites, and all Muslims were required to make a pilgrimage, which is called a **Hajj**, to Mecca once in their lifetime.

Publication of the Quran - Also called the **Koran**, this book was the holy book for adherents to Islam. The current version was published around 656 CE. It was compiled, written and canonized shortly after the prophet Muhammad's death. All earlier versions were destroyed so only one version would be copied and distributed.

Umayyad Caliphate - A caliphate was a region under Muslim rule that followed Sharia law. The Umayyad Caliphate became the first **Muslim dynasty** around 661 CE. It has always been controversial because many thought that the leadership should be descendants of Muhammad and selected by the people, not inherited. Thus the **Sunni** and **Shi'ite** sects evolved.

The Umayyad dynasty won several battles and took control. They changed the language to **Arabic**. Thus, Greek was no longer the main language of Syria or Egypt. They spread throughout the Middle East and into northern Africa and Spain, bringing Islam with them. The Umayyad dynasty was destroyed by civil war, and the **Abbasid dynasty** took over around 750 CE.

Khmer Empire - The Khmer people migrated to present-day Cambodia along the Mekong River. In 802 CE, the region was united by **Jayavarman II**. The Khmer dominated the southern half of the present-day **Indochina Peninsula**. Khmer art was influenced by India, as was their religion, which was predominantly **Hindu**. The temple complex of **Angkor Wat** covered an area larger than Manhattan and could support one million people.

. . . .

TOMB RAIDER - A temple at Angkor Wat, famous for the large vines that strangle the ruins, was the location for the movie Tomb Raider. *The movie studio paid $10,000 per day for seven days to film there.*

- **End of Khmer Empire**
- *Rubaiyat*
- **Shogun Rule in Japan**
- **Mongol Empire**

Empires & Dynasties

End of the Khmer Empire - Many improvements were made under the Khmer rule, such as canal and reservoir systems that were designed so water was available for farming all year, including the dry season. The empire faced a serious defeat by the **Cham** of present-day Vietnam in the 12th century, but recovered. Ultimately, the Thai migration succeeded in overrunning the kingdom in 1431. This established **Siam**, which became present-day **Thailand**. The capital city of Angkor Wat was abandoned to the jungle.

Rubaiyat - **Omar Khayyam** was a Persian astronomer and mathematician who contributed much to both sciences. However, he became most noted as the poet who wrote *The Rubaiyat* around 1120.

Shogun rule in Japan (1192-1868) - A shogun was a Japanese military ruler and was originally under the authority of the emperor. The military nobility were called **samurai**. Their ethical code was known as the **Bushido**. Gradually, the shoguns increased their power, and the emperor acted as a mere puppet figure. The last shogun, **Yoshinobu,** relinquished power in 1868, and the new centralized government that had arisen during the **Edo period** formed a basis for the Japanese imperial government. Japan's monarchy, also called the **Chrysanthemum Throne**, was the oldest continuous, hereditary monarchy.

Mongol Empire - **Genghis Khan**, whose original name was **Temüjin**, rose from poor beginnings to unify **Mongolia** and conquer lands across central Asia to the Adriatic Sea between 1206 and 1227. His tactics were often brutal. His sons and his grandson, **Kublai Khan**, conquered even more territory, and only the **British Empire** of the 19th century was larger. Genghis Khan was a brilliant strategist and cavalry officer. The Mongol's affinity with and mastery of horses can only be compared to that of the **Comanche** nation of the U.S. Genghis Khan brought the **Uyghur** script to the Mongols, encouraged religious tolerance and promoted people based on merit rather than kinship. This empire lasted until 1368.

. . . .

OUTSPOKEN - *"The moving finger writes; and, having writ; / Moves on: nor all thy piety nor wit; / Shall lure it back to cancel half a Line; / Nor all thy Tears wash out a Word of it."* ~ *Omar Khayyam from* The Rubaiyat

- Consolidation of Silk Road
- *Travels of Marco Polo*
- Ottoman Empire
- *Rihla*
- Ming Dynasty in China

Empires & Dynasties

Consolidation of Silk Road - Though the routes from the Far East to the Mediterranean were present from the 2nd century, the routes were consolidated under Genghis Khan. This became a series of trade and cultural transmission routes that connected the West and East by linking traders, merchants, soldiers, pilgrims and others. Over 4,000 miles long, the route derived its name from the lucrative trade in Chinese silk.

Travels of Marco Polo - This book was written by Italian **Marco Polo** around 1300. Polo had learned the trade of a merchant from his father and uncle. The three embarked on a 24-year journey. When they returned to Venice, the city was at war with Genoa, and Polo was imprisoned. He dictated his book to an inmate. He was later released and became a wealthy merchant.

Beginning of the Ottoman Empire - The Ottoman Empire began as a small state in northwest Turkey around 1300 and rose to prominence when it conquered **Constantinople** in 1453. At its height, the empire controlled the North African coast, coasts of the Red Sea, Iraq, the Anatolian Peninsula and the Balkans.

Rihla - This book's title means *journey*. It was written around 1354. **Ibn Battuta**, a Moroccan scholar and geographer dictated this travelogue of his 29-year journey. His travels took him through most of the world's Islamic regions, as well as many other lands throughout Africa, the Middle East and Asia.

Ming dynasty in China - Beginning in 1368, this was the last ethnic Han dynasty to rule China, although the Han have continued to be the predominant ethnicity in China to present times. During the Ming dynasty, the **Forbidden City** was constructed, and the **Great Wall of China** was fortified. During this period, **Zheng He**, the great Chinese admiral, made voyages throughout the Indian Ocean to Arabia and Africa. Porcelain, lacquer ware and cloisonné were exported to Europe and Japan. The Ming dynasty gradually declined and ended in the mid-1600s.

• •

DON'T DRAW THAT SWORD - *A samurai had several swords, but the largest was called a katana. The samurai belief was that one should never ever draw his katana without drawing blood.*

- Timurid Dynasty
- Fall of the Byzantine Empire
- Expulsion of Mongols from Russia

Empires & Dynasties

Timurid dynasty - **Timur the Lame**, who was also known as **Tamerlane**, was often considered the last of the nomadic conquerors. Of Mongol descent, he conquered much of Central Asia and his reign, which began in 1370, was known for its revival of the arts and scholarship. **Gur-e Amir**, his mausoleum in Samarkand in Uzbekistan, was an outstanding example of the intricate blue and turquoise tile work of the time.

Much of the **Timurid Empire** was lost after Timur's time, but the dynasty continued to rule smaller states until around 1500.

Fall of the Byzantine Empire - After a series of civil wars, the Byzantine Empire had dwindled down to **Constantinople** and **Morea**, a section of present-day Greece. Following the **Battle of Kosovo** in 1389, the **Ottoman Empire** claimed most of the **Balkans**, leaving the remaining part of the Byzantine Empire surrounded. Constantinople fell in 1453 after a two-month siege. The last emperor, **Constantine XI Palaiologos**, disappeared in the fighting.

Expulsion of Mongols from Russia - The Mongols had invaded much of Asia and Russia in the 13th century and in the years following. For almost 300 years, the Mongols held portions of Eastern Europe and Russia as a territory called the **Golden Horde**. This Mongol invasion of Russia had transformed the East Slavic people into three separate groups, which became **Russia**, **Ukraine** and **Belarus**. A series of battles between 1380 and 1480 triggered the decline of Mongol influence and resurrection of Russian princes.

Ivan III was the Grand Prince of Moscow and called **Ivan the Great**. He led Rus forces in the **Great Standoff** on the Ugra River. When **Akhmat**, who was the ruler of the Mongols, faced off against the Russians, he was concerned about the Crimeans on his south flank. Both the Mongols and the Russians retreated, which was seen as a victory for the Russian, or Muscovite, ruler. The Mongols were attacked and defeated by the Crimeans a year later.

••

LONG GRAVEYARD - While it was being built, the Great Wall of China was called 'the longest cemetery on earth.' Reportedly, more than one million people died during its construction and are buried within the wall.

173

- Easter Island Moai
- Beginning of Sikhism
- Ottoman Empire
- Mughal Empire

Empires & Dynasties

Easter Island moai - Between 1250 and 1500, monolithic human figures were carved from volcanic tuff. About 900 statues, known as *moai*, were created by peoples of Polynesian descent. The statues were from four to 33 feet tall, though the average statue was 13 feet tall. The average weight was about 14 tons. In 1774, British Captain **James Cook** was the first European to see them.

Beginning of Sikhism - The first Sikh community was founded by **Guru Nanak** in the 16th century **Punjab** district, which is modern-day northwestern India and eastern Pakistan. Sikhism was monotheistic and stressed the importance of good acts and active involvement in the world.

Ottoman Empire - The empire's greatest leader was **Suleiman I**, who was also called **Suleiman the Magnificent**. His rule began around 1520. The empire had been operating since around 1300. Suleiman broadened his realm via military strength and helped to create its civilized law, literature, art and architecture. Suleiman successfully besieged Vienna to end Habsburg intervention and nearly overran the city. He waged three campaigns against Prussia. After his conquests, the Byzantine city of Constantinople became known as **Istanbul**, a name that had been used interchangeably for many years.

Mughal Empire - A Chagatai Turkic prince, **Babur**, invaded India and founded the **Mughal dynasty** in 1526. From the early 16th to the 18th centuries, this Muslim dynasty ruled most of northern India. Its apt rulers and administrative structure were notable for their attempt to meld a united Indian state via integration of the Hindi and Muslim populations.

In 1556, **Akbar the Great**, one of the greatest rulers of this dynasty, tripled the size and the empire's wealth, raised an impressive army, and established significant social and political reform. He also amassed an impressive library, loved the arts and built luxurious walled cities, such as the empire's capital, **Agra**. The Mughal Empire became one of the largest medieval empires.

• •

HOLD ONTO THE REINS - Early sultans of the Ottoman typically imprisoned or executed all of their brothers in order to secure their claim to the throne.

- Invasion of Korea by Japan
- Edo Period in Japan
- End of Mughal dynasty

Empires & Dynasties

Invasion of Korea by Japan - In 1592, a Japanese general, **Toyotomi Hideyoshi**, deployed forces, aiming to infiltrate the Korean peninsula to reach and invade China. Though land battles did not go well for Korean forces due to the superior weaponry of the Japanese samurai, Korean admiral **Yi Sun-shin** reigned dominant on the sea and later, on land. Korean forces employed guerrilla tactics. Korean people of all stations were inspired to defend their country, and the Ming leaders in China sent aid, forcing Japan to retreat. The Japanese tried again in 1597, but Hideyoshi died during the campaign and, with him, the Japanese invasions. Korea was destroyed during the course of these invasions.

Edo Period in Japan - In 1598, a five-year-old child named **Hideyori** inherited rule of Japan when Toyotomi, his father, died. Due to his age, a group of counselors led by **Tokugawa Ieyasu** ruled. Tokugawa became **Shogun** in 1603 and shifted the government from Kyoto to Edo, modern day Tokyo, and assumed complete power by 1615. After this, 250 years of national unity, referred to as the Tokugawa or Edo period, began. The government was a mix of military shoguns and **daimyo**, who were powerful feudal lords. The ideology was a form of neo-Confucianism that promoted a strict social hierarchy and an agrarian economy. The merchant class grew, and tension increased over the years.

End of the Mughal dynasty - Gaining the throne in 1628, **Shah Jahan** was the fifth ruler of the Mughal dynasty in present-day India. He greatly expanded the empire, but he was most remembered for building the **Taj Mahal**, a majestic and ornate mausoleum constructed in memory of **Mumtāz Mahal**, his favorite wife. The dynasty ultimately declined and ended in 1857.

SOUND THE ALARM - In 1241, Mongols approached Kraków in Poland. A trumpeter sounded the alarm from a high tower. He continued until a Mongol arrow struck him down. Today, every 24th of March, a trumpeter from the Kraków fire department sounds the alarm from a tower on the cathedral. The alarm ends suddenly at the exact time that the original trumpeter was struck by the Mongol arrow.

175

- Manchu Dynasty
- Battle of Plassey
- Colonization of Australia

Empires & Dynasties

Manchu dynasty - Also called the **Great Qing** or **Qing dynasty**, this was the last imperial dynasty of China, and it lasted from 1644 to 1912. The Manchus were from **Manchuria**, north of China. They secured control of China in 1644 when, due to an invasion of **Beijing**, the Ming dynasty sought their assistance, but the Manchus chose to overthrow the empire instead. Choosing to assimilate into Chinese culture, the Manchus allowed many officials of the Qing family to remain in place and kept many traditional Chinese institutions.

Key achievements of their reign include tripling the empire's size, a flourishing artistic community and an integrated national economy. However, the Manchus spelled the end of Chinese imperial rule. The end of their reign was plagued by foreign intervention, government corruption and the birth of a nationalist revolution led by the Han majority.

Battle of Plassey - In 1757, troops of the **East India Company**, a British joint-stock company, fought in this battle to establish British control of India. The troops were led by **Robert Clive**, who bribed **Mir Jafar** to join forces with the British. Thus, **Siraj ud-Daulah**, who was ruler of the Principality of Bengal, and his troops were defeated, establishing the British control of India.

Colonization of Australia - Though the first known landing in Australia was in 1616 by a Dutch explorer, it was not colonized until 1788. The first colony was a penal group established by Britain to relieve overcrowding in prisons. The **British First Fleet** consisted of 11 ships that brought convicts, seamen, marines, their families, government officials and stores to Australia. The Aboriginal Australians were the original inhabitants. They had arrived more than 45,000 years before the British. Europeans introduced diseases and conflict which greatly weakened the number of Aborigines.

. . . .

GUESS WHAT'S FOR DINNER? - When Europeans reached Australia, they didn't find available food. They soon learned what the Aborigines were eating, and this included bat and lizard meat. The natives considered kangaroo-tail soup a delicacy.

- **Opium Wars**
- **Taiping Rebellion**

Turmoil & Conflict

Opium Wars - There were two wars fought in a 20-year period over the distribution of opium, which Britain imported from India and sold in China in the late 18th and early 19th century. The opium addiction in China was alarming and had a dramatically negative effect on the Chinese economy and state of affairs. The Chinese ruler decided to regulate its trade. This decreased profits of British traders and angered them.

The **First Opium War** was fought in 1839 between China and Britain and resulted in the **Treaty of Nanking** in 1842. China was forced to pay a sizable indemnity, grant Britain five ports for trade and allow British citizens to be tried in British courts rather than in Chinese courts.

Conflict was reignited as the **Second Opium War**, or **Arrow War**, when several Chinese boarded a British ship called the **Arrow** and lowered its flag. The French joined in this war, allying with the British, and, at its close, China was forced to sign the **Treaty of Tianjin** in 1858. This treaty was repressive and was also referred to as the **Unequal Treaty**.

Taiping Rebellion - This rebellion was led by **Hong Xiuquan**, a man who believed himself to be the younger sibling of **Jesus Christ**, against the **Qing dynasty**. Xiuquan compiled a **Heavenly Army** composed of peasants, who were impressed by his expressions of equality and common property ownership. The uprising began in the Guangxi province in 1850 and was followed by 15 years of fighting. The rebels formed a kingdom in **Nanjing**, hoping to eradicate the Qing dynasty. War continued until 1860, when Europeans determined that Hong Xiuquan was a threat to their commercial interests and allied with the Qing dynasty, which they considered corrupt, to quell the rebellion.

. . . .

FOLLOW THE YELLOW BRICK ROAD - Opium, or the poppy from which it is derived, has been mentioned in many movies. In The Wizard of Oz, the wicked witch used poppies to put Dorothy and her friends to sleep to try to prevent their reaching the Emerald City.

- Sino-American Treaty of Wanghia
- Colonization of Vietnam
- Meiji Restoration
- Suez Canal
- Boxer Rebellion

Turmoil & Conflict

Sino-American Treaty of Wanghia - This was a diplomatic agreement in 1844 between China's Qing dynasty and the U.S. The treaty dictated that U.S. citizens could only be tried by U.S. consular officers. It fixed tariffs on trade in certain ports and allowed Americans to purchase land in such treaty ports. The U.S. also received a most-favored-nation status. The opium trade was declared illegal, and the U.S. agreed to turn offenders over to China.

French colonization of Vietnam - Seeking new markets and expansion of France's Asian landholdings, **Napoleon III** decided to invade Vietnam. The French colony established there was called **Cochinchina**. This acquisition set the stage for the **Vietnam War** in 1954, which lasted until 1975.

Meiji Restoration - In 1868, the **Tokugawa shogunate** and its last shogun, **Tokugawa Yoshinobu**, fell. Prompted by unrest due to foreign intervention and domestic problems, a restoration was led by a young samurai, and imperial rule was restored under Emperor **Meiji**. His reign, referred to as the **Meiji period**, was characterized by change, and it continued until 1912. During this time, Japan was modernized and Westernized.

Suez Canal - In 1869, this canal was opened, connecting the Mediterranean and Red Seas. It was the shortest trade route between the East and West.

Boxer Rebellion - This was a two-year rebellion against the rise of Western influence and privilege in China led by a group called the **Boxers**, members of **Righteous and Harmonious Fists**. Though against the Manchu dynasty, they were convinced to unite with it to expel foreign influence in 1898. The rebellion began in northern China, but swept across the country. More than 100,000 died; most were civilians; and many were Christians. International forces ended the rebellion and forced China to pay reparations. It failed to accomplish its goal, but succeeded in creating Chinese national pride.

. . . .

MISNOMER - Members of the Righteous and Harmonious Fists were dubbed Boxers *because they performed physical exercises that they believed would let them withstand bullets. The Western media popularized the name, Boxer Rebellion, but this was not an accurate term.*

- Philippine Independence
- Iranian Oil Discovery
- Russo-Japanese War
- Decline of the Manchu Dynasty

Turmoil & Conflict

Philippine independence - Three hundred years as a Spanish colony were ended by the **Philippine Revolution**. Catalysts for an independence movement included the corruption of the Spanish in Manila and the propaganda movement led by Dr. **José Rizal**, who was executed and became a martyr. Revolutionaries successfully gained independence from Spain but the Philippines became property of the U.S. in a treaty that ended the **Spanish-American War** in 1898. As a result of the treaty, the U.S. paid Spain 20 million dollars for the Philippines.

Iranian oil discovery - In 1901, Englishman **William D'Arcy** purchased a 60-year oil concession in Persia, which is present-day Iran. Large quantities of oil were discovered on this concession in 1908.

Russo-Japanese War - This conflict between Russia and Japan over Korea and Manchuria occurred because Russia had occupied the countries, and Japan drove them out. This stopped Russian expansion in the Far East, and Japan became the first Asian country to defeat a European one in modern history. The war ended in 1905 with the **Treaty of Portsmouth**, mediated by **Theodore Roosevelt**, U.S. president, who earned the **Nobel Peace Prize** for his efforts. Japan's claims to Korea were recognized. Russia evacuated Manchuria. The island of Sakhalin was divided, and no reparations were paid.

Decline of the Manchu dynasty - This dynasty, which had occupied and ruled China since the 1600s, was spiraling down. When the Empress Dowager **Cixi** died in 1908, the throne was passed to a three-year-old child, **Puyi**, and his incapable regency. This, combined with foreign intervention and rising nationalism, further weakened the Manchu and set the stage for conflict.

. . . .

ANIMAL FARM - The Theodore Roosevelts had more than 40 pets while they lived in the White House. These included birds, cats, dogs, a pony, guinea pigs, a badger, a one-legged rooster, a pig, a raccoon, rats and snakes. His daughter Alice would wear a snake named Emily Spinach around her neck to greet and shock visitors.

- Chinese Revolution
- Fall of the Ottoman Empire
- Republic of China
- Indian Independence

Turmoil & Conflict

Chinese Revolution of 1911 - Revolutionary **Sun Yat-sen** and the **Tongmenghui** formed a Revolutionary Alliance and conflict ignited in 1911 with an uprising in **Wuchang**. Though the Qing dynasty had begun the transition from authoritarian imperialism to a constitutional monarchy with **Yuan Shikai** as premier, the revolutionaries were unsatisfied. The seven-year-old emperor abdicated in 1912. The **Republic of China** was created, led by Yuan Shikai.

Fall of the Ottoman Empire - By the early 19th century, this empire had been considered the *sick man of Europe* and was on the decline. **Mustafa Kemal Atatürk** led the **Turkish National Movement**, which was their war for independence. The sultanate was overthrown and modern Turkey was created in 1923.

Republic of China - **Chiang Kai-shek** of the nationalist **Kuomintang** party assumed power in 1928. Between 1931 and 1946, China was threatened by Japanese occupation. Communist leader, **Mao Zedong**, began his rise near the end of this period. After years of civil war between Chinese Communists and Nationalists, Mao Zedong proclaimed the **People's Republic of China** in 1949.

Indian independence - India was occupied by foreigners for most of its history. When the British took control, they did not assimilate to Indian practices as former rulers had done, and turmoil built. British racism, their unwelcome introduction of Christianity and the inability of Indian people to participate in their own politics resulted in a buildup of nationalism in a once fragmented population. **Mohandas Gandhi** became known worldwide as **Mahatma Gandhi**. *Mahatma* is a title of respect that meant *great soul* in Sanskrit. Gandhi created a unified effort beginning in 1915. He used nonviolent tactics, including fasting and marches, to gain independence from Britain in 1947.

. . . .

SIXTH TIMES THE CHARM - Gandhi never received the Nobel Peace Prize, though he was nominated five times. Decades later, the Nobel Committee publicly declared its regret for the omission. He was to again be nominated in 1948, but was assassinated before the close of nominations. The group awarded no peace prize and explained that "there was no suitable <u>living</u> candidate." When the 14th Dalai Lama was awarded the Prize in 1989, the committee said that this was "in part a tribute to the memory of Mahatma Gandhi."

- Anglo-Iraqi War
- WWII Pacific Theatre
- Atomic Bombs
- Partition of India

Turmoil & Conflict

Anglo-Iraqi War - This 30-day conflict occurred between Britain and Iraq during WWII. A rebel Iraqi government supported the Axis powers. Iraq, which had gained independence from Britain in 1932, was invaded by the British who succeeded, despite their support from the **German Luftwaffe**. Thus, Britain occupied the country again, reinstalling Prince **'Abd al-Ilah**.

WWII Pacific theatre - The Japanese mounted a war against European nations and the U.S. in the Pacific by bombing **Pearl Harbor** in 1941. Two battles became the turning points for this theatre. The **Battle of the Coral Sea** was a Japanese tactical victory but a U.S. strategic victory. The **Battle of Midway** was a decisive U.S. victory. From here, Allies practiced island-hopping tactics to regain territory and stall the Japanese advance. By 1945, the U.S. made the fateful decision to drop two atomic bombs on Japan; Emperor **Hirohito**, who was also known as Emperor **Shōwa**, was forced to surrender.

Atomic bombs - The **Manhattan Project** had been researching atomic bombs since 1942 at **Los Alamos National Laboratory**. It was led by **J. Robert Oppenheimer** with support of Britain and Canada. After WWII had ended in 1945 in the European theatre, a B-29 bomber, dubbed the *Enola Gay* dropped the first atomic bomb on **Hiroshima** in **Japan**. Around 70,000 were immediately killed. The final death toll rose to 135,000. Two days later, a more powerful bomb was dropped on **Nagasaki**, killing 40,000 people instantly, with death tolls ultimately around 50,000. The U.S. was successful in quickly ending the war. Five days later, Japan surrendered.

Partition of India (1947) - The post-British partition of India was based on the premise that Muslims and Hindus were inherently different. India was divided into the **Dominion of Pakistan**, which was primarily Muslim, and the **Union of India**, which was mainly Hindu. The result was genocidal violence.

SECOND PLACE - A B-29 bomber, named Bock's Car, *was scheduled to drop an atomic bomb on Kokura in Japan. The crew was told to drop the bomb only after a positive visual identification of the arms factory, which was the target. Three times, the plane passed over Kokura with bomb bays open, but clouds obscured the factory. The plane then headed to its secondary target, Nagasaki, to drop the bomb.*

- Israel Independence
- People's Republic of China
- Taiwan

Independence & Conflict

Israel independence - The Jewish people considered Israel their homeland, even though they had been exiled from it for 1,900 years. In the 1880s, Jewish people begin to migrate to **Palestine** as anti-Semitism grew in Europe. Due to pressure from **Zionists**, who were those supporting the movement to reestablish a homeland for Jews, the British government issued the **Balfour Declaration** in 1917. It pledged to help make a Jewish homeland in Palestine.

WWI saw the defeat of the **Ottoman Empire**, which had controlled the area. The **League of Nations** put Palestine under British mandate. Arabs were unhappy with this decision and violence between them and Jewish immigrants ensued. During the extreme persecution that the European Jewish community had suffered during WWII, emigration increased. Escalating violence between Jewish immigrants and Palestinian Arabs resulted in a division of Palestine ordered by the UN in 1947. This dictate, along with the Zionist movement, resulted in Israel's gaining statehood.

People's Republic of China (PRC) - At the end of WWII, civil war raged in China, and Chiang Kai-shek and the Kuomintang party were ousted by Mao Zedong and the **Communist Party**, which Mao had formed in 1921. Mao established the PRC in 1949 and instituted many changes, including centralization of the state, collectivization of farming, and state owned industry. Mao disagreed with policies of Russian leader **Nikita Khrushchev**, and split from the Russian form of communism to create his own format termed **Maoism** in the 1950s.

Taiwan - After the PRC was formed on the mainland of China, remnants of the former Chinese government fled to the island of Taiwan in 1949. The island was formerly called **Formosa**. The leaders of the defunct **Republic of China** (**ROC**) reestablished its government on the island. Relations between the PRC and ROC have remained strained, as each claimed to be the one true China.

. . . .

GOING DOWN? - *In the U.S., the number 13 is considered unlucky, but in China, the number four is the one to avoid since it sounds similar to the word for death. Many Chinese buildings do not have a fourth floor.*

- Great Leap Forward   • First Indochina War
- Cambodian Independence   • Vietnam Divided

Independence & Conflict

Great Leap Forward - Between 1958 and 1961, Mao devised this project, which was intended to catapult China from an agrarian society to an industrialized and collectivized country. It failed and ultimately caused the **Great Chinese Famine**. It also led to a brutal purge known as the **Cultural Revolution**, which was intended to preserve the *true* communist ideology in China by purging capitalist and traditional elements. This failed and paralyzed China politically and affected it negatively on economic and social fronts.

Cambodian independence - After Japan's surrender ended WWII, they no longer occupied Cambodia. France reestablished its past claims in their stead. A guerrilla campaign was launched against this French protectorate and, by 1953, Cambodia became independent. The **Kingdom of Cambodia**, led by King **Norodom Sihanouk**, was established in its place. He ruled until 1955, when he became prime minister in Cambodia's first parliamentary election.

First Indochina War - Vietnam had been a French colony since the 1880s. Imperialist Japan had invaded **French Indochina** in 1940 during WWII. Seeking independence, communist **Ho Chi Minh** led the **Viet Minh** guerrilla organization and joined with Allied forces during the invasion. Though Ho declared Vietnam independent after the Axis defeat, France reoccupied the country. The fighting continued until the **Geneva Accords** in 1954 split Vietnam into a communist North Vietnam and non-communist South Vietnam at the 17th parallel.

Vietnam divided - The division of Vietnam was meant to be temporary, but the elections were never held. Prime Minister **Ngo Dinh Diem** took over the government in the south. Communists occupied the north. Both sides committed atrocities, and North Vietnam signed a military support treaty with the Soviet Union alarming those opposed to the spread of communism.

PERSIAN CATS - These cats are one of the oldest breeds of domesticated cats in the world. They originated in the high plateaus of Persia, which is now Iran. Their long, silky hair protected them from the cold temperatures. Italian traders took them to Europe, and they became exotic status symbols.

- Vietnam War
- Legislation Favoring Aborigines
- Beginning of OPEC
- Rise of Arab Socialism
- Beginning of the PLO

Independence & Conflict

Vietnam War - The **Vietcong** and their leader **Ho Chi Minh** in North Vietnam worked to overthrow South Vietnam's government in 1955. Fearing the spread of communism, the U.S. sent aid and eventually joined the war efforts in the early 1960s. Material costs and casualties of the war were high for the U.S. in this exceedingly unpopular war. U.S. forces withdrew, and, in 1975, North Vietnam was victorious, and the **Socialist Republic of Vietnam** was formed.

Legislation favoring Aborigines - During the 1960s, the Australian government began to reverse oppressive and discriminatory legislation concerning the Aboriginal people. **Aborigines** had occupied the continent for nearly 50,000 years before British explorer **James Cook** arrived in 1770. The Aboriginal society was a nomadic culture of primarily hunters and gatherers. Many tribes were displaced and decimated by disease brought by the British and by maltreatment and conflict with the colonial government and its citizens. These legislative changes were an attempt to acknowledge past mistakes.

Beginning of OPEC - The **Organization of Petroleum Exporting Countries** (OPEC) was founded in 1960. This cartel was organized to regulate oil policy and prices. The initial group included Venezuela, Iran, Iraq, Kuwait and Saudi Arabia. Many more have since joined.

Rise of Arab Socialism - This term was coined in 1960 by **Michel Aflaq**, a founding member of both **Ba'athism** and the **Ba'ath Party**. It described a blend of socialism and **pan-Arabism**, which was an ideology encouraging unification of the countries of North Africa and West Asia.

Beginning of the PLO - The **Palestinian Liberation Organization** (PLO) was established in 1964 to create a **State of Palestine** for displaced Palestinians. Their goal was to secure Palestinian self-determination and destroy Israel, often engaging in guerrilla military conflicts with Israelis, whose **State of Israel** was established in 1948.

USEFUL SLINKY - During the Vietnam War, the Slinky was used as an antenna for mobile radios. It was a popular cylindrical wire toy of the 1950s and 1960s.

- Division of Pakistan and Bangladesh
- Coup in Afghanistan
- Killing Fields
- Restructuring in China

Independence & Conflict

Division of Pakistan and Bangladesh - After the **Partition of India**, Pakistan was intended to be home to Indian Muslims. **East** and **West Pakistan** were separated by India, dividing the Pakistan Muslim community. West Pakistan dominated the country, resulting in unrest and the **Bangladesh Liberation War**. India allied with East Pakistan in the nine-month war, during which millions were displaced. **Bangladesh** became an independent state in 1971.

Coup in Afghanistan - In 1973, **Mohammed Zahir Shah** was deposed in a coup led by his cousin, **Mohammed Daoud Khan**. Daoud, who was connected to both the Soviet Union and **Afghan Communist Party**, turned the kingdom into a republic. However, the Afghan Communist Party deposed Daoud in a 1978 coup, and Soviet influence in Afghanistan increased.

Killing Fields - Between 1975 and 1979, more than two million people were executed or starved to death by the communist **Khmer Rouge** regime under **Pol Pot**. Pot had the reputation of being the 'Hitler of Cambodia.' This purge was an ethnic cleansing and an attempt to eliminate all who had been connected to the former government or to foreign governments. Cambodian journalist **Dith Pran** escaped from the area and exposed this atrocity, coining the term *killing fields*. The regime collapsed, and turmoil ensued in the area.

Economic restructuring in China - When Mao died in 1976, a power struggle began. **Deng Xiaoping** became leader in 1978. Under him, an **open-door policy** that encouraged a market economy set China on the road to prosperity. A **one-child policy** was instituted to control the population. It allowed married couples to have only one child, but there were many exceptions. During this period, students were encouraged to go abroad to study. Along with these social and cultural changes, Xiaoping's regime was also brutal. He reigned with an authoritarian iron fist.

- -

CHAMELEON QUARTERS - The Taj Mahal appears to be different colors at various times of the day. It has a pinkish hue in the morning, a chalky white color in the evening and a golden glow at night when lit by the moon. It is said that the changing color resembles the changing mood of females, in particular the queen, which it memorialized.

- Conflict in Afghanistan
- Islamic Revolution
- Iran-Iraq War
- Tamil Tigers

Independence & Conflict

Conflict in Afghanistan - Between 1979 and 1989, the Soviets supported the newly installed communist government fighting against anti-communist Muslim guerrillas. The U.S. sent aid to anti-communist troops, resulting in a stalemate. The Soviets were forced to withdraw by 1989 after a costly and unsuccessful war.

Islamic Revolution - Also known as the **Iranian Revolution**, this conflict was characterized by expressions of social discontent and rebellion. Rallying behind organizer Ayatollah **Ruhollah Khomeini**, **Madrasa** students and Iranian youths began to protest. A cycle of violence and martyrdom was initiated. The revolution resulted in the overthrow of the **Shah of Iran** and in the creation of a conservative, theocratic republic led by the Ayatollah. This prompted a nervous Iraq to invade Iran. The Ayatollah ruled from 1979 to 1989.

Iran-Iraq War - Also called the **First Persian Gulf War**, this invasion of Iran in 1980 was ordered by **Saddam Hussein**, Iraq's president and a member of the **Arab Socialist Ba'ath Party**. While his official reasoning was a waterway dispute, Hussein truly fought the threat of the **Islamic Revolution**. This war, coupled with the Revolution, exacted an horrific human cost on both, and it eventually drew the intervention of U.S. and Soviet forces. In 1988, Iran lost and both nations suffered economically.

Tamil Tigers - To establish **Eelam** as an independent Tamil state in north and east **Sri Lanka**, **Velupillai Prabhakaran** created a group that was named the **Liberation Tigers of Tamil Eelam** (**LTTE** or Tamil Tigers). Their campaign resulted in the **Sri Lankan Civil War** between 1983 and 2009. They employed bloody guerrilla and suicide tactics, were considered a terrorist organization and were still very active in the early 2000s. The civil war ended when they were defeated by Sri Lanka's military, and the group ceased to exist in 2009.

• •

BANNING OBESITY - In 2008, Japan passed legislation that made it illegal to be overweight. Companies conduct regular checkups and those who are deemed overweight must undergo counseling, etc. The standard required waistline measurements are 33.5 inches for men and 35.4 inches for women.

- Imperial House of Japan
- Tiananmen Square
- Gulf War

Independence & Conflict

Imperial House of Japan - Emperor **Shōwa**, better known as Hirohito or Japan's political head during WWII, died in 1989. Emperor **Akihito**, Hirohito's son, inherited the throne. This signaled the end of the **Shōwa era.** Japan had become a totalitarian, fascist empire, had suffered defeat in WWII and had become the **State of Japan** with a largely ceremonial imperial house. The **Heisei era** began. Its name was picked from Chinese history and philosophy books and meant *peace everywhere*.

Tiananmen Square - This was the site of student-led protests in Beijing in China that were forcibly suppressed by armed troops and tanks directed by **Deng Xiaoping**. Estimates of deaths were unclear, but ranged between a few hundred to a few thousand. Deng retired after this incident in 1989, and **Jiang Zemin** took control. The growth of China's economy continued through reform, and China has become a superpower.

Gulf War - This conflict was initiated in 1990, when forces of Iraqi dictator Saddam Hussein invaded **Kuwait**, attempting to gain the vast oil fields located there. Thirty-four nations, led by the U.S., participated in the two-phase conflict. The military build-up was code-named **Operation Desert Shield**.

The second phase of the conflict was code-named **Operation Desert Storm**. The **Iraqi Revolutionary Guard** was defeated in 42 days. The Iraqi troops set fire to 700 Kuwaiti oil wells during their retreat, a typical scorched-earth military tactic. Texas oil fire fighter **Red Adair** was called as a specialist to contain the fires. It took ten months to suppress the fires, and it caused enormous widespread destruction and serious pollution. The air and land offensives were successful, but tension remained in the region.

. . . .

JUST FISHY - Hirohito, better known as Emperor Shōwa in Japan, published several books on ichthyology. His son Aki-hito is a part-time ichthyologist and has published almost 40 peer-reviewed papers, as well as having a species of goby fish named after him.

- Commonwealth of Independent States
- *Mabo v. Queensland* Case
- Taliban in Afghanistan
- Shanghai Cooperation Organization (SCO)

Independence & Conflict

Commonwealth of Independent States (CIS) - The USSR fell in 1991, and 15 new nations emerged. Immediately, Russia, Belarus and Ukraine decreed that they were forming a commonwealth. Confronted with sudden independence, the remaining states were unprepared to govern themselves. The **Central Asian Republics**, including Kazakhstan, Kyrgyzstan, Tajikistan, Turkmenistan and Uzbekistan aligned themselves with Russia. By 2010, the CIS contained nine full member nations and two participating nations.

Mabo v. Queensland* Case** - In 1992, **Eddie Mabo** and several other **Torres Strait Islanders**, who had fought for their people's land rights in a 1982 court case, won this case. Australia's High Court decision recognized native title to land in Australia. British colonists considered much of the land to be ***terra nullius, that is *land belonging to no one*. They considered that the Aborigines had no civilized society and, hence, no property rights. This case overturned this doctrine in favor of a common law doctrine of Aboriginal title.

Rise of Taliban in Afghanistan - A civil war between the north and south areas of Afghanistan and government defections aided the **Taliban**, a Muslim fundamentalist organization, in getting a solid foothold in Afghani politics. Through a mixture of force, arbitration, and bribes, the Taliban took over the capital, **Kabul** and then Afghanistan itself in 1996. Their short reign was characterized by intolerance and the imposition of **Sharia** laws. U.S. forces toppled the government in 2001, in the wake of the 9/11 attacks. The U.S. felt that the Taliban regime protected the terrorist organization **al-Qaeda** and its leader, **Osama Bin Laden**, who perpetrated the 9/11 terrorism.

Shanghai Cooperation Organization (SCO) - This Eurasian organization, originally titled the **Shanghai Five**, consisted of China, Russia, and all of Central Asia's five nations except Turkmenistan. Several more nations were later given partial membership. The purpose of this organization was to discuss joint security, military, economic and cultural interests.

∙ ∙

FITTING END - *Acting on intelligence gathered by the CIA, a Navy SEAL unit killed Bin Laden and two other men at a compound in Abbottabad, Pakistan. DNA tests confirmed Bin Laden's identity, and he was buried at sea.*

- Second Gulf War
- Chinese Space Program
- SARS Outbreak
- Indian Ocean Earthquake
- Arab Spring

New Millennium

Second Gulf War - In the wake of 9/11 and with the belief that Iraq possessed biological weaponry and supported terrorist organizations, President **George W. Bush** delivered an ultimatum to Saddam Hussein, the president of **Iraq**. When Hussein refused to step down, a coalition of primarily U.S. and British troops successfully invaded Iraq in 2003, toppling Hussein's authoritarian regime with the **Fall of Baghdad**, and the country began to destabilize.

Hussein escaped, but was captured and executed. His brutal dictatorship was marked by more than a million deaths through war and ethnic and political cleansing. U.S. forces did not withdraw until 2011. Almost 4,500 Americans died in this conflict. Iraqis suffered between 100,000 and 500,000 casualties.

Chinese space program - The **China National Space Administration (CNSA)** successfully placed **Yang Liwei** in orbit in 2003. Thus, he became China's first astronaut, and China became the third country to achieve space travel.

SARS outbreak - In 2003, an outbreak of **severe acute respiratory syndrome** (SARS) originated in China and spread across international borders. It resulted in panic and the deaths of more than 800 people before the virus was contained.

Indian Ocean earthquake - This was the third-largest earthquake in recorded history with a magnitude of 9.2. It hit **Indonesia** and **Sri Lanka** in 2004 and caused the planet to vibrate. The resulting **tsunami** killed more than 280,000.

Arab Spring - In 2010, a frustrated Tunisian vegetable salesman chose to set himself on fire in protest. He became a martyr, unleashing civilian unrest and, ultimately, the deposition of **Zine El Abidine Ben Ali**, president of Tunisia. This event sparked a series of rebellions in North Africa and the Middle East. Other countries involved in this pro-democracy, anti-oppressive government movement included Egypt, Yemen, Syria and Libya.

· ·

MAKING WAVES - *Greek historian Thucydides in his* History of the Peloponnesian War *was the first to associate tsunamis with underwater earthquakes. This was in the 1st century BCE. The word* tsunami *means* harbor wave *in Japanese.*

2010 - Present

- Indonesian Volcanic Eruption
- Earthquake in Japan
- Malaysia Airlines

New Millennium

Indonesian volcanic eruption - In 2010, an active volcano, **Mount Merapi**, erupted several times. These eruptions released ash plumes, lahars, pyroclastic flows and toxic sulfur dioxide gas. More than 350 people were killed.

Earthquake in Japan - In 2011, the **Tōhoku** earthquake struck Japan's main island, **Honshu**. Its coastline was then battered by a resulting tsunami that damaged much of coastal Japan. This hit 9.0 on the Richter scale and was the fourth-largest earthquake in recorded history; there were 15,885 reported fatalities. The Tōhoku region was hit particularly hard. The tsunami resulted in damage to the **Fukushima I Nuclear Power Plant**. This was the largest nuclear disaster since **Chernobyl** and resulted in a series of explosions and a desperate effort to cool the reactors.

Malaysia Airline problems - Flight 370 from Kuala Lumpur to Beijing disappeared mysteriously over the South China Sea in March 2014. The flight vanished from radar screens about one hour after take-off. International search efforts found no evidence of the plane. Searches have continued in a larger and larger area and now has expanded to a comprehensive search of the seafloor, which will take nearly another year.

Four months later, Flight 17 from Amsterdam to Kuala Lumpur was thought to have been shot down in 2014 by Ukrainian separatists, killing all 283 passengers and 15 crew members. Early reports indicated Russian involvement, though the investigation was incomplete as of 2015. Russia recently overran Crimea, and Ukrainians have feared this kind of invasion.

. . . .

MAKE ME MARIO - The Nintendo company started as a playing card maker in 1898. In the 1960s, the owners decided to diversify the business and tried several directions. The company moved into the Japanese toy industry in 1966, started producing video games in 1977 and has become a household name.

EASTERN HEMISPHERE

Part 5
Africa

- Earliest People
- African Migrations
- Central Africa

Prehistoric Period

Earliest people - Africa has been home to some of the oldest archeological sites in the world. Scientists have extracted volumes of information from such sites about the development of human beings and their progression out of Africa.

A fossil of the ***Australopithecus*** species found in a cave in South Africa and fossil fragments from Ethiopia, which have been called **Lucy**, were estimated to be 3½ million years old. An example of the human species ***Homo habilis*** was found in **Olduvai Gorge** in Tanzania by **Dr. Louis S. B. Leakey** and his wife **Mary**, who were both British anthropologists. This species has been found along with primitive stone tools and lived about two million years ago.

Homo erectus probably lived between two million and 100,000 years ago and was among the first group of early humans to leave Africa, as indicated by the **Java Man** and **Peking Man** fossils which have been found in present-day Indonesia and China respectively. ***Homo sapiens*** evolved in Africa about 200,000 years ago. There was some overlap with the *Homo erectus* group, but *Homo sapiens* eventually prevailed. The *Homo sapiens* species also left Africa.

African migrations - Roughly 160,000 years ago, four groups of people began to spread from east-central Africa across the continent in different directions. They reached the **Ivory Coast**, the **Cape of Good Hope**, the **Congo** and the **Horn of Africa**.

Central Africa - The migration from Central Africa scattered into all regions of Africa. The Central Africa region included what is currently Chad, Congo, and others. Of this group of countries, only Chad was partly covered by the **Sahara Desert**, which is also called the **Great Sahara**. This desert covered over ten percent of the entire continent. It encompassed about half of its current area in ancient times. Today it is 3½ million square miles, and it has continued to expand.

. . . .

HOMO HABILIS - *This name literally means* skillful man. *It was used because of the evidence of small tools, which included hand axes and other stone and bone tools made for various uses. Of course, it has been recently observed that man is NOT the only animal which makes or uses tools, for some of the great apes do, as well.*

- **Northern Africa**
- **Western Africa**
- **Eastern Africa**

Prehistoric Period

Northern Africa - Egypt was in this region, which included the countries on the **Mediterranean Sea** and **Atlantic Ocean** as well as much of the huge Sahara desert. Present-day countries in this region are Morocco, Algeria, Tunisia, Libya and Sudan.

Western Africa - The Ivory Coast was in this region, along with such countries as Liberia, Sierra Leone, Mali, Senegal, Nigeria, Côte d'Ivoire and more. Côte d'Ivoire meant *Ivory Coast* in French. It was so named when the ivory trade flourished through settlements along this western coastal area of Africa. The Sahara also covered more than half of the countries along the northern part of this region.

Eastern Africa - This area included the Horn of Africa, which was seen as a jutting rhino horn on the eastern edge of the continent. The area included present-day Ethiopia, Somalia, Kenya, Tanzania, Mozambique, Zimbabwe and the island of Madagascar. The **Serengeti**, which in the Maasai language means *endless plains,* was a geographic region of this area that covered much of present-day Tanzania and Kenya. It was similar to the Great Plains in the central U.S. and has been the location of the largest animal migrations in the world. It has remained to the present time.

Between 135,000 BCE and 115,000 BCE, the group near the Horn of Africa traveled north to **Egypt** and east to the **Levant** area, which was along the Eastern Mediterranean and included present-day Cyprus, Israel, Jordan, Lebanon, Palestine, Syria, and part of Turkey. There were also multiple waves of migration that crossed the mouth of the Red Sea and moved to the south coast of the **Arabian Peninsula**. Recent evidence has suggested that the earliest of these was around 100,000 years ago. These were thought to be ancestors of all non-African people.

· ·

DIAMOND IN THE ROUGH - The archeologist team that named Lucy, one of the very early skeletons, picked the name after a celebration of their find during which they listened to the then popular song, "Lucy in the Sky with Diamonds" recorded by the Beatles.

- Southern Africa
- Khoisan People

- Egypt United

Prehistoric Period

Southern Africa - The Cape of Good Hope is on the southern tip of this region. Countries included are South Africa, Swaziland, Botswana and Namibia.

Khoisan people - This ancient people dated to the early **Stone Age** or perhaps before that. The earliest culture was the **Sangoan** group in Southern Africa. The present-day **San** and **Khoikhoi** resembled the **Sangoan** people. They have inhabited the Northern Cape province of South Africa for hundreds of years.

It was believed that the Sangoan were related to the Khoisan people who lived in the **Kalahari Desert** of southern Africa in Botswana, Namibia and part of South Africa. The Khoisan later domesticated cattle and sheep, which skill they learned from the **Bantu**.

The **San** were hunter-gatherers. The **Khoikhoi** were a pastoral society, who migrated into this area later. Though almost entirely destroyed by later settlers, these people were famous for their rock art. They used a distinct, click-based language, sounds from which have been assimilated into other African languages. The Khoikhoi were called **Hottentots** by the early Dutch settlers, and the **San** were called **Bushmen**. Both of these have become derogatory terms.

Egypt united - Egypt was originally separated into two kingdoms along the **Nile River**. This river was the lifeblood of Egypt, and early Egyptian settlements clustered around it. The Nile has held the distinction of being the longest river in the world. The northern **Upper Kingdom** and the southern **Lower Kingdom** were united under **Menes** about 3100 BCE, which was the beginning of the **Early Dynastic Period** during the **Bronze Age**. He made the city of **Memphis** in Egypt his capital. With the region united, opportunity arose for a single culture to develop. Advances from the distant **Sumer** civilization were adopted and refined for the Nile region.

CAT WORSHIP - *The ancient Egyptians worshiped felines and imposed punishments on those who injured or killed them. Why? One of their goddesses, Bastet, was depicted as half feline and half woman.*

- Three Kingdoms of Egypt
- Old Kingdom
- Middle Kingdom
- New Kingdom

Early Civilizations

Three kingdoms of Egypt - These periods began during the **Bronze Age** and survived for more than a thousand years. Egyptian culture was divided into three periods. Actual dates of these periods were not recorded and often differ from source to source. These periods were interrupted by brief episodes of disunity and strife often triggered by drought, famine or civil war.

Old Kingdom - This first of the three kingdoms lasted between around 2650 BCE to around 2150 BCE. This kingdom saw the emergence of a complex society along with the building of monuments and great intellectual and artistic achievements. **Khufu**, an Egyptian pharaoh who was also known as **Cheops**, built the **Great Pyramid** at **Giza** during this period. The nearby **Great Sphinx** was probably built at the same time.

Middle Kingdom - This period spread from around 2050 BCE to around 1700 BCE. This period saw art and jewelry design reach new heights. The pyramid at **Hawara** was called **Labyrinth** by **Herodotus**. It was built during this period, and it contained 3,000 rooms. The Middle Kingdom fell to **Hyksos** invaders, who used a new style of warfare, which included bronze weapons and horse-drawn chariots that were superior to the Egyptian weapons.

New Kingdom - This last kingdom dated from around 1550 BCE to around 1050 BCE. The period started after the Hyksos were routed. By the time Egypt had entered the **Iron Age**, **Amenhotep**, who changed his name to **Akenhaton**, was ruler. He believed in only one god, the sun god **Aton**. His wife was the famed **Nefertiti**. Together, they changed the religion from a multi-god system to **monotheism**. The most famous pharaoh of this period was **Tutankhamun**, also called **King Tut** or the boy king. He was famous mainly because his tomb was found intact with a tremendous wealth of artifacts in 1922.

. . . .

ANCIENT NOSE JOB - Early drawings of the Sphinx, which is half lion and half human, indicate that the damage to the nose occurred in the 14th or 15th century. It has been determined that vandals hammered rods into the face to pry off the nose, but no one knows why.

- **Karnac & Luxor**
- **Kingdom of Kush**
- **Bantu People**

Early Civilizations

Karnac and Luxor - The last great pharaoh was **Ramses II**, who ruled for 67 years. He added to the great building complexes at **Karnak** and **Luxor**. His death in 1213 BCE marked the beginning of Egypt's decline.

Kingdom of Kush - People of this area were **Kushites**, or **Nubians**. They lived in what was called **Kush**, or **Nubia**, in present-day Sudan. Some legends described the Kush as one of the oldest races on earth. The **Bible** made reference to this group, and some have associated the region with **Eden**.

This culture predated that of the Egyptians, though it became an Egyptian colony around 1500 BCE. When the New Kingdom of Egypt collapsed, the people of Kush united under a local ruler, **Alara**, their founder. For a short period, the Kush ruled Egypt when King **Piye** established the 25th Egyptian dynasty, which was also known as the **Nubian Dynasty** or as the **Black Pharaohs**. This dynasty lasted until 653 BCE.

The Kush moved their capital to **Meroë** when forced out of Egypt. *Pharaoh* remained the title of their leaders, but a new script in the **Meroitic language** replaced **Egyptian hieroglyphics**. The region became a successful commercial center, with extensive ironworking and gold mining. Women often ruled. The decline began around 100 CE, and they disappeared around the 4th century.

Bantu people - Around 1000 BCE to 500 BCE, a migration of people from what is now Nigeria and Cameroon brought people into the southeastern part of Africa. These people spoke the **Bantu language**, and they displaced many of the **Khoisan** people. They included groups, such as the **Zulu** of South Africa and **Kikuyu** of **Kenya**. All spoke a Bantu language. The Zulus spoke **Swahili**, which has survived to become one of the official languages of Tanzania, Kenya and Uganda.

. . . .

VITAL ORGANS - Before burial, ancient Egyptians used a special tool to scoop out brain matter from the skull through the nasal openings. They didn't value this organ. Other organs were saved in jars. The heart was thought to be the center of intelligence and feeling. The body was packed with resins and spices and covered with cloth strips.

c. 1000 BCE - c. 300 BCE

- Phoenicians & Carthage
- Death of Alexander
- Ptolemaic Dynasty
- Alexandria

Early Empires

Phoenicians and Carthage - The Phoenicians were traders and merchants who colonized the **Mediterranean** region around 1000 BCE. Located in what is now Tunisia, the ancient city of Carthage was established in 814 BCE by Queen **Elissa**, a Phoenician who was better known as **Dido**. Over the years, it developed into a significant trade center and became one of the most powerful pre-Roman, Mediterranean cities. The Phoenicians' most famous contribution was development of a script with 22 letters that was later adopted by the Greeks.

Death of Alexander the Great - In 323 BCE, the great leader died. The Byzantine Empire went through a period of conflict. The empire was weakened and lost Egypt, Syria and Palestine.

Ptolemaic dynasty - A former general in the army of **Alexander the Great**, **Ptolemy I Soter**, began this dynasty in 305 BCE after Alexander's death. He was from **Macedonia**, a region of Northern Greece that had been part of Alexander's empire. He declared himself Pharaoh of Egypt and proceeded to maintain a **Hellenist**, or Greek, type of empire in northern Africa. His empire, or the **Ptolemaic Kingdom**, stretched from Syria in the east, to what is now Libya in the west. It ranged southward to **Nubia**, in present-day southern Egypt and Sudan.

Members of this dynasty adopted many Egyptian customs, including marrying their siblings. They built numerous monuments and temples to the Egyptian gods. However, they retained the Greek language and laws and insisted on a Greek education for their children. Intermarriage of Greek citizens with local Egyptians produced a large class of educated people. This dynasty continued for 275 years with **Cleopatra VII Philopator** being the last dynastic ruler.

. . . .

HANNIBAL'S MOUNTS - War elephants were trained and guided by humans for combat. They were primarily used to charge the enemy, break their ranks and instill terror. Military units with elephant-mounted troops are called elephantry.

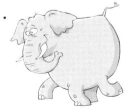

- Alexandria
- Three Punic Wars
- First Punic War
- Second Punic War

Early Empires

Alexandria - This city was built by Alexander the Great in 332 BCE as the capital of Egypt. It remained the capital after his death under the Ptolemaic dynasty until the city surrendered to Arab forces in 642 CE. It was one of the Mediterranean's greatest cities, a hub of science and learning. The great lighthouse built on the island of **Pharos** was considered one of the **Seven Wonders of the World** and reportedly over 350 feet tall. It stood until the 14th century. The **Library of Alexandria** was the most famous of the time and was part of a research institute in Alexandria. It was destroyed around 48 BCE.

Three Punic Wars - These wars were fought between **Rome** and **Carthage** over trading rights in the Mediterranean Sea. Rome controlled most of present-day Italy, and Carthage controlled the coastal region of northern Africa, southern Spain and many of the islands in the Mediterranean.

First Punic War - This initial war lasted from 264 BCE to 241 BCE and was triggered over control of **Sicily**. The Romans won the war, in spite of their inferior navy. They developed tactics and strategies new to naval warfare. The **Ebro Treaty** set the boundary between Rome and Carthage, and this awarded Rome much of the Carthaginian territory.

Second Punic War - This segment began in 218 BCE. **Hannibal**, a Carthaginian leader, made his famous march across the Alps with a number of elephants. He won victory after victory, until reaching central Italy where he hit a stalemate. As in the first war, the government of Carthage refused to send reinforcements or extra money to hire mercenaries. Rome used their navy and attacked Carthage directly. With the capital at risk, Hannibal was forced to surrender in 201 BCE.

. . . .

SERIOUS STUDY - Dedicated to the Muses, which are the nine goddesses of the arts, the Library of Alexandria was a major center of scholarship from its construction in the 3rd century BCE until it was burned in 30 BCE. King Ptolemy II Philadelphus was said to have set 500,000 scrolls as an objective for the library. Some accounts credit Mark Antony as giving Cleopatra more than 200,000 scrolls as a wedding gift, but this is conjecture.

- Third Punic War
- End of the Ptolemies

Early Empires

Third Punic War - This last of the three wars was short. It began in 149 BCE and ended three years later. Carthage, after paying their war debt to Rome after the second war, attacked **Numidia**. Rome declared Carthage a danger to regional peace and began a three-year siege. Carthage surrendered, and Rome burned everything to the ground. During this period, Rome continued to develop its navy and build ships to become the undisputed top naval power of the Mediterranean.

End of the Ptolemies - The last ruler of the dynasty was **Cleopatra VII Philopator**, whose reign began in 51 BCE when she was 18 years old. She ruled briefly with her younger brother until his death in battle. She succeeded in keeping other siblings off the throne, including her surviving brother, although he was nominally considered a co-ruler.

Cleopatra was most famous for her affairs with Rome's leading men, **Julius Caesar** and **Mark Antony**. She was seldom given credit for her strategies to keep Egypt independent and out of Roman hands. Cleopatra was multi-lingual and seldom needed an interpreter.

During Rome's civil war between **Octavian** and Antony, Cleopatra remained with Antony, which was a strategic mistake. Octavian defeated Antony at the **Battle of Actium** in 31 BCE. When Octavian marched into Alexandria a year later, the terms he offered Cleopatra were unacceptable to her, and she ultimately committed suicide. Egypt remained part of the Eastern Roman or Byzantine Empire until the Arabs conquered it by 645 CE.

NOT A LOCAL - *Cleopatra's heritage was not Egyptian, but Greek and Macedonian. She was a descendent of one of Alexander the Great's lieutenants. Though the myth of her beauty has been disputed, it is apparent that she was intelligent and a skillful politician. The 1963 movie* Cleopatra *starred Elizabeth Taylor and Richard Burton. The film was a box office flop initially, but it was well known for its monstrous budget for that time.*

- **Kingdom of Aksum**
- **Edict of Milan**
- **Fall of Roman Empire**

Early Empires

Kingdom of Aksum in Ethiopia - This kingdom thrived between the 1st and 8th century in present-day **Ethiopia**. The Aksum, or Axum, Empire was a powerful state located between the **Eastern Roman Empire** and **Persian Empire** below southern Egypt. The kingdom controlled the **Red Sea** and **Gulf of Aden**. They had a monopoly on **ivory trade** with **Sudan**.

Christianity arrived in the 4th century. **Makeda**, the **Queen of Sheba**, reportedly began a journey to visit **King Solomon** in Jerusalem. They produced a son, **Menelik I**, who began the **Solomonic dynasty** in the Aksum Kingdom.

Edict of Milan - Portions of Africa became a part of the Roman Empire when Rome was victorious over Carthage. In the 1st and early 2nd century, Christianity arrived in northern Africa. From there, its reach expanded east to Ethiopia and west to Alexandria. However, Christians were often persecuted within the Roman Empire, and events like the **Diocletian Persecution** were common until the **Edict of Milan** in 313 CE established a principle of religious tolerance toward Christians within the Roman Empire.

Fall of the Roman Empire - In 476 CE, **Odoacer** deposed the emperor of the Western Roman Empire, and this ended its existence. He became king of Italy. The **Eastern Roman Empire** survived as the **Byzantine Empire**, but it was never as large and continued shrinking until the 13th century.

The ethnic origin of Odoacer was never determined. He was thought to be a German soldier and probably of the **Sciri** tribe. He joined the Roman army and rose to power. The Roman general **Orestes** overthrew the Western emperor, **Julius Nepos**. Odoacer then overthrew Orestes. However, recent studies have suggested the Odoacer might have been a **Hun**. He was later ousted and killed by **Theodoric**, a Goth who had been appointed king of Italy by **Zeno**, the emperor of the **Eastern Roman Empire**, or **Byzantine Empire**.

. . . .

HIDDEN AWAY - *Tradition credited Menelik I with taking the Ark of the Covenant chest, which reputedly contained the Ten Commandments on stone tablets, from Jerusalem to Ethiopia to the church of St. Mary of Zion, where it is believed to have remained to the present time.*

- Arab Invasion of Egypt
- African Slave Trade
- Decline of Aksum Kingdom

Early Empires

Arab invasion of Egypt - The Arabs, who were **Muslims**, invaded Egypt, which was part of the **Byzantine Empire** in 639 CE. The Byzantine fleet supported the Egyptians, but it was defeated at Alexandria in 645 CE. The native Egyptians, **Copts**, did not support the Byzantines, but they did not actively support the **Muslim** armies either.

A treaty between Copts and the Arabs provided for the security of the Copts, freedom from religious persecution and the preservation of their churches and farms in return for a tax payment. The Arabs built **Al-Fusṭāṭ**, rather than use Alexandria as the capital for their governmental operations. Arab cultural influences came to Egypt slowly. Greek remained the official language until the 8ᵗʰ century, but **Coptic** was still widely spoken.

African slave trade - Slavery played an integral part in African history. African natives had slaves throughout history, and Arabs enslaved Africans as early as 700 CE. Beginning in the 1400s, Europeans kidnapped Africans from the western, central and southeastern regions of the continent to fill the demand of the burgeoning Atlantic slave trade. Millions of Africans were displaced and subjected to abject cruelty. African history was altered dramatically by the impact of the slave trade, which has continued to present times, but has never again been legalized.

Decline of the Aksum Kingdom - As the **Islamic Empire** gained control of the Red Sea and the northern Nile area, this empire declined. The Solomonic dynasty led the Aksum Kingdom and then Ethiopia until 1974 when **Emperor Haile Selassie I**, the last ruler of the **House of Solomon**, was deposed.

. . . .

LOST IN TRANSLATION - In 1799, a stone slab was discovered near Rosetta, Egypt, by a group of Napoleon's soldiers who were digging a fort. Its inscriptions were a decree written in three scripts, including Egyptian hieroglyphics and Greek. Due to this discovery, which was called the Rosetta Stone, *scholars were able to translate Egyptian hieroglyphs for the first time, and much of the language was decoded.*

- Ghana Kingdom
- Madagascar
- Morocco

Early Empires

Ghana Kingdom - This was an ancient kingdom of western Africa, not to be confused with present-day **Ghana**. It occupied part of what became **Mali** and **Mauritania**. It flourished around 700 CE, when the **Soninke** people united.

This region was a crossroads of trade and rich in gold, which was traded for a more valuable commodity of the time, salt. The town of **Timbuktu** became a trading center. The Soninke people developed an army with superior weapons. The kingdom expanded, but finally fell to Muslim invaders in the 11th century.

Madagascar - This island was located off the southeastern coast of Africa. It was settled around 700 CE and has only been inhabited for about 1,300 years. Despite its proximity to Africa, its peoples, the **Malagasy**, are primarily of Polynesian descent.

The island's flora and fauna also differed from that of mainland Africa, and it was renowned for unique evolvements of primitive species, including well over 30 species of lemur. Madagascar was invaded in 1894 and colonized by the French in 1896. Though it gained independence in 1960, it has continued to have close ties with countries in western Africa that speak French.

Morocco - The **Idrisid** family, which rose to power in 788 CE, founded the **Kingdom of Morocco**. This family traced their ancestry back to the Prophet **Muhammad**. The Idrisids welcomed Arab settlers, and this transformed much of the **Maghreb** region. The cultural shift worked both ways, and many **Berber** influences were seen. Though the nation experienced a succession of dynasties, they were never overrun by outside nations. Portugal was able to occupy a few areas, including **Cueta**, in 1415.

· ·

BLUE PEOPLE - The Taureg are a Berber people who are nomadic pastoralists in the Sahara of northern Africa. The indigo dye of their traditional robes stains their skin, which is the source of their nickname, the Blue People. *In Taureg society, men, not women, are traditionally veiled, and this is thought to ward off evil spirits.*

1000 - 1350

- Mali Empire
- Great Zimbabwe
- Travels of Ibn Battuta

Early Empires

Mali Empire - Also called the **Malinke Kingdom**, this arose from the remnants of the **Ghana Kingdom** about 1235 under the leadership of **Sundjata**. The kingdom expanded from central Africa westward to the coast, which allowed them to trade more easily with Europeans. They used the **Niger River**, in addition to camels and horses, to transport goods, and they farmed in the river valley. With this secure food source, stability in the kingdom was increased. The Niger also gave them access to the **Gulf of Guinea** for trade.

Mali, like Ghana, heavily taxed goods entering and leaving the region. The Mali Empire was famous for its wealth and gold. Their ruler, **Mansa Musa,** made a pilgrimage to **Mecca** along with thousands of people, free and enslaved. They carried many goods, such as gold bars, silk fabric, exotic spices and animals. He returned from Mecca with scholars who settled in Timbuktu, which became a center for learning. He built the **Great Mosque**. Revolts occurred in the Mali Empire, which began to crumble after Musa's death.

Great Zimbabwe - This capital city of the **Kingdom of Zimbabwe** was built by ancestors of the **Shona** people who thrived in this area between the 11th and 15th centuries. Stone buildings and houses of this city covered more than 1000 acres. The city walls were 15-feet high and built without mortar. On top of monoliths along the wall were birds carved of soapstone. The **Zimbabwe Bird**, which was later depicted on the Zimbabwe flag, originated from these carvings. Evidence suggested distant trading from this city, as with China.

Travels of Ibn Battuta - Battuta's travels began in 1325 from Tangier as a **Hajj**, which was a pilgrimage to **Mecca** that all Muslims were required to make. After three years in Mecca, he continued traveling the world. During his journey, he trekked roughly 75,000 miles and visited the lands of 44 modern-day countries. He dictated an account of his travels to a scholar before his death, producing one of the world's most famous travel books, *Rihla*, or *Travels*. This book has been a significant source of history about the period.

. . . .

WAMPUM? - *The* ensuba *is a heavy iron potato masher that once was used as an ancient form of currency in Bafia in Cameroon. In Mali, snakes made of copper and other metals served as money.*

1350 - 1700

- Songhai Empire
- Cape of Good Hope
- Slave Traffic
- Battle of Three Kings
- Kingdom of Ashanti

Early Empires

Songhai Empire - This short-lived empire developed east of the Mali Empire. In the 1400s, **Sonni Ali** was the first king of this empire. He conquered much of the Mali Empire, and moved the capital to **Gao**. The empire fell with the rise of **Morocco** and arrival of Portuguese, who altered the control of trade.

Cape of Good Hope reached - Seeking a trade route to India, Portuguese navigator **Bartolomeu Dias** sailed around southern Africa and landed at the Cape of Good Hope in 1488. This discovery revolutionized travel and allowed for the establishment of trade between Europe and Asia.

Slave traffic - In 1510, King **Ferdinand** of Spain approved a systematic transfer of slaves from Africa to work the gold mines in **Hispaniola** in the **Caribbean**. Slave trade had long existed between conquerors and the vanquished, but this marked the first time a continent was seen as a steady source of slaves. The result was the transportation of millions of Africans across the seas until the 19th century. In 1530, **Juan de la Barrera** of Spain began taking slaves directly from Africa to the New World without stopping in Europe.

Battle of Three Kings - This battle in 1578 enhanced Morocco's stature among European nations. During the battle, the former king of Morocco united with **Sebastian**, the king of Portugal, to overthrow ʻ**Abd al-Malik**, the current king of Morocco. All three kings died, but al-Malik's brother survived and claimed the remains of the Portuguese army as a prize. By the 17th century, the ʻ**Alawite dynasty** came into power and has remained in power since.

Kingdom of Ashanti - Located in modern-day **Ghana**, this kingdom was forged and first ruled by King **Osei Tutu** in the late 17th century. The Ashanti conquered surrounding areas and created an empire. They exchanged gold and war slaves for guns and other goods from Europeans. During the 1800s, they fought the British, who tried to abolish slave trade and control the area. A century later, the region fell to the British and was colonized. The Ashanti have remained one of the largest ethnic groups in Ghana.

. . . .

ON THE GO - *"Traveling--it leaves you speechless, then turns you into a storyteller."* ~ *Ibn Battuta*

- South African Nguni
- Bantu Languages
- Sierra Leone

Colonial Period

South African Nguni people - The Nguni are a group of people that speak Bantu and dwell in southern Africa. The **Zulu, Swazi** and **Ndebele** make up the northern Nguni, while the **Xhosa**, Thembu, Bomvana, Mpondo, and Mpondomise constitute the southern Nguni. The Zulu are South Africa's largest ethnic group and tied to the Swazi and Xhosa.

In the early 1800s, **Shaka** waged war to become king and, once head of the Zulu, united many tribes through war and formed an empire. Slaughter and migrations resulted from his campaigns but the empire survived after his assassination. In 1879, conflicts with European settlers culminated in the **Anglo-Zulu War**. By 1883, the Zulu Kingdom was dismantled and much of it was divided between the British and Dutch.

Bantu languages - There were over 250 dialects of this ancient language of Africa. It was developed primarily in Central, Southeast and Southern Africa by native speakers. The **Swahili** language was one of the dialects with the largest number of speakers. In this dialect, many Arabic words were incorporated due to this culture's trading with the Middle Eastern countries.

Sierra Leone - Archeological evidence indicated that Sierra Leone has been inhabited for over 2,500 years. Its dense tropical rainforest and swampy environment made it impenetrable and subject to tsetse flies which carried disease that was fatal to cattle and horses. It became a slave-trading center for Europeans to obtain slaves brought from the interior by African traders.

After the Revolutionary War, the British organized a settlement in Sierra Leone called the **Province of Freedom** to resettle many of the African Americans freed by the British during the war. Many migrated here from Nova Scotia as well, developing **Freetown** in the area around 1800.

IN HIS FOOTSTEPS - *"When you follow in the path of your father, you learn to walk like him."* ~ *Ashanti Proverb*

- Liberia
- Slave Trade Banned
- Invasion of Algeria
- Voortrekkers
- Discovery of Victoria Falls

Colonial Period

Liberia - Next to Sierra Leone, Liberia became a country distinct from other African countries. It was the sole African country to avoid European imperialism. In the late 1700s and early 1800s, Britain and the U.S. created colonies of freed African-Americans and Caribbean slaves in this region. Liberia is Africa's oldest republic.

Slave trade banned - The Britain Empire banned the slave trade in 1807. The U.S., which had imported slaves from Africa since 1619, followed and abolished the slave trade via a Congressional vote in 1808. This did not end slavery in the southern U.S. Both the U.S. and British Empire continued to allow descendants of imported slaves to remain as chattels. Illegal trafficking of slaves continued.

Invasion of Algeria - In 1830 during the **Bourbon Restoration**, France used a previous political slight as an excuse to invade and occupy **Algiers**. By 1847, resistance was defeated, and Algeria became a French colony.

Voortrekkers - The Voortrekkers were **Boers**. These descendants of Dutch settlers that migrated from Britain's **Cape Colony** in South Africa to the southern African interior in 1834. They founded the colony of **Natal** and two independent states, the **Orange Free State** and the **South African Republic** (or **Transvaal**). This is often called the *Great Trek*, thus the name Voortrekkers.

Discovery of Victoria Falls - In 1855, Scottish missionary and explorer **David Livingstone** became the first European to lay eyes on **Victoria Falls**. He named it after Queen **Victoria**. Its common name was **Mosi-oa-Tunya**, which meant *smoke that thunders*. Both names have been in continual use since.

· ·

HIP, HIP, HIPPO - The most dangerous animal in Africa is not the lion or crocodile; it is the hippopotamus. The hippo is very territorial and protective of its young, and its canine teeth can be up to 20 inches long.

- Source of the Nile River
- Building the Suez Canal
- Scramble for Africa

Colonial Period

Source of the Nile River - Many explorers searched for the source of the Nile River. The first to reach and name **Lake Victoria** was British explorer **John Hannin Speke** in 1858. He claimed it to be the source of the Nile.

Sir **Henry Morton Stanley**, a Welsh journalist, was tasked with going to Africa to find Livingstone, who had been out of communication for six years. Stanley found Livingstone, continued exploring the area, and ultimately verified that Lake Victoria was truly the Nile's source.

Building the Suez Canal - French diplomat **Ferdinand de Lesseps** convinced the Viceroy of Egypt, **Mohamed Said**, to allow a shipping canal to be built between Africa and Asia. Construction of this canal to connect the **Mediterranean** and **Red Sea** began in 1859, opening a significant trade route.

Scramble for Africa - The second period of colonialism, sometimes called **New Imperialism**, exploded in Africa and Asia. While it began as early as 1830, the period between 1885 and 1910 was the greatest period of colonization. Britain, France and Germany were the prime participants.

The colonization was encouraged by what **Rudyard Kipling** described in the poem, **"White Man's Burden."** The poem's title and message emphasized the superiority of the white man and his obligation to rule over those from other cultural backgrounds. Many considered this a satiric poem, not representative of Kipling's actual views. Most of Africa was ultimately subjected to colonization and exploited mercilessly for its raw resources.

. . . .

DR. LIVINGSTONE, I PRESUME? This was supposedly the greeting from Stanley when he strode into Livingstone's camp in the wilds near Lake Tanganika. Livingstone had been on the Dark Continent *for more than six years, when Stanley with 200 men spent eight months searching for him. Livingstone had ignited an interest in the public after his first trip to Africa with his writings and lectures. He had become something of a national hero, and public curiosity is what encouraged the publisher of the* New York Herald *to send a reporter to search for him.*

- Congo Exploitation
- South African War
- Afrikaans Language

Colonial Period

Congo Exploitation - In 1867, **Sir Henry Morton Stanley** returned to Africa to become the first European to explore the Congo. **Leopold II** was elected to the Belgian throne in 1865 and harbored imperialist notions. Through political scheming, Leopold managed to consolidate private control of the **Congo Basin** and exploited its natural resources, particularly ivory and rubber.

Leopold's claim of the **Congo Free State** was recognized at the **Berlin Conference** in 1884 and 1885. He was charged with improving the lives of the natives. Instead, he brutally exploited the region and its people. In 1908, international concern over atrocities in the area caused the Belgian government to annex the **Congo Free State**, ending Leopold's private venture and his genocide of millions of Congolese.

South African War - Also called the **Second Boer War**, these clashes broke out between the British and **Boers**, who were the South African descendants of the original Dutch colonists. Britain had controlled the **Dutch Cape Colony** since 1806. Finding diamonds and gold caused the conflicts from 1899 through 1902. The Boers had created two independent Dutch states, **Transvaal** and the **Orange Free State**, and both resisted the British. They were also unhappy with the British anti-slavery stance. Guerrilla fighting resulted and, by 1902, the British were victorious and the **Peace of Vereeniging** was signed. The region later became part of the **Union of South Africa**.

Afrikaans language - This language, also referred to as **Cape Dutch** or **Netherlandic**, was a West Germanic language spoken in South Africa. It was developed in the Dutch colony at the Cape of Good Hope by descendants of European colonists, indigenous peoples, and slaves of both African and Asian origin. Afrikaans is similar to Dutch. The three official languages of the **Union of South Africa** have been designated as Dutch, English and Afrikaans.

• •

LEOPOLD THE HEARTLESS - *"They were conquerors, and for that you want only brute force--nothing to boast of, when you have it, since your strength is just an accident arising from the weakness of others."* ~ *Joseph Conrad from* Heart of Darkness *(This was written about the brutal period of Leopold.)*

- Ivory Trade
- Division of Morocco
- Independence for African Countries

Conflict & Independence

Ivory trade - Ivory, a material found in elephant tusks, has been used for everything from piano keys to jewelry and works of art. In the early 20th century, demand for ivory soared and large-game recreational hunting safaris became popular. Enormous numbers of elephants were killed. The elephant population numbered 26 million in 1800, and less than a million have remained to current times. A ban on ivory sales was instituted in 1989, but it was upset by later sanctions. Poaching has remained a serious problem.

Division of Morocco - France, Britain and Italy competed for influence in northern Africa, and Spain maintained its districts in Morocco. The king, in an effort to westernize and bring Morocco out of isolation, made changes too fast, triggering unrest. France's war with neighboring Algeria also caused political unrest. By 1912, the sultan signed the **Treaty of Fez**, making Morocco a French protectorate and giving Spain a protectorate in the northern region.

Throughout the following period, France continued to appoint sultans from the ʿ**Alawite dynasty**. The tumultuous years after WWII left France weary of dealing with Morocco, and their demands for independence were answered in 1956.

When the French Protectorate was dissolved without warning, Spain soon followed and turned over the majority of its Moroccan holdings in 1956. The protectorate of **Tarfaya** returned to Morocco in 1958, but Spain has retained its districts of **Ceuta** and **Melilla**.

Independence for African countries - Liberia and Ethiopia escaped the menace of colonialism, though Ethiopia was briefly invaded by Italy prior to WWI. The two World Wars significantly weakened the European hold on Africa. The first African country to gain independence of Western domination was the **Union of South Africa** in 1910 and the last was the **Republic of Zimbabwe** in 1980.

ANCIENT PROVERB - *"You do not teach the paths of the forest to an old gorilla."* ~ *Congolese proverb*

- Germany & Italy Surrender
- Apartheid in South Africa
- Field Biology

Conflict & Independence

German and Italian surrender - In 1943, the **North African Front** of WWII was closed by the surrender of the German and Italian **Afrika Axis Korps** there.

Apartheid in South Africa - In 1948, the **National Party**, an all-white political party, controlled the government in South Africa. By 1950, the party passed apartheid legislation, which started racial segregation policies. These policies included forcing anyone who was not white to live in separate areas and use different facilities. **Soweto**, which was an acronym for <u>So</u>uth<u>we</u>st <u>To</u>wnship was one such region. There were other social and political injustices.

Field biology - Inspired by *The Story of Dr. Dolittle* and Tarzan books and movies, young **Jane Goodall** dreamed of visiting Africa and worked to make that dream a reality. After arriving in Africa, Goodall became assistant to anthropologist and paleontologist Dr. **Louis S. B. Leakey**. He sent her to Tanzania in 1960, where she devoted years to studying **chimpanzees**. She was the first to observe chimps eating meat and making and using tools, such as their pulling leaves off a stick to use for digging termites to eat.

Like Goodall, **Dian Fossey** worked to get to Africa and, there, met Dr. Leakey. Eventually, he helped her to gain sponsorship for a research project to study **mountain gorillas** in Rwanda. Her methods altered the technique for studying animals in their natural habitat. *Gorillas in the Mist* was published in 1983 and was a first-hand account of her adventures and studies. Fossey was later murdered at her study compound, and her killer was never identified.

Both women were sponsored by *National Geographic*, and both were influential in the development of field behavioral study techniques and significant contributors to animal conservation efforts.

. . . .

FIXER-UPPER? - *"The tragedy is not that things are broken. The tragedy is that things are not mended again."* ~ *Alan Paton from* Cry, The Beloved Country *(This book was written about his native South Africa during a tumultuous time and published in 1948.)*

• Civil Rights in South Africa • Libya

Conflict & Independence

Civil rights movement of South Africa - This movement was intertwined with **Nelson Mandela**, a civil rights leader of the **apartheid** resistance movement. At the **Rivonia Trial**, Mandela was received a life prison sentence for his activities in 1963. The result of the trial was the conviction of leaders of the **African National Congress** who were accused of inciting a revolution.

In 1976, the **Soweto Uprising** began with thousands of high school students protesting against the **Afrikaans Medium Decree of 1974**, which required all black schools to use both English and Afrikaans in their teaching. Violence erupted and many children were injured and killed. The uprising lasted a few days, but it received worldwide condemnation. Many called for Mandela's release from prison and for an end to the apartheid policy.

Mandela was not released until 1990. He worked with South African President **F.W. de Klerk** to end apartheid. They won the **Nobel Peace Prize** for their efforts. In 1994, Mandela voted in his first democratic election and became South Africa's first democratically elected president and served for one term.

Libya - Italy had invaded Libya in 1911. During WWII, the Allies defeated and removed the Italians from the country. After WWII, Britain's foreign minister and a later UN vote promised Libya independence. A constitution was penned and newly chosen King **Idris I** headed the **Libyan National Assembly**. He declared the country's independence in 1951.

In the 1960s, oil became a major resource. Unrest followed, and a coup in 1969 ousted the king. Revolutionary leader **Muammar Gaddafi** came to power of the **Great Socialist People's Libyan Arab Jamahiriyah**. After the bombing of a Pan American plane over **Lockerbie** in Scotland in 1988, Libya was shunned by much of the world until 2003 when Gaddafi turned over the terrorists. He ruled with an iron fist. He was ousted after the civil war of 2011.

· ·

MAGNETIC COUNTRY - *"All I wanted to do was get back to Africa. We had not left it, yet, but when I would wake in the night I would lie, listening, homesick for it already."*
~ *Ernest Hemingway from* Green Hills of Africa *(In 1933, Hemingway went on a safari in Africa. The 10-week trip provided a backdrop for this book as well as some short stories.)*

- Kenya
- Nigeria
- Algeria

Conflict & Independence

Kenya - The **Mau Mau Uprising** was also called the **Kenya Emergency**. This movement occurred in the 1950s in colonial Kenya. The Mau Mau were a militant, nationalist organization composed primarily of **Kikuyu** tribesmen. Their ultimate goal was to rid Kenya of British rule and expel European settlers. The Mau Mau were radical and violent, forcing other Kenyans to pledge an oath to join their society and help them kill Europeans.

British troops responded. Through an oppressive campaign involving detention camps and four years of military operations, the British ended the violence. However, in spite of outlawing the Mau Mau and efforts to convert detainees to British political views, the seeds of independence had been sewn. Ten years after the uprising, **Jomo Kenyatta**, a formerly jailed Mau Mau leader, became independent Kenya's first prime minister in 1963.

Nigeria - This country had been in a state of unrest off and on since the early 19th century, when Fulani leader **Usman dan Fodio** began a holy war to spread proper Islam into the region. Numerous small monarchies crumbled under the assault, including the **Oyo Empire**. The **Yoruba Wars** followed and continued for 56 years, until 1886. Internal slaves kept the economy running by producing palm oil. Slavery increased with the price of palm oil.

Britain eventually established rule over the country in an effort to stabilize the palm oil industry and eliminate the internal slave drives. Within 70 years, a new type of oil would dominate the economy. In 1956, after 50 years of European exploration, commercial quantities of oil were discovered in Oloibiri by Shell-BP. Oil has remained vital to the Nigerian economy.

Algeria - Algeria had been occupied by the Roman Empire, an assortment of **Arab-Amazigh dynasties**, and the Ottoman Empire. After the decline of the Ottomans, Algeria briefly experienced independence before France invaded. Algeria remained a part of colonial France from 1847 to 1962.

. . . .

SIGN OF RESPECT - Among members of the Maasai tribe of Kenya and Tanzania, spitting on your hand before greeting someone who is older is a sign of respect.

- Algerian Independence
- Botswana
- Congo

Conflict & Independence

Algerian War of Independence - This war between France and the Algerians ended with the **Évian Accords** in 1962, which declared a cease-fire, after a dozen years of civil war. Through this, Algeria gained independence. This agreement formed a cooperative exchange between the two countries.

Congo - The **Belgian Congo** became the **Democratic Republic of Congo** in 1960, when the country gained its independence. In its early days of independence, chaos ensued. Belgian troops in **Katanga** attempted to suppress a revolt. The result was that UN forces entered at the request of Prime Minister **Patrice Lumumba** who objected to foreign troops aiding the Katanga area. The U.S. and USSR watched the turmoil, trying to determine whether the Congo would become pro-Western or pro-Soviet.

Believing that Lumbaba was in Soviet sway, the U.S. helped to depose him and worked to create a Congolese government aligned with U.S. views. Military leader **Joseph Mobutu Sese Seko**, an anti-communist, initiated several coups, gained the seat of power, and retained it until the mid-1990s. The country has remained unstable with limited development to present times.

Botswana - Botswana gained independence in 1966. The next year, a large diamond cache was found in Orapa. Quickly, Botswana transitioned from very poor to one of Africa's wealthiest nations. This was partly due to the fact that the mining company involved, **De Beers**, chose not to exploit Botswana for its resources, as many African nations had experienced at the hands of foreign business and internal corrupt government officials. Instead, it founded a 50-50 joint venture. Botswana thus produced **conflict-free diamonds**.

De Beers is a cartel of companies that dominate diamond mining in Botswana, Namibia, South Africa and Canada.

. . . .

ONE STEP AT A TIME - *The highest peak in Africa is Kiliman-jaro, which is between Kenya and Tanzania. It was first successfully climbed in 1889 by Hans Meyer, a German geology professor, and Ludwig Purtscheller, an Austrian mountaineer. They were the first to determine that the mountain was truly a volcano.*

- Blood Diamonds
- New Heart
- Civil War in Nigeria
- Uganda

Conflict & Independence

Blood diamonds - In parts of Africa, such as Zimbabwe, Angola and others, economic monies have come from blood diamonds, which are diamonds mined in war zones and sold to finance insurgencies by warlords. They have provided income to profiteers, gangs and marauding armies and have resulted in the deaths and maiming of thousands of people, including children. The **Kimberley Process Certification Scheme** was enacted by world governments and industry leaders in 2003 to stem the flow of diamonds that fund rebels and their wars, but it has failed to stop the flow of blood diamonds.

New heart - The first human heart transplant was performed in a Cape Town hospital in 1967 by **Christiaan Barnard**. The heart recipient lived 18 days until he succumbed to pneumonia.

Civil war in Nigeria - In 1966, many Nigerian **Igbo** people, who were Christian, were massacred by Muslim **Hausa**. Thousands sought refuge in eastern Nigerian states. Though not of their religion, Lieutenant Colonel **Odumegwu Ojukwu** announced that three of these eastern Nigerian states were seceding, forming the **Republic of Biafra**, to protect them. The Nigerian government initiated a civil war. Though Biafran forces gained initially, they were overtaken by Nigerian forces. Lost oil fields meant lost food supplies and millions starved. Biafra surrendered in 1970 and was absorbed back into Nigeria.

Uganda - Uganda became independent of Britain in 1962, giving way to an unstable republic. In 1971, Prime Minister **Milton Obote** was deposed in a military coup orchestrated by **Idi Amin Dada**, who became a brutal dictator. His eight-year reign was bloody and full of ethnic persecution under the guise of a policy of **Africanization**. Amin was deposed during the **Uganda-Tanzania War** in 1979, when Tanzanian forces and Ugandan exiles invaded. Uganda's history continues to be plagued by political instability and armed rebel forces such as the **Lord's Resistance Army** led by **Joseph Kony**.

. . . .

LOST IN TRANSLATION? - There are over 2,000 recognized languages spoken in Africa, which is one of the reasons most countries have three or more official languages. The exception is Somalia, the only country in Africa where all citizens speak one language, Somali.

- Ethiopia
- Rwandan Massacre
- Current Ecology Problems

Conflict & Independence

Ethiopia - The emperor of Ethiopia was **Haile Selassie** from 1930 to 1974. He ended Ethiopia's 3000-year rule by emperors. Selassie worked to modernize Ethiopia gradually and to centralize his authority by taking an anti-feudal stance. He also joined the **League of Nations** and, later, the **UN**. He helped to create the **Organization of African Unity** in 1963. Italy temporarily occupied the country, and Selassie drove the Italians out with British aid. Famine and other internal problems prompted a mutiny, and he was deposed in a 1974 coup by Marxist military officers, and this was followed by years of turmoil.

Rwandan Massacre - This was a conflict primarily between the **Hutu** and **Tutsi**, the main ethnic groups of Rwanda. Tutsi, though the minority, were considered the elite and occupied most government positions. The Hutus overturned the Tutsi monarchy in 1959, and many of the Tutsi became refugees, fleeing to surrounding countries. The **Rwandan Patriotic Front** (RPF) was formed in Uganda by a group of these refugees.

In 1994, the plane of the Hutu president in Rwanda, **Juvenal Habyarimana**, was shot down. Blaming this act on the Tutsi, the presidential guard began executions and initiated three months of violence and slaughter. UN negotiations to end the conflict were unsuccessful, the RPF was finally able to overthrow Habyarimana, and a multi-ethnic government led by the Tutsi was created. Nearly a million died during the purge, and conflict has continued between these groups to the present.

Current ecology problems - Africa was home to more than 5,615 endangered species. This included the African elephant, lion, cheetah, black rhinoceros, pygmy hippopotamus and many more. These animal populations have been affected by poaching, over hunting, and growth of the wild game meat trade, which has become a multi-billion dollar industry. Sale of rhino horns for medicinal use in Asia have caused their decimation. Poverty has remained a factor that has driven many to hunt endangered species for sustenance.

· ·

WORKING TOWARD - *"Peace is a day-to-day problem, the product of a multitude of events and judgments. Peace is not an 'is,' it is a 'becoming.'"* ~ *Haile Selassie*

- African Union
- Arab Spring
- Ebola Epidemic

New Millennium

African Union - In 2002, the African Union replaced the Organization of African Unity, which was founded in 1963 and in need of revision. Some of its main objectives included the achievement of African unity and the defense of member states. Other objectives were to retain sovereignty and to develop a sound economic system similar to the **European Union**, which would encourage prosperity of all African nations.

Arab Spring - In 2011, numerous Arab nations across Africa and the Middle East saw the rise of large-scale citizen protests calling for more freedoms and, in some cases, new governments. These protests started in Tunisia with the self-immolation of a fruit cart owner. Some governments completely fell, some protests were overwhelmingly crushed, and others saw some gains and others have remained in conflict.

Tunisia, Egypt and Libya have witnessed destruction of their governments and the overthrow of oppressive leaders. Zine el Abidine Ben Ali was run out of Tunisia. **Hosni Mubarak** stepped down from his 30-year rule of Egypt after demonstrations in the 2011 revolution. Muammar Gaddafi was killed in Libyan uprisings, and the government was overthrown. The governments of Algeria and Morocco stood fast with limited violence and minor gains for their citizens.

Ebola epidemic in Liberia - In 2014, the largest recorded Ebola epidemic in history broke out in Western Africa. This virus has been associated with a high incidence of death, particularly in underdeveloped countries. The most extensive outbreaks were in Guinea, Liberia and Sierra Leone. The entire globe watched news of the epidemic with concern over cases transmitted to other countries, including the U.S., by travelers who did not realize they carried the potentially fatal virus.

. . . .

THE FORCE BE WITH YOU - *The deserts of Tunisia served as a backdrop for the planet Tatooine during the making of the original* Star Wars *movie. Today, Luke Skywalker's house is a tourist attraction.*

BIBLIOGRAPHY

"About Dr. King." The King Center. Web. 2014. <http://www.thekingcenter.org/about-dr-king>.

"About the Crisis | Cuban Missile Crisis." Cuban Missile Crisis. Web. 2014. <http://www.cubanmissilecrisis.org/background/>.

"Alhambra De Granada. Entradas, Visitas Guiadas, Información, Fotografías, Guía De Granada." Alhambra De Granada. Web. 2014.

"Almagest - A Multimedia Database for Teaching & Learning." Almagest. Web. 2014. <http://etcweb.princeton.edu>.

"Alpha History: Because the past Matters." Alpha History. Web. 2014. <http://alphahistory.com>.

American Presidents: Life Portraits. Web. 2014. <http://www.americanpresidents.org/>.

"Ancient Civilizations." UShistory.org. Independence Hall Association. Web. 2014. <http://www.ushistory.org/civ>.

Ancient Greece. Web. 2014. <http://www.ancient-greece.org>.

"Ancient History Encyclopedia." Ancient History Encyclopedia. Web. 2014. <http://www.ancient.eu>.

Asia Society. Web. 2014. <http://asiasociety.org/>.

BBC. Web. 2014. <http://www.bbc.co.uk>.

Biographical Directory of the United States. Web. 2014. <http://bioguide.congress.gov/>.

Biography – Nelson Mandela Foundation. Web. 2014. <http://www.nelsonmandela.org/content/page/biography>.

Chicago History Museum | Chicago History Museum. Web. 2014. <http://chicagohs.org/history>.

Chinese Revolution of 1911 - 1899–1913 - Milestones - Office of the Historian. Web. 2014. <https://history.state.gov/milestones/1899-1913/chinese-rev>.

Clarence Darrow Collection (The). Web. 2014. <http://darrow.law.umn.edu>.

"Classroom Materials." Classroom Materials. Web. 2014. <http://www.loc.gov/teachers/classroommaterials>.

CNN. Cable News Network. Web. 2014. <http://www.cnn.com>.

"Collections." Smithsonian's National Air and Space Museum Home Page. Web. 2014. <http://airandspace.si.edu>.

"Congress of Vienna." Princeton University. Web. 2014. <http://www.princeton.edu/~achaney/tmve/wiki100k/docs/Congress_of_Vienna.html>.

"Elizabeth I." Elizabeth I. Web. 2014. <http://tudorhistory.org/elizabeth/queen.html>.

Encyclopedia Britannica Online. Encyclopedia Britannica. Web. 2014. <http://www.britannica.com>.

"Experience Monticello." Thomas Jefferson's Monticello. Web. 2014. <http://www.monticello.org>.

"Father Junipero Serra (1713-1784)." Web. 2014. <http://www.sfmuseum.net/bio/jserra.html>.

"First Americans Arrived As Two Separate Migrations, According To New Genetic Evidence." ScienceDaily. Web. 2014. <http://www.sciencedaily.com/releases/2009/01/090108121618.htm>.

Founders & Patriots of America. Web. 2014. <http://www.founderspatriots.org>.

Galileo Project (The) | Chronology | Gregorian Calendar. Web. 2014. <http://galileo.rice.edu/chron/gregorian.html>.

"George Washington's Mount Vernon." George Washington's Mount Vernon. Web. 2014. <http://www.mountvernon.org>.

"Gulf Oil Spill." Smithsonian Ocean Portal. Web. 2014. <http://ocean.si.edu/gulf-oil-spill>.

"Hinduism Facts | Facts about Hindu Religion." Web. 2014. <http://hinduismfacts.org>.

History Learning Site. Web. 2014. <http://www.historylearningsite.co.uk>.

History of Macedonia and the Macedonian Nation. Web. 2014. <http://www.historyofmacedonia.org>.

History Sites by Knox. Web. 2014. <http://europeanhistory.boisestate.edu/>.

"History Timelines." Web. 2014. <http://www.datesandevents.org>.

"History Topics." History.com. A&E Television Networks. Web. 2014. <http://www.history.com/topics>.

HistoryWorld - History and Timelines. Web. 2014. <http://www.historyworld.net>.

Ipl2: Information You Can Trust. Web. 2014. <http://www.ipl.org>.

"Irish Free State Declared." History.com. A&E Television Networks. Web. 2014. <http://www.history.com/this-day-in-history/irish-free-state-declared>.

John Nance Garner Biography Page 3 - Briscoe-Garner Museum - Dolph Briscoe Center for American History. Web. 2014. <http://www.cah.utexas.edu/museums/garner_bio_three.php>.

Journey of Mankind - The Peopling of the World. Web. 2014. <http://www.bradshawfoundation.com/journey/>.

Judaism 101. Web. 2014. <http://www.jewfaq.org/>.

"League of Nations." History Learning Site. Web. 2014. <http://www.historylearningsite.co.uk/leagueofnations.htm>.

Lesson 2: The Strategy of Containment, 1947–1948 | EDSITEment. Web. 2014. <http://edsitement.neh.gov/lesson-plan/strategy-containment-1947-1948>.

Mali, PWNET. Web. 2014. <http://mali.pwnet.org/>.

Medici Family (The). Web. 2014. <http://galileo.rice.edu/lib/student_work/florence96/alexc/medici.html>.

Middle Ages - Medieval Resources. Web. 2014. <http://www.themiddleages.net/>.

Miller Center. Web. 2014. <http://millercenter.org>.

Musée Canadien De L'histoire - Canadian Museum of History. Web. 2014. <http://www.historymuseum.ca>.

NASA. Web. 2014. <http://www.nasa.gov/>.

National Geographic Magazine. Web. 2014. <http://ngm.nationalgeographic.com>.

National Geographic Society Atlas of World History, National Geographic Society, 1997

"National Geographic: Lewis & Clark." National Geographic: Lewis & Clark. Web. 2014. <http://www.nationalgeographic.com/lewisandclark>.

"National Institute of Culture and History." National Institute of Culture and History. Web. 2014. <http://www.nichbelize.org>.

New Mexico Genealogical Society. Web. 2014. <http://www.nmgs.org/artcuar4.htm>.

New World Encyclopedia. Web. 2014. <http://www.newworldencyclopedia.org>.

"Office of the Historian." Office of the Historian. Web. 2014. <https://history.state.gov>.

Oneida Nation Museum. Web. 2014. <http://oneidanation.org/museum>. "National Geographic Society Atlas of World History," Noel Grove, 1997.

PBS. Web. 2014. <http://www.pbs.org>.

PBS. Web. 2014. <http://www.pbs.org/empires/martinluther/about_driv.html>.

PBS. Web. 2014. <http://www.pbs.org/empires/medici/renaissance/michelangelo2.html>.

PBS. Web. 2014. <http://www.pbs.org/faithandreason/gengloss/revolution-body.html>.

Phoenicia Canaanite Encyclopedia. Web. 2014. http://phoenicia.org

"Presidents of the United States (POTUS)." Web. 2014. <http://www.ipl.org/div/potus>.

Princeton University. Web. 2014. <http://www.princeton.edu>.

"Science and Space Facts, Science and Space, Human Body, Health, Earth, Human Disease-National Geographic." National Geographic. Web. 2014.<http://science.nationalgeographic.com>.

Smithsonian. Web. 2014. <http://www.smithsonian.com>.

"Songhai Empire." New World Encyclopedia. Web. 2014. <http://www.newworldencyclopedia.org/entry/Songhai_Empire>.

"Suleyman I | Biography - Ottoman Sultan." Encyclopedia Britannica Online. Encyclopedia Britannica. Web. 2014. <http://www.britannica.com/EBchecked/topic/572395/Suleyman-I>.

"Texas State Historical Association (TSHA) | A Digital Gateway to Texas History." Texas State Historical Association (TSHA) | A Digital Gateway to Texas History. Dec. 2014. <http://www.tshaonline.org>.

"The Big Read." The Grapes of Wrath. Web. 2014. <http://www.neabigread.org/books/grapesofwrath/>.

"The Borgias - History of the Powerful Italian Family." Robert Wilde. Web. 2014. <http://europeanhistory.about.com/od/italyandthecitystates/a/The-Borgias_2.htm>.

"The First Council of Nicaea." The Catholic Encyclopedia. H. Leclercq. 1911. Web. 2014. <http://www.newadvent.org/cathen/11044a.htm>

"The Galileo Project." The Galileo Project. Web. 2014. <http://galileo.rice.edu/>.

"The May 4 Shootings at Kent State University." Kent State University. Jerry M. Lewis and Thomas R. Hensley. Web. 2014. <http://dept.kent.edu/sociology/lewis/lewihen.htm>.

"The Navigation Act, 1651." The Navigation Act, 1651. Web. 2014. <http://bcw-project.org/church-and-state/the-commonwealth/the-navigation-act>.

"The Real Robinson Crusoe." Smithsonian. Web. 2014. <http://www.smithsonianmag.com/history/the-real-robinson-crusoe-74877644/?no-ist>.

"The Religious World of the Cherokees." Maintaining Balance: The Religious World of the Cherokees. Web. 2014. <http://www.learnnc.org/lp/editions/nchist-twoworlds/1839>.

The United States. Follet Educational Services, Social Studies. Pearson Education, Inc. Scott Foresman 2003.

"The War of 1812." NMAH. Web. 2014. <http://amhistory.si.edu/starspangledbanner/the-war-of-1812.aspx>.

The Washington Post. Web. 2014. <http://www.washingtonpost.com>.

"Tribal History." Mashantucket (Western) Pequot Tribal Nation. Web. 2014. <http://www.mashantucket.com/tribalhistory.aspx>.

UCMP - University of California Museum of Paleontology. Web. 2014. <http://www.ucmp.berkeley.edu>.

"UNESCO World Heritage Centre." UNESCO World Heritage Centre. Web. 2014. <http://whc.unesco.org>.

United States Holocaust Memorial Council. Web. 2014. <http://www.ushmm.org/>.

United States. National Park Service. "St. Augustine Town Plan Historic District--American Latino Heritage: A Discover Our Shared Heritage Travel Itinerary." National Parks Service. U.S. Department of the Interior. Web. 2014. <http://www.nps.gov/nr/travel/American_Latino_Heritage/St_Augustine_Town_Plan_Historic_District.html>.

University of Washington. Web. 2014. <https://depts.washington.edu.>

US Department of State. Web. 2014. <http://www.state.gov>.

"US History." UShistory.org. Independence Hall Association. Web. 2014. <http://www.ushistory.org>.

"Vienna - A City with History and a Melting Pot of Nations." Vienna Business Agency. Web. 2014. <http://www.expatcenter.at/fileadmin/upload/Texte/Vienna_a_city_with_history_A_melting_pot_1804-1918.pdf>.

"Welcome to the Division of Chemical Education." Purdue University College of Science Welcome. Web. 2014. <http://chemed.chem.purdue.edu>.

"What Every American Should Know About American History," Dr. Alan Axelrod and Charles Phillips, 1992.

"What Was Colonial Life Like in Early America?" Kid Info. Web. 2014. <http://www.kidinfo.com/american_history/colonization_colonial_life.html>.

Wikimedia Foundation. Web. 2014. <http://en.wikipedia.org>.

World History International: World History Essays From Prehistory To The Present. Web. 2014. <http://history-world.org/>.

Images

George Washington to James Polk; engraved portraits by The Bureau of Engraving and Printing

"Zachary Taylor" and (Willard) "Fillmore" by Unknown.

"Franklin Pierce" and "James Buchanan" and "President Andrew Johnson" by Mathew Brady, Library of Congress.

"Abraham Lincoln November 1863" by Alexander Gardner, <http:www.britannica.com>.

"UlyssesGrant" by Brady-Handy Photograph Collection. Library of Congress Prints and Photographs online collection.

"President Rutherford Hayes 1870 - 1880" by Mathew Brady - This image is available from the United States Library of Congress's Prints and Photographs division.

"James Abram Garfield, photo portrait seated" by Unknown; part of Brady-Handy Photograph Collection. - This image is available from the United States Library of Congress's Prints and Photographs division.

"Chester Alan Arthur" Wikimedia Commons, public.

"Stephen Grover Cleveland" by Unknown. Library of Congress Prints and Photographs online collection.

"Pach Brothers - Benjamin Harrison" by Pach Brothers - photograph Adam Cuerden - restoration. Library of Congress Prints and Photographs online collection.

"William McKinley 1" by Barnett McFee Clinedinst(1862-1953). Library of Congress Prints and Photographs online collection.

"President Theodore Roosevelt, 1904" by Pach Brothers. Library of Congress Prints and Photographs online collection.

"William Howard Taft, Bain bw photo portrait, 1908" by George Grantham Bain; (c): Moffett Studio. Wikimedia Commons, public.

"President Woodrow Wilson portrait December 2 1912" by Pach Brothers, New York. Library of Congress Prints and Photographs online collection.

"Warren G Harding-Harris & Ewing" by Harris & Ewing. <http://www.old-picture.com/american-legacy/003/President-Harding-Warren.htm. Wikimedia Commons, public.

"John Calvin Coolidge, Bain bw photo portrait" by George Grantham Bain - This image is available from the United States Library of Congress's Prints and Photographs division.

"Herbert Hoover" by Underwood & Underwood, Washington. Library of Congress Prints and Photographs online collection.

"Harry S. Truman" by Frank Gatteri, United States Army Signal Corps. Wikimedia Commons, public.

"Dwight D. Eisenhower, White House photo portrait, February 1959" by Presumably a White House photographer, since it is in the Presidential years collection and no assertion of copyright is made. Wikimedia Commons, public.

John F. Kennedy. Unknown. Scanned from 1964 Warren Commission report (Government printing office).

"Lyndon B. Johnson, photo portrait, leaning on chair, color" by Arnold Newman, White House Press Office. Library of Congress Prints and Photographs online collection.

"Richard M. Nixon, ca. 1935 - 1982 - NARA - 530679" by Unknown or not provided. Wikimedia Commons, public.

"Gerald Ford" by David Hume Kennerly. <http://www.fordlibrarymuseum.gov.>

"JimmyCarterPortrait" by Department of Defense. Department of the Navy. Naval Photographic Center - This media is available in the holdings of the National Archives and Records Administration. Wikimedia Commons, public.

"Official Portrait of President Reagan 1981" by Unknown. Library of Congress Prints and Photographs online collection.

"George H. W. Bush, President of the United States, 1989 official portrait" by POTUS.

"Bill Clinton" by Bob McNeely, The White House.

"George-W-Bush" White House photo by Eric Draper. This image was released by the United States Department of Defense.

"President Barack Obama, 2012 portrait crop" by Official White House Photo by Pete Souza.

Photos of Anne Frank, Martin Luther King, and Babe Ruth - United States Library of Congress's Prints and Photographs division.

Cover - "The Discovery of King Tut" reproduction by Premier Exhibitions <http://www.premierexhibitions.com>

INDEX

9/11, 69, 188, 189
Abbasid dynasty, 170
Abd al-Ilah, 181
Aborigines, 176, 184, 188
Academy, 108, 134
Acadia, 29
Achaemenid, 164
Acoma, 12
Act of Succession, 126
Act of Supremacy, 126, 128
Act of Uniformity, 128
Act of Union, 133
Adair, 187
Adams, 22, 23, 24, 25, 26, 28, 32, 33, 72, 73
Adams-Onís Treaty, 32
Adena, 12
Administration of Justice Act, 22
Adobe Walls, 46
Adolf Hitler, 59, 146
Adolphus, 130
Aegean, 104, 105
Aesop, 106
Afghan Communist Party 185
AFL, 49
Aflaq, 184
African Nat'l Congress, 211
African Union, 216
Afrika Axis Korps, 210
Afrikaans, 208, 211
Age of Enlightenment, 129, 137
Age of Reason, 127, 129
Agra, 174
Agricultural Adjustment Act, 58
Akbar, 174
Akenhaton, 195
Akhmat, 173
Akihito, 187
Akkadian script, 163
Aksum, 200, 201
Alamo, 36
Alara, 196
Alaric, 113
Alaska, 4, 12, 20, 33, 44, 67, 84
Alba, 116
Albany Congress, 21
Alberti, 118
Albigensian Crusade, 117
Aldrin, 65
Alexander, 26-7, 36, 45-6, 108-9, 120, 124, 133, 153, 163-5, 197-9
Alexandria, 197-201
Alfonso, 114
Alfred, 68, 116
Al-Fusṭāṭ, 201
Algerian War, 213
Algiers, 206
Algonquin, 14, 21
Alhambra, 114
Alien and Sedition Acts, 28
Allied Powers, 55, 59
Allies, 55, 60, 61, 142, 145, 148, 150, 151, 181, 211
al-Qaeda, 69, 71, 188
Althing, 115
Álvarez, 13
Amaru, 92
Amazon, 84, 92, 102
Amendment 27-8, 37, 43, 45, 54-5, 57-8, 63, 65-6, 98

Amenhotep, 195
American Civil War, 34, 39
American Federation, 49
American Indian Movemt, 50
American Promise, 66
American Red Cross, 48
American Revolution, 23
Amin, 214
Amundsen, 99
Anasazi, 12
Anastasia, 145, 155
Anatolia, 158, 169
Andalusia, 114
Andersen, 138
Anderson, 39
Andes Mountains, 90, 97
Andros, 18
Angevin Empire, 118
Angkor Wat, 170, 171
Anglo-Iraqi War, 181
Anglo-Saxons, 116
Anglo-Zulu War, 205
Anne of Cleves, 126
Anthony, 37
Antinomian Controversy, 16
Antonius, 111, 112
Antony, 109, 110, 198, 199
Apache, 14, 49
Apartheid, 210
Apollo 11, 65
Appalachian Mountains, 21
Arab Socialism, 184
Arab Spring, 189, 216
Aramaic script, 163
Arapaho, 20, 41, 46, 47
Arawak, 88
Archaic Era, 84
Archimedes, 107
Ardennes, 148
Argentina, 96, 100, 101
Aristotle, 106, 108
Armstrong, 47, 65
Arnold, 25
Arthur, 74, 77, 113
Articles of Confederation, 23, 25, 26
Aryabhata, 168
Aryan, 60, 149
Ashanti, 204, 205
Ashoka, 166
Assyrian Empire, 163
Atacama Desert, 97
Atahualpa, 91
Atatürk, 180
Athens, 107, 108
Atlantic Ocean, 100, 142, 193
atomic bomb, 61-2, 150, 181
Aton, 195
Attila, 168
Attlee, 150
Augustulus, 113
Aurelius, 112
Auschwitz, 149
Australopithecus, 192
Austria, 38, 61, 122, 131, 133-6, 138, 141-2
Austro-Hungarian, 122, 138, 142, 143
Axis power 59, 147, 151, 181
Ayamara, 88
Azocar, 101
Aztec, 86, 87, 89, 90, 91
Babur, 174
Babylonia, 161, 163
Babylonian Empire, 163

Bach, 130
Bacon, 18, 55, 129
Baghdad, 155, 189
Bailey, 36
Balfour Declaration, 182
Baltimore & Ohio Railroad 37
Bangladesh, 185
Bantu, 194, 196, 205
Barbarossa, 117
Bard, 128, 129
Barnard, 4, 214
Baroque, 130, 135
Barton, 48
Batista, 100
Battle of Actium, 199
Battle of Adobe Walls, 46
Battle of Agincourt, 120
Battle of Antietam, 40
Battle of Appomattox, 42
Battle of Bad Axe, 34
Battle of Berlin, 61
Battle of Bosworth Field, 122
Battle of Britain, 148
Battle of Bunker Hill, 24
Battle of Chaeronea, 108
Battle of Chancellorsville, 40
Battle of Fort McHenry, 31
Battle of Fort Sumter, 39
Battle of Fredericksburg, 40
Battle of Hastings, 116
Battle of Issus, 164
Battle of Kosovo, 173
Battle of Lützen, 130
Battle of Marathon, 107
Battle of Midway, 60, 181
Battle of New Orleans, 31
Battle of Plassey, 176
Battle of Saratoga, 25
Battle of Stalingrad, 148
Battle of Stamford, 116
Battle of the Boyne, 133
Battle of the Bulge, 61, 148
Battle of the Coral Sea, 181
Battle of the Thames, 30
Battle of Three Kings, 204
Battle of Trafalgar, 137
Battle of Trenton, 24
Battle of Waterloo, 139
Battle of Watling Street, 110
Battle of Yorktown, 25
Battles at Bull Run, 40
Battles of Lexington and Concord, 23
Battuta, 172, 203, 204
Bayonet Constitution, 51
Beatles, 38, 153, 193
Beauregard, 39
Beethoven, 137
Beijing, 176, 187, 190
Belgian Congo, 213
Bell, 46
Ben Ali, 189, 216
Benet, 50
Bergen-Belsen, 149
Bering, 12, 20, 84
Berkeley, 18
Berlin Wall, 152, 153
Bessemer, 52
Biafra, 214
Bible, 16, 122, 126, 160, 162, 167, 196
Bienville, 19
Bill of Rights, 27, 63
Bingham, 43, 99
Bismarck, 141, 142

Bissel, 38
Black Death, 121
Black Hawk, 34
Black Kettle, 41
Black Sea, 105, 115
Black Shirts, 146
Black Tuesday, 57
Bland-Allison Act, 48
Bleeding Kansas, 38
blood diamonds, 214
Blue Jacket, 25
Boccaccio, 119
Boer, 208
Boleyn, 128
Bolívar, 93
Bolivia, 88, 93, 97, 100, 102
Bolshevik, 144
Bomvana, 205
Boone, 22
Boonesborough, 22
Booth, 42
Borgia, 120, 124, 125
Bosnia and Herzegovina, 151
Boston Marathon, 71
Boston Massacre, 22
Boston Port Act, 22
Boston Tea Party, 22, 70
Boudicca, 110
Bourbon, 133, 139, 206
Boxer Rebellion, 178
Boyle, 127
Bozeman, 44
Brackenridge, 22
Bradford, 15
Brahms, 137
Bramante, 125
Branch Davidians, 68
Brandenburg Concertos, 130
Brandenburg Gate, 153
Brezhnev, 152
Brihadratha, 166
British Commonwealth, 59, 151
British East India Co., 132
British Petroleum, 70
British Royal Air Force, 148
British Virginia Company, 15
Brontë, 138
Bronze Age, 9, 12, 104-5, 159, 194-5
Brothers Grimm, 138
Brown, 39, 50, 51, 63
Brown v. Board, 51, 63
Brutus, 106, 109
bubonic plague, 121, 166
Buchanan, 75
Buchenwald, 149
Buddhism, 165, 166
Buenos Aires, 93, 100
Buna, 149
Buonarroti, 118, 120
Bureau of Alcohol, Tobacco and Firearms, 68
Burgoyne, 25
Burr, 28
Bush, 69, 82, 155, 189
Bushido, 171
Byzantine, 112-14, 169, 173, 174, 197, 199-201
Cabot, 13
Cabral, 122
Caesar, 106, 108-10, 199
Cajuns, 29
Calcutta, 132
Caligula, 110

INDEX

Calvin, 56, 79, 126, 132
Cambodia, 170, 183, 185
Campana Admirable, 93
Canadian Arctic, 84
Candide, 129
Canterbury Tales, 121
Cape Colony, 206
Cape of Good Hope, 122, 132, 192, 194, 204, 208
Cape Verde Islands, 90, 124
Carib, 88
Caribbean Islands, 29
Carlos, 49, 96, 150
Carnegie, 52
Carter, 81
Carthage, 197, 198, 199, 200
Cartier, 13
Cartwright, 36
Carver, 56
Cassidy, 97
Cassius, 109
Castile, 114, 123
Castro, 100, 101
Çatalhöyük, 158
Cathars, 117
Catherine, 46, 120, 126, 128, 135
Cave of Altamira, 104
Cayuga, 14
Central Africa, 192
Central Asian Republics, 188
Central Park, 38, 51
Central Powers, 142
Céspedes, 96
Ceuta, 209
Cézanne, 142
Chaco, 100
Chalcolithic, 9
Challenger, 67
Cham, 171
Champlain, 14
Chandragupta, 165, 166
Chapultepec, 89
Charbonneau, 29
Charlemagne, 115
Charles I, 115, 131, 133, 139
Chaucer, 121
Chavín, 85, 88
Cheops, 195
Chernobyl, 154, 190
Cherokee, 31, 34
Cheyenne, 20, 41, 44, 46, 47
Chicago Fire, 46
Chichen Itza, 89
Chief Joseph, 47
Chinese Famine, 183
Chinese space program, 189
Chiricahua Apache, 49
Chivington, 41
Chopin, 137
Christ Redeemer Statue, 99
Churchill, 61
Civil Rights, 43, 65, 211
Civil War, 28, 34, 36, 39, 40, 41, 42, 43, 44, 45, 48, 55, 56, 131, 147, 186, 214
Classic Era, 85, 87
Classical Age, 106, 168
Classical Period, 135
Claudius, 110
Clay, 30, 33, 37
Clayton Antitrust Act, 54
Cleisthenes, 107
Clement VII, 121
Cleopatra, 110, 197, 198, 199

Clermont, 30
Cleveland, 49, 51, 77
Clinton, 82
Clive, 176
Clovis, 12
Cochinchina, 178
Cold War, 62, 101, 150-52
Coleridge, 138
Collins, 145
Columbia Shuttle, 70
Columbian Exchange, 12
Columbian Exposition, 51
Columbine High, 69
Columbus, 12, 51, 84, 115, 118, 123
Comanche, 18, 20, 44, 46, 171
Committee of Safety, 51
Commodus, 112
Common Sense, 24
Commonwealth of Independent, 155, 188
Communist Manifesto, 139
Communist Party, 100, 146, 152, 154, 182, 185
Compromise, 32, 37, 38, 43, 47
Concentration camps, 149
Concordat of Worms, 117
Confederate States of America, 40
Confederation of the Rhine, 138
Confucianism, 164, 165, 175
Confucius, 163, 164
Congo, 91, 192, 208, 213
Congress of Vienna, 139
Connecticut Colony, 16
conquistadors, 91
Conservative Movement, 63
Constantine, 112, 125, 173
Constantinople, 89, 112, 117, 119, 169, 172, 173, 174
Constitution, 26, 27, 28, 43, 51, 72, 129
Continental Army, 23, 24
Convention of 1818, 32
Cook, 98, 174, 184
Coolidge, 56, 79
Copernicus, 127
Copts, 201
Corcovado, 99
Corinth, 105
Coronado, 13
Cortés, 92
Council of Constance, 121
Council of the Indies, 91
Cradle of Civilization, 158-9
Creek Wars, 31
Crete, 104, 105
Crime of the Century, 57
Croatia, 122, 151
Cromwell, 131
Crusades, 114, 117
Cuban, 64, 96, 100-1
Cultural Revolution, 183
Cumberland Gap, 22
cuneiform, 105
Custer, 47
Cuzco, 90
Cyprus, 117, 193
Czech Republic, 154
da Gama, 122, 123
da Vinci, 118, 120, 124

Dachau, 149
daimyo, 175
Dál Riata, 116
dan Fodio, 212
Dante, 119
Daoud, 185
Dare, 14
Darius, 164
Dark Ages, 114
Darwin, 141
Dawes, 23
Dawson City, 98
D-Day, 61, 80, 148
De Beers, 213
de Grasse, 25
de Klerk, 211
de la Barrera, 91, 204
de Lesseps, 207
de Soto, 13
Dead Sea, 158
Declaration of Independence, 24, 72
Declaration of Rights and Resolves, 23
Declaration of the Causes, 23
Deepwater Horizon, 70
Deere, 35
Defenestration of Prague, 130
Defense of Marriage Act, 69
Defoe, 133
Degas, 142
Dekanawidah, 14
Delaware, 17, 19, 24, 26
Democratic National Committee, 66
Democratic Republic of Congo, 213
Deng, 185, 187
Dewey, 62
Dias, 122, 123, 204
Díaz, 99, 114
Dickens, 140
Dickinson, 23
Dido, 197
Diem, 183
Diocletian, 112, 200
Diplomatic Revolution, 134
Directory, 136
Dirty War, 101
Divine Comedy, 119
Dolce Stil Novo, 119
Dominion Police, 97
Dorian, 105
Douglas, 37, 39
Douglass, 36
Dred Scott v. Sanford, 38
Drug cartels, 102
Dubček, 153
Dublin, 115, 127, 143
DuBois, 53
Dull Knife, 47
Dutch East India Co., 15, 132
Dutch West India Co., 16
Earhart, 58
East Berlin, 152
East India Co 15, 22, 132, 176
Easter Island, 167, 174
Easter Rebellion, 143
Eastern Africa, 193
Ebola, 216
Ebro Treaty, 198
Ecuador, 85, 90, 92, 93, 102
Ecumenical Council, 112
Edict of Milan, 112, 200

Edo period, 171, 175
Edward, 20, 116, 119-20, 128
Edwards, 20
Eelam, 186
Egypt united, 194
Einstein, 62
Éire, 145
Eisenhower, 80, 148
El Cid, 114
El Duce, 59
El Niño, 87, 88
Elba, 136, 139
Eleanor, 118, 120
Elissa, 197
Elizabeth I, 122, 128, 131
Elizabethan Era, 128, 129
Emancipation, 41
Emerson, 23
Emmanuel, 146
Engel v. Vitale, 63
English Civil War, 131
Enlightenment, 119, 129, 130-4, 137
Enola Gay, 150, 181
Erik the Red, 115
Erikson, 12, 115
Etruscans, 106
Euclid, 107
Euphrates River, 159
European Economic Community, 156
European Union, 156, 216
Eurozone crisis, 156
Évian Accords, 213
Excalibur, 113
Executive Order, 61, 66
Exodus, 161
Exxon Valdez, 67
Falkland War, 101
Fall, 55, 173, 180, 189, 200
Fascist, 59, 146
Faust, 137, 138
February Revolution 139, 144
Federal Bureau of Investigation, 68
Federal Meat Inspection, 53
Federal Reserve, 54
Federal Trade Commission 54
Federalist Papers, 26
Federalists, 30, 31
Ferdinand, 12, 90, 123, 130, 142, 204, 207
Ferris, 51
Fillmore, 75
Finney, 26
First Continental Congress, 23
First Crusade, 117
First Fleet, 176
Fitzgerald, 56, 80
Five Nations, 14
Florentine, 124
Folsom, 12
Food and Drug Administration, 53
Forbidden City, 172
Ford, 42, 52, 66, 74, 81
Formative Era, 85
Formosa, 182
Forsyth, 50
Fort Amsterdam, 16
Fort Christina, 17
Fort Duquesne, 20
Fort McHenry, 31
Fort Orange, 15

221

INDEX

Fort Sumter, 39, 40
Fossey, 210
Fountain of Youth, 13
Four Corners, 12
Fourteen Point Plan, 55
Francis I, 13, 115, 138
Francis II, 115, 138
Franco, 140, 147, 150
Franco-Prussian War, 140
Frank, 60, 75, 149
Franklin, 20, 21, 24, 25, 58, 60, 61, 75, 79, 149
Franks, 115
Frederick the Great, 134
Free Silver Movement, 48
Freetown, 205
French and Indian War, 20, 92
French Indochina, 183
French Revolution, 93, 134, 136, 139
Freneau, 22
Freud, 141
Führer, 147
Fukushima, 190
Fulton, 30
Gaddafi, 154, 211, 216
Galapagos Islands, 141
Galileo, 127
Galtieri, 101
Gandhi, 141, 180
Ganges Plain, 161
Gao, 204
Garfield, 48, 76
Gates, 25
Gaul, 109, 168
Gautama, 165
Geneva, 48, 145, 183
geoglyphs, 87
George I-IV, 21, 23, 25, 134
Geraldine Rebellion, 127
German Empire, 141
Geronimo, 49
Gettysburg, 40, 42
Ghana Kingdom, 202, 203
Gilded Age, 45
Gilgamesh, 160
Glorious Revolution, 133
Godwinson, 116
Goethe, 138
Gold Standard Act, 48
Golden Age, 9, 135
Golden Horde, 173
Golden Period, 111
Gompers, 49
Goodall, 210
Goodnight, 44
Goodnight-Loving, 44
Gorbachev, 152, 153, 155
Goth, 113, 200
Granada, 114
Grand Alliance, 132
Grant, 42, 46, 76
Great Awakening, 20, 26
Great Binding Law, 14
Great Depression, 57-59, 61
Great Lakes, 12, 32, 37
Great Leap, 183
Great Migration, 35
Great Plains, 12, 18, 20, 35, 44, 47, 193
Great Schism, 121
Great Society, 65
Great Sphinx, 195
Great Trek, 206

Great Wall of China, 172, 173
Greco-Persian Wars, 107
Greenland, 84, 115, 121, 125
Gregorian calendar, 109, 129
Grey, 128
Grito de Dolores, 93
Groseilliers, 132
Guantanamo Bay, 98
Guatemala, 88, 89
Guerroro, 95
Guevara, 100, 101
Gulf of Mexico, 13, 68, 70
Gulf War, 67, 70, 155-6, 186-89
Gunpowder Plot, 131
Gupta, 168
Gur-e Amir, 173
Gutenberg, 126
Habsburg, 115, 122, 131, 133, 134, 174
Habyarimana, 215
Hadrian, 111, 112, 113
Hagia Sophia, 169
Haiti, 90, 92, 93
Hale, 24
Hamilton, 26, 27
Hammurabi, 161
Han dynasty, 166, 172
Handel, 130
Hannibal, 198
Hanover, 134, 140
Harald Hardrada, 116
Harappa, 160
Harding, 55, 79
Harold, 116
Harris, 69
Harrison, 30, 49, 74, 77
Hartford, 16, 31
Hausa, 214
Havana, 51
Hawaii, 60, 148, 167
Hawara, 195
Haydn, 135, 137
Hayes, 47, 76
Heavenly Army, 177
Heisei era, 187
Hellenes, 105
Hemingway, 96, 211
Henry, 13, 117-18, 120, 122, 126-129
Hephthalites, 168
Heraclius, 169
Herbert, 79, 82, 98
Herculaneum, 111
Herodotus, 106, 113, 195
Hesiod, 9
Hessian, 23, 24
Hiawatha, 14
Hidalgo, 36, 93, 96
Hideyori, 175
Hideyoshi, 175
hieroglyphics, 196, 201
Himalaya Mountains, 161
Hindenburg, 59, 143, 147
Hindu, 158, 165, 168, 181
Hinduism, 158, 161, 165
Hippocrates, 107
Hippocratic Oath, 107
Hirohito, 59, 181, 187
Hiroshima, 62, 150, 181
Hispaniola, 12, 90, 92, 204
Hitler, 59, 60, 61, 146, 147,

148, 149, 185
HMS Beagle, 141
HMS Dreadnought, 143
HMS Leopard, 29
Ho Chi Minh, 183, 184
Hobbes, 129
Holocaust, 60, 149
Holy Roman Empire, 115, 122, 130, 132, 134, 138, 139
Homer, 105, 106, 162
Homestead Act, 41
Hong, 177
Honorius, 113, 117
Honshu, 190
Hooker, 16
Hoover, 79
Hopewell, 12
Horn of Africa, 192, 193
Hudson, 13, 15, 30, 132
Huguenots, 131, 132
humanism movement, 119
Hundred Days, 139
Hundred Schools of Thought, 163
Hundred Years' War, 120, 121
Huns, 113, 168
Hurricane Katrina, 70
Hussein, 67, 70, 155-6, 186-9
Hutchinson, 17
Hyksos, 195
Iberia, 114
Iceland, 115, 121, 125
Idris I, 211
Idrisid, 202
Impressionism, 142
Inca, 88, 90, 91, 99
Incheon, 62
Indian Citizenship Act, 56
Indian Ocean, 172, 189
Indian Removal Act, 34, 35
Indian Territory, 35, 49
Indochina War, 183
Indus River, 160
Industrial Revolution, 33, 127, 135
International Brigades, 147
International Space Station, 71
Intolerable Acts, 22
Inuit, 84, 102
Investiture Controversy, 117
Iran hostage crisis, 67
Iranian oil, 179
Iran-Iraq War, 186
Iraq War, 70, 156, 186
Irish Free State, 145
Irish Republican Revolution, 143
Iron Age, 9, 106, 162, 165, 166, 195
Iroquois, 14
Isabella, 12, 123
Islam, 123, 161, 166, 169, 170, 212
Islamic Revolution, 186
Israel, 161, 163, 182, 184, 193
Israel and Judah, 163
Istanbul, 174
Italian Wars, 119
Iturbide, 95
Ivan, 141, 173
Ivory, 192, 193, 209
Jackson, 31, 33, 34, 40, 43, 51, 73
Jackson Park, 51
Jacobins, 136

Jacobs, 44
Jainism, 165
James, 131, 133
Jamestown, 15, 18
Japanese Internment, 60, 61
Java Man, 192
Jay, 25, 26, 27
Jayavarman, 170
Jazz Age, 56
Jericho, 158
Jerusalem, 117, 163, 170, 200
Jesus, 128, 167, 169, 177
Jiang, 187
Jim Crow Laws, 43
Joan of Arc, 120, 121
John I, 118
Johnson, 42-3, 45, 64, 74, 76, 80
Jolliet, 18
Judaism, 123, 161
Judea, 167
Judiciary Act, 28
Julian calendar, 109
July Revolution, 139
Justinian, 169
Kabul, 188
Kai-shek, 180, 182
Kalahari Desert, 194
Kālidāsa, 168
Kalmar Agreement, 121
Kansas-Nebraska Act, 38
Kant, 129
Karnak, 196
Katanga, 213
Kazakhstan, 159, 188
Keats, 138
Kennedy, 64, 78, 80, 101, 152
Kent State, 66
Kenyatta, 212
Kepler, 127
Key, 16, 31, 142, 176
Khan, 118, 171, 172, 185
Khayyam, 171
Khmer, 167, 170, 171, 185
Khoikhoi, 194
Khoisan, 194, 196
Khomeini, 186
Khrushchev 64, 101, 152, 182
Khufu, 195
Kikuyu, 196, 212
Killing Fields, 185
Kimberley Certification, 214
King Arthur, 113
King Philip's War, 18
kingdoms of Egypt, 195
Kiowa, 46
Kipling, 207
Klebold, 69
Klondike Gold Rush, 98
Knickerbocker Rules, 36
Knights Hospitaller, 117
Knights Templar, 117
Knossos, 105
Knox, 74, 126
Kony, 214
Korea, 62, 160, 169, 175, 179
Korematsu v. U.S, 61
Koresh, 68
Ku Klux Klan, 43
Kulturkampf, 142
Kuomintang, 180, 182

INDEX

Kush, 196
Kuwait, 67, 70, 155, 184, 187
La Venta, 86
Lafayette, 25
Lake Ponchartrain, 70
Lake Texcoco, 89
Lake Titicaca, 88, 90
Lakota, 20, 44, 47, 50
Lancaster, 122
Laozi, 163, 164
Lapita, 162
las Casas, 90
Lascaux Cave, 104
League of Augsburg, 132
League of Nations, 55, 139, 143, 145, 151, 182, 215
Leakey, 192, 210
Lebensraum, 147
Lech Wałęsa, 154
Lee, 39, 40, 42, 64
Lenin, 144, 146
Leninism, 152
Lenni Lenape, 17, 19
Leopold, 132, 208
Lepidus, 109
Leutze, 24
Levant, 160, 193
Lewis and Clark, 29
Igbo, 214
Liberia, 193, 206, 209, 216
Liliuokalani, 51
Lincoln, 4, 36, 39-42, 48, 65, 75
Lindbergh, 57, 58
Lindisfarne, 115
Lister, 48
Liszt, 137
Little Ice Age, 125
Little Turtle, 25
Little Wolf, 47
Livingston, 24, 29
Livingstone, 206, 207
Locke, 129
Lockerbie, 154, 211
Longfellow, 23
López, 95, 96
Lord Byron, 138
Lost Colony, 14
Louis, 118, 120, 131-33,139
Louisiana, 19, 29, 32, 36, 70
Loving, 44
Lucy, 76, 192, 193
Lumumba, 213
Lusitania, 54, 142
Luther, 63, 65, 126, 141
Luxor, 196
Lyceum, 108
Lysell, 141
Maastricht Treaty, 156
Mabo v. Queensland, 188
MacAlpin, 116
Macedonia, 108, 151, 197
Machiavelli, 125
Machu Picchu, 90, 99
Mackenzie, 46, 47
Madagascar, 193, 202
Madison, 26, 28, 30, 72
Magna Carta, 4, 118
Mahal, 175, 185
Makeda, 200
Malagasy, 202
Malay Peninsula, 159
Malaysia Airline, 190
Mali Empire, 203, 204
Malinke Kingdom, 203

Manaus, 92
Manchu dynasty, 176-9
Manchuria, 176, 179
Mandate of Heaven, 162
Mandela, 211
Manhattan, 16, 61, 62, 181
Manifest Destiny, 36, 95
Mansa Musa, 203
Mao, 180, 182, 183, 185
Marbury v. Madison, 28
March to the Sea, 41
Maria Theresa, 122, 134
Marian Persecution, 128
Marie Antoinette, 134, 136
Marlowe, 138
Marquette, 18
Marshall, 28, 32
Martin Luther King, 63, 141
Marx, 139
Marxism, 144
Mary I, 122, 128
Mary, Queen of Scots, 128
Massachusetts Bay, 15-16
Matthew Shepard Act, 71
Mau Mau, 212
Maurya Empire, 165, 166
Maya, 85, 86, 87, 88
Mayflower, 15
McCormick, 35
McCulloch v. Maryland, 32
McKinley, 51, 52, 78
McVeigh, 68
Mecca, 170, 203
Medes, 163
Medici, 124
Medicine Lodge, 46
Megaliths, 104
Meiji, 178
Melilla, 209
Memphis, 67, 194
Menelik I, 200
Menéndez, 14, 123
Menes, 194
Mensheviks, 144
Merlin, 113
Meroë, 196
Meroitic language, 196
Mesoamerica, 84, 86, 87
Mesolithic, 9
Mesopotamia, 105, 110, 159, 160, 161, 163
Metacomet, 18
Mexica, 89
Mexican Revolution, 99
Mexican War of Independence, 93
Mexican-American War, 36, 95, 96
Miami, 25
Middle Ages, 106, 114, 119, 121, 129
Middle Kingdom, 195
Midway, 60, 181
Miles, 15, 47, 50
Ming dynasty, 172, 176
Minoan, 104, 105, 160
Minotaur, 105
Minuit, 16, 17
Mir Jafar, 176
Miranda, 65, 93
Miranda v. Arizona, 65
Mississippi, 12, 13, 18, 19, 25, 31, 34, 37, 79
Missouri Compromise, 32, 38
Mixtec, 87, 89

moai, 174
Mobutu, 213
Moctezuma, 91
Mohawk, 14
Mohenjo-Daro, 160
Moluccas, 132
Monet, 142
Mongols, 171, 173, 175
Monroe, 29, 33, 73, 95
Monroe Doctrine, 33, 95
Montana Territory, 44
Monte Albán, 86
Montenegro, 151
Montesquieu, 129
Moors, 114
Mormon, 37
Morocco, 193, 202, 204, 209, 216
Morris, 35
Moses, 161, 169
Mosi-oa-Tunya, 206
Mott, 37
Mound Builders, 12
Mount Merapi, 190
Mount Sinai, 161
Mozart, 135
Mozi, 163
Mpondo, 205
Mpondomise, 205
Mubarak, 216
Mughal, 174, 175
Muhammad, 169, 170, 202
Mussolini, 59, 61, 146
Mycenae, 105
NAACP, 53, 65
Nagasaki, 62, 150, 181
Nahuatl, 89
Nanak, 174
Napoleon, 74, 78, 136, 137, 138, 139, 140, 178, 201
NASA, 65
Naṣrid, 114
Natal, 206
Nathaniel Bacon Rebellion 18
National Aeronautics and Space Administration, 65
National Assembly, 136, 211
National Fascist Party, 59
National Labor Union, 43
National Party, 210
Navigation Act, 18
Nazca, 87
Nazi, 59, 147, 148, 149
Ndebele, 205
Nebuchadnezzar, 163
Nefertiti, 195
Nelson, 47, 50, 137, 211
Neo-Babylonian Empire, 163
Neolithic, 9, 104, 158
Nepos, 200
Nero, 111
Nerva, 111
New Amsterdam, 16
New Deal, 58
New England Confederate 17
New England Federalist, 31
New Kingdom, 195, 196
New Netherland, 16
New Orleans, 19, 29, 31, 40, 70
New Sweden Company, 17
Newton, 127
Nez Perce, 47
Nguni, 205
Nicea, 112

Nicene Creed, 112
Nicholas, 144
Nichols, 68
Niger River, 125, 203
Nile River, 194, 207
Ninety-Five Theses, 126
Nineveh, 163
Nixon, 64, 66, 81
Nobel, 63, 66, 81, 82, 149, 179, 180, 211
Norman, 116
Normandy, 61, 115, 116, 148
Norse, 12, 116
Norte Chico, 85
North American Free Trade, 68
North Pole, 98
Northern Africa, 193
Northwest Indian War, 25
North-West Police, 97
Northwest Ordinance, 26
Northwest Territory, 25, 27, 102
Nubia, 196, 197
Nullification Crisis, 28, 34
Oaxaca, 86, 89
Obama, 82
Obote, 214
Oceania, 159, 167
Octavian, 109, 110, 199
October Revolution, 144, 145
Odoacer, 112, 113, 200
Oglethorpe, 19
Ojukwu, 214
Oklahoma City bombing, 68
Oklahoma Land Rush, 49
Old Kingdom, 195
Oldenburg dynasty, 121
Oldham, 17
Olduvai Gorge, 192
Olive Branch Petition, 23
Olmec, 84, 85, 86
Olmsted, 38, 51
Olympia, 105, 106
Olympics, 106, 107, 182
Oñate, 14
Oneida, 14
Onís, 32
Onondaga, 14
Operation Desert Shield, 155, 187
Operation Desert Storm 67,187
Operation Neptune Spear, 71
Operation Overlord, 61, 148
Opium War, 177
Oppenheimer, 181
Orange Free State, 206, 208
Ordinance of Nullification, 34
Oregon Trail, 35, 44
Orellana, 92, 102
Orestes, 200
Organization of African Unity, 215, 216
Organization of American States, 97
Organization of Petroleum Exporting Countries, 184
Orléans, 139
Osama bin Laden, 69, 71
Osei Tutu, 204
Oswald, 64
Otis, 21
Ottawa, 21
Oyo Empire, 212

INDEX

Pachacuti, 90
Pacific Northwest, 29, 33
Pact of Steel, 146
Paine, 24
Pakenham, 31
Pakistan, 71, 160, 164, 174, 181, 185, 188
Paleo-Indian period, 84
Paleolithic, 9, 104
Palestine 161, 182,184,193,197
Palestinian Liberation, 184
Pan American, 154, 211
Panama Canal, 53
Pan-American Union, 97
Panic, 32, 45
Pantheon, 111
Paraguay, 96, 100
Paris Peace, 55, 145
Parker, 42, 46
Parks, 65
Parr, 126
Parris, 19
Pax Romana, 112
Peace of Vereeniging, 208
Peace of Westphalia, 130
Pearl Harbor, 60, 61, 148, 181
Peary, 98
Pedro, 14, 97, 122, 123
Peking Man, 192
Penn, 17, 19
Pequot, 17
Perón, 100
Persepolis, 109
Persian, 67, 70, 107, 109, 155-6, 159, 164, 171, 186, 200
Petrarch, 119
Pharos, 198
Pheidippides, 107
Philadelphia, 19, 20, 23
Philip 14, 108, 117,120,128,133
Philippe, 75, 139, 140
Philippine Revolution, 179
Phoenician alphabet, 105
Pict, 116
Pierce, 75
Pilgrim, 15, 126
Pilgrim-Wampanoag treaty, 15
Pinochet, 101
Pinta, 12
Piye, 196
Pizarro, 91, 92
Plan of Iguala, 95
Plan of the Union, 21
Plantagenet, 118, 120, 122
Plato, 108
Platt Amendment, 98
Plessy v. Ferguson, 51, 63
Plutarch, 106, 108
Plymouth, 15, 72, 123
Pocahontas, 15
Pol Pot, 185
Polk, 74, 95
Polo, 118, 172
Pompeii, 111
Ponce de León, 13
Pontius Pilate, 167
Poor Richard's Almanack, 20
Pope Alexander, 120, 124
Pope Benedict, 121
Pope Calixtus, 117

Pope Gregory, 117, 129
Pope Honorius, 117
Pope Julius, 125
Pope Leo, 115, 126, 142
Pope Martin, 121
Pope Urban, 117
Portsmouth, 17, 179
Portuguese Empire, 122
Postclassic, 84, 87, 89
Potsdam Conference, 150
Powhatan, 15
Prabhakaran, 186
Praetorian Guard, 110
Prague Spring, 153
Pran, 185
Pre-Classic, 85
pre-Columbian, 84, 99
Prescott, 23
Presley, 67
Proclamation of 1763, 21
Progressive, 50
Prohibition, 55, 58
Promontory Point, 45
Province of Freedom, 205
Ptolemaic dynasty, 197, 198
Ptolemy, 109, 197, 198
Pueblo, 12, 19, 87
Punic War, 198, 199
puquios, 87
Pure Food, 53
Puritan, 16, 17, 20
Puyi, 179
pyramid, 195
Pythagoras, 107
Qeswachaka, 91
Qin dynasty, 166
Qin Shi Huang, 166
Qing dynasty, 176-8, 180
Quaker, 19, 51
Quartering Act, 22
Quebec, 14, 92
Quechua, 91
quipu, 90
Quito, 90, 92
Quran, 170
Radical Republican, 42, 45
Radisson, 132
Raleigh, 14
Ramses II, 196
Raphael, 125
Rasputin, 143
Ravenna, 113
Reagan, 63, 67, 81, 153
Reconquista, 114
Reconstruction, 40, 42, 43, 45
Red Cloud, 44
Red River War, 46
Red Sticks, 31
Reformation, 119, 126, 130
Reign of Terror, 136
Renaissance, 87, 114, 118-21, 124, 126-7
Renoir, 142
Republic of China, 180, 182
Rescript of Honorius, 113
Revere, 23
Rhode Island, 16, 17, 19, 26
Richard, 117, 122, 123
Richelieu, 131
Ride, 23, 67
Right to Life, 66
Rihla, 172, 203
Riis, 50
Rio Grande River, 36

Rivonia Trial, 211
Rizal, 179
RMS Lusitania, 142
Roanoke Colony, 14
Roaring Twenties, 55
Robespierre, 136
Rodrigo, 114
Roe v. Wade, 66
Rolfe, 15
Roman Catholic Church, 117, 126
Roman Kingdom, 106
Roman Republic, 106, 109
Romanov dynasty, 144
Romantic period, 137
Roosevelt, 50-3, 58, 60-2, 78-9, 149-50, 179
Rosetta Stone, 201
Rough Riders, 51
Rousseau, 129
Royal Academy of Arts, 134
Royal Canadian Mounted Police, 97
Royal Dutch Shell, 99
Royal Society of London, 127
Royalist, 131
Ruby, 64
Russian Communists, 144
Russo-Japanese War, 179
Rwanda, 210, 215
Sacajawea, 29
Sahara, 192, 193, 202
Said, 207
Saint-Domingue, 92
Saladin, 117
Salem witch trials, 19
Salt Lake, 37
Samoset, 15
samurai, 171, 172, 175, 178
San Juan Hill, 51, 78
San Lorenzo, 86
Sand Creek Massacre, 41
Sangoan, 194
Sanhedrin, 167
Sanskrit, 161, 165, 168, 180
Santa Anna, 36, 95
Santa Fé, 14
Santa María, 12
Santiago, 90
Santo Domingo, 92
Sargon, 160
Sauk, 34
Saxon, 116, 122
Scandinavia, 112, 121
Scientific Revolution 119, 127
Sciri, 200
Scopes Trial, 56
Scott, 31, 36, 38, 56, 75
Scramble for Africa, 207
Sebastian, 130, 204
Secession, 40
Second Continental Congress 23
Secret Service, 52, 81
Selassie, 201, 215
Selective Service Act, 54
Seleucus, 109
Selkirk, 133
Seneca, 14, 37, 42
Seoul, 62
Separatists, 15
Serbia, 142, 151
Serengeti, 193

Service, 52, 54, 81, 98
Seven Cities of Cibola, 13
Seven Days Battle, 40
Seven Wonders of the World, 198
Seven Years' War, 134
Seward, 45
Seymour, 126
Shah Jahan, 175
Shaka, 205
Shakespeare, 109, 120, 123, 128, 129
Shanghai Organization, 188
Sharia, 170, 188
Shawnee, 25, 30, 31
Shelley, 138
Sherman, 24, 41, 50, 54
Shiva, 158
shogun, 171, 178
Shona, 203
Shoshone, 29
Shōwa, 181, 187
Shuttle Atlantis, 71
Siam, 171
Siege of Yorktown, 25
Sierra Leone, 193, 205-6, 216
Sihanouk, 183
Sikhism, 174
Silk Road, 121, 166, 172
Silla dynasty, 169
Silverites, 48
Simpson, 76
Sinclair, 53
Sino-American Treaty, 178
Sioux, 44, 47
Siraj, 176
Sistine Chapel, 120
Sitting Bull, 50
Six Nations, 14
Slovenia, 151
Smith, 15, 37
Snowden, 71
Socrates, 108
Solidarity, 154
Solomon, 159, 163, 200, 201
Solon, 107
Songhai Empire, 204
Soninke, 202
Sons of Liberty, 21, 22
Sooners, 49
Sopwith Camel, 143
South African Republic, 206
South Pole, 99
Southern Africa, 194, 205
Soviet Republic, 144, 146
Soweto, 210, 211
Space Shuttle Columbia, 70
Spanish Armada, 128, 129
Spanish Civil War, 147
Spanish flu, 55, 143
Spanish Inquisition, 123
Spanish-American War, 51, 98
Sparta, 105
Speke, 207
Spirit of St. Louis, 57
Sputnik, 152
Squanto, 15
Square Deal, 52
Sri Lankan Civil War, 186
St. Augustine, 13, 14, 123
St. Lawrence River, 12, 13, 14
St. Patrick, 113

INDEX

St. Peter's Basilica, 125
Stalin, 146, 149, 150, 152
Standish, 15
Stanley, 207, 208
Stanton, 37
Steinbeck, 59
Stone Age 9, 12, 104, 158-9, 194
Stonehenge, 104
Storm of the Century, 68
Storming of the Bastille, 136
Stowe, 38
Strangers, 15
STS-135, 71
Stuart, 131
Suez Canal, 178, 207
Sugar Act, 21
Suleiman, 174
Sumer, 84, 159-61, 194
Sun Tzu, 163
Sun Yat-sen, 180
Sundance Kid, 97
Sundjata, 203
Sunni, 170
Supreme Court, 28, 32, 38, 51, 56, 63, 65, 66, 69, 78
Swahili, 196, 205
Swazi, 205
Switzerland 122,126,130,145
Taft, 78
Taino, 90
Taiping Rebellion, 177
Taiwan, 182
Taj Mahal, 175, 185
Taliban, 69, 188
Talleyrand, 28, 73
Tamerlane, 173
Tamil, 186
Taoism, 164, 165
Tarfaya, 209
Tarquin, 106
Taylor, 74, 199
Tchaikovsky, 138
Tea Act, 22
Tea Party, 22, 70
Teapot Dome Scandal, 56
Tecumseh, 25, 30, 31, 41
Ten Commandments 161,200
Tennessee Vly Authority 58
Tenochtitlan, 86, 89
Teotihuacan, 85, 87, 89, 90
Territory of Nunavut, 102
Teutonic Knights, 117
Thames River, 125
Thatcher, 101, 153
Thembu, 205
Theodoric, 200
Theodosius, 106
Third Reich, 147, 148
Third Republic, 140
Thirty Years' War, 130
Tiananmen Square, 187
Tiber River, 106
Tiglath-Pileser, 163
Tikal, 88
Tilden, 47
Timbuktu, 125, 202, 203
Timur, 173
Tippecanoe, 30, 74
Titanic, 54
Titicaca, 88, 90
Tito, 151
Tiwanaku, 88, 90
Tlaxcalan, 91
Tōhoku earthquake, 190

Tokugawa, 175, 178
Tolstoy, 141
Toltec, 86, 89
Tongmenghui, 180
Torah, 162
Torquemada, 123
Townsend, 38
Townshend Acts, 21
Trail of Tears, 34, 35
Trajan, 111
Transcontinental Railroad, 45
Transvaal, 206
Treaty of Easton, 20, 21
Treaty of Fez, 209
Treaty of Fontainebleau, 136
Treaty of Fort Jackson, 31
Treaty of Ghent, 31
Treaty of Guadalupe Hidalgo, 36, 96
Treaty of Horseshoe Bend, 31
Treaty of Hubertusburg, 134
Treaty of Lisbon, 156
Treaty of Nanking, 177
Treaty of Paris 19, 25, 27, 134
Treaty of Picquigny, 120
Treaty of Portsmouth, 179
Treaty of Ryswick, 92
Treaty of Tianjin, 177
Treaty of Tordesillas, 90, 124
Treaty of Versailles, 55, 143-4
Triple Alliance, 96
Triumvirate, 109, 110
Trojan, 105, 162
Trotsky, 144, 146
Troy, 105, 162
Truman, 61, 62, 80, 150
Tsarnaev brothers, 71
Tubman, 33
Tudor, 122, 128, 131
Tula, 89
Turkish Nat'l Movement, 180
Turner, 34
Tuscarora, 14
Tuskegee Institute, 48, 56
Tutankhamun, 195
Twain, 45
Twelve Tables, 107
Tyler, 74
U. S. Steel, 52
U.S. Space Transportation, 71
U-boats, 142
Uganda-Tanzania War, 214
Ukraine, 110, 154, 159, 173, 188
Umayyad Caliphate, 170
Underground Railroad, 33
UNESCO, 162
Union Army, 39
Union of India, 181
Union of South Africa, 208-9
Union of Soviet Socialist Republics, 144, 146
Union Pacific, 45
United Nations, 59, 62, 139, 145, 151, 162
Upper Kingdom, 194
Ur, 161

USS Arizona, 60
USS Chesapeake, 29
USS Maine, 51
USSR, 62, 144, 146, 147, 148, 150, 152, 153, 155, 188, 213
Uyghur script, 171
Valdivia culture, 85
Valois, 120
Valparaiso earthquake, 98
Van Buren, 73
Vandals, 112, 113, 168
Vaux, 180
Vedic period, 161
Velvet Revolution, 154
Veneziola, 94
Venezuela, 88, 93, 94, 99, 102, 184
Vergil, 105, 162
Verrazano, 13
Versailles, 55, 131, 143, 144
Vespucci, 94
Victoria, 140, 206, 207
Viet Minh, 183
Vietnam, 64, 66, 151, 171, 178, 183, 184
Vikings, 115, 116
Vishnu, 158, 168
Vivaldi, 130
Voltaire, 129
Voortrekkers, 206
Waco siege, 68
Wagner, 137
Wallenstein, 130
Wampanoag, 15, 18
War Hawks, 30
War of 1812, 30, 31, 32, 73
War of Austrian Succession, 134
War of Spanish Succession, 133
War of the Pacific, 97, 100
War of the Roses, 122
War of the Triple Alliance, 96
War on Terror, 69
Warren, 55, 63, 65, 79
Warsaw Pact, 153
Washington, 20, 23-4, 26, 27, 31, 35, 48, 56, 65-6, 72, 78
Watergate, 66
Weimar Republic, 144
Welsh, 122, 207
Wesley, 20
West Berlin, 152, 153
West Germany, 151, 152
West Point, 25
Western Africa, 193, 216
Western Roman Empire, 112, 113, 114, 200
Westminster, 100
Whiskey Rebellion, 27
White, 14, 51, 168
White Sticks, 31
Whitman, 35
Whitney, 27
Wiesel, 149
Wilderness Road, 22
Wilhelm, 141
William Howe, 24, 25

William, 116, 120, 133
Williams, 16
Wilson, 31, 54-5, 78, 81, 145
Wordsworth, 138
World Trade Center, 66, 69
World War I, 54, 57, 59, 122, 142, 145, 147
World War II, 57, 59, 145, 147
World Wide Web, 68
Wounded Knee Massacre, 50
Wright, 52
Wuchang, 180
Wuti, 166
Xhosa, 205
Yalta Conference, 149, 150
Yang, 189
Yangtze River, 159
Yellow River, 158
Yellowstone Nat'l Park, 46
Yi, 175
yin and yang, 164
Yoruba Wars, 212
Yoshinobu, 171, 178
Young, 37, 74, 75
Yuan, 180
Yucatán, 88
Yugoslavia, 59, 151, 156
Yukon, 98
Zahir Shah, 185
Zapotec, 85, 86, 87
Zeno, 113, 200
zeppelin, 59
Zheng He, 172
Zhou Dynasty, 162
Zimbabwe 193,203, 209, 214
Zimmerman, 54, 142
Zionists, 182
Zoroastrianism, 164
Zulu, 196, 205

225

Study the past if you would define the future.

~ Confucius